Greenhill Books

Omdurman 1898:
THE EYE-WITNESSES SPEAK

Omdurman 1898:

THE EYE-WITNESSES SPEAK

THE BRITISH CONQUEST OF THE SUDAN AS DESCRIBED BY
PARTICIPANTS IN LETTERS, DIARIES, PHOTOS, AND DRAWINGS

EDITED BY:

PETER HARRINGTON AND FREDERIC A. SHARF

Greenhill Books, London
Stackpole Books, Pennsylvania

Omdurman 1898:
THE EYE-WITNESSES SPEAK

First published 1998 by:

Greenhill Books,
Lionel Leventhal Limited, Park House,
1 Russell Gardens, London NW11 9NN

and

Stackpole Books,
5067 Ritter Road, Mechanicsburg, PA 17055, USA

in association with

Anne S.K. Brown Military Collection
Brown University Library

British Library Cataloging in Publication Data available

ISBN: 1-85367-333-1

Library of Congress Cataloging-in-Publication Data available

Designed by Dianne Tine, Newburyport Press, Inc.
Printed by Newburyport Press, Inc. in the United States of America

Front Cover Illustration:
Kitchener & Staff Arriving at Omdurman, Richard Caton Woodville, 1898.
ASKB Collection
Back Cover Illustration:
Dervish Spearman, Lieutenant Angus McNeill, 1898.
Barbara McNeill Collection

ACKNOWLEDGEMENTS

Acquisition of manuscripts and artwork, together with research support, was provided by Colin Brown, Jim Clancey and Glenn Mitchell of Maggs Ltd., London.

Transcribing of manuscripts of Maud's and James' reports was organized by Ms. Nancy TenBroeck, Salem, Massachusetts, who also provided overall editorial assistance.

Transcribing of Angus McNeill's Diary was organized by Colonel David Fanshawe, Andover, England.

Access to the Angus McNeill Diary and Drawings was arranged by Colonel David Fanshawe, Andover, England.

Original drawings by Lieutenant Angus McNeill come from the Collection of Mrs. Barbara McNeill. These drawings were commissioned by Winston Spencer Churchill for use in his account of the British Expeditions to the Sudan, which was published in two volumes under the title *The River War*. Volume I was published in 1899; Volume II was published in 1900.

Permission to use the drawings by Angus McNeill was granted by the Churchill Estate, London.

Biographical information and photos of Alfred Edward Hubbard were provided by David Lickman, Nottingham, England.

Research support was provided by Professor Edward M. Spiers, University of Leeds, Leeds, England.

Research support, editorial advice, and inspiration were all provided by Dr. Timothy Kendall, Associate Curator, Museum of Fine Arts, Boston, MA.

Book Designed and Assembled by Dianne Tine, Newburyport Press, Inc., Newburyport, Massachusetts.

● ● ● ● ●

The Authors would like to recognize two events of August, 1998 which provided a sense of urgency for this publication:

Ninth International Conference of Nubian Studies, Museum of Fine Arts, Boston, Massachusetts.

Exhibition Entitled "Empire of the Warrior Prophet: The Sudan in the Age of the Mahdi, 1881-1898" at the Museum of the National Center for Afro-American Artists, Boston, Massachusetts.

THEATRE OF OPERATIONS IN THE SUDAN

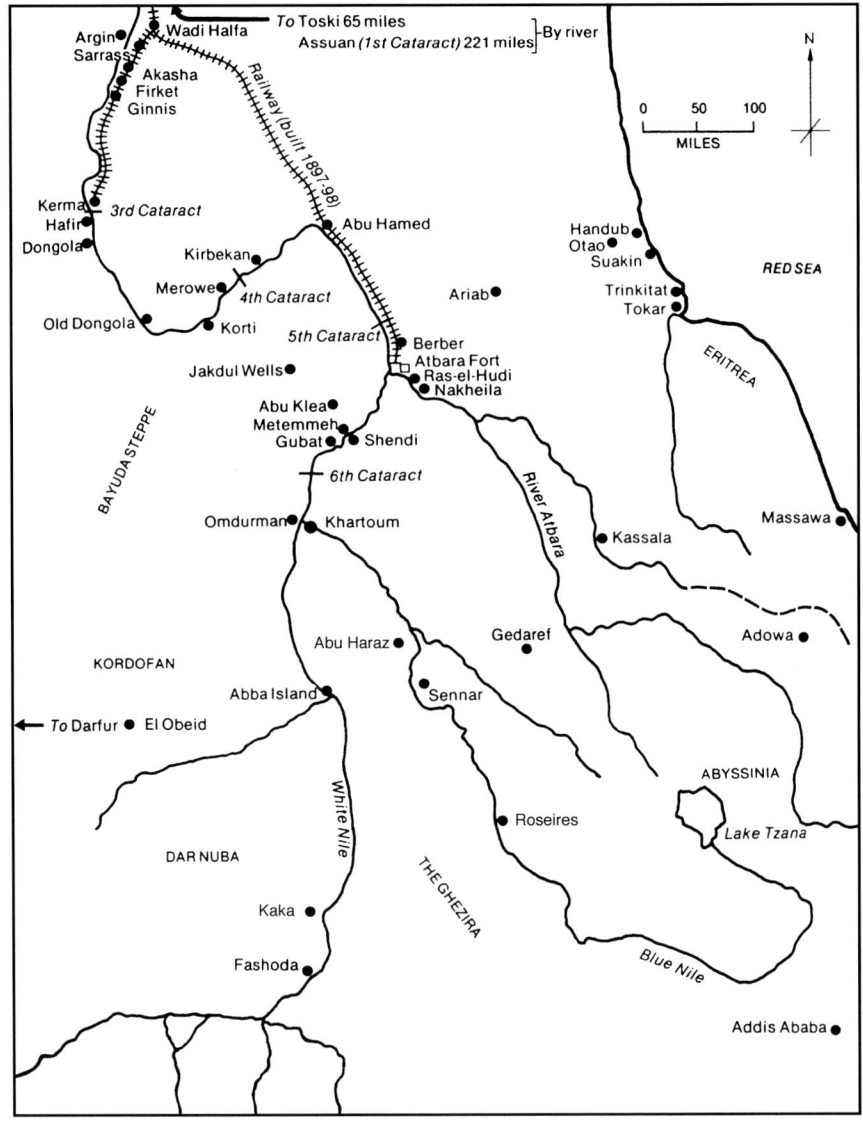

TABLE OF CONTENTS

Preface: Frederic A. Sharf . . . . p. 5

Introduction: Peter Harrington . . . . p. 7

Chapter One: Preparing for the Campaign . . . . p. 11
   A series of reports by William T. Maud, accompanied by drawings.

Chapter Two: Diary . . . . p. 43
   Captain A. E. Hubbard of the Lincolnshire Regiment.

Chapter Three: The Omdurman Campaign . . . . p. 75
   *Letter sent by Lieutenant Hamilton Hodgson of the Lincolnshire Regiment
   to his father.*

Chapter Four: The Omdurman Campaign . . . . p. 87
   Telegrams from Lionel James, the Reuters correspondent, to his London office.

Chapter Five: The Omdurman Campaign and the Charge of the 21st Lancers . p. 107
   A series of letters written by Major Harry Finn to his wife.

Chapter Six: The Battle of Omdurman and the Charge of the 21st Lancers . . . p. 123
   Letter written by Lieutenant Robert Napier Smyth to his sister.

Chapter Seven: The Battle of Omdurman . . . . p. 133
   *Extracts from the Diary of Lieutenant Angus McNeill of the Seaforth
   Highlanders, accompanied by drawings.*

Chapter Eight: The Battle of Omdurman . . . . p. 151
   *A letter written by General Sir Archibald Hunter to his brother, containing
   detailed descriptions of the military campaign.*

Chapter Nine: The Capture of Gedaref . . . . p. 161
   Letter from Major Henry Merrick Lawson to his sister.

Chapter Ten: Return to Omdurman, 1899 . . . . p. 167
   *Journal of Lieutenant Colonel Harry Finn, traveling up the Nile exactly one
   year after the campaign.*

Chapter Eleven: The Kaka Expedition, October 1899 . . . . p. 211
   *A detailed account written by Captain Arthur Pirie to Finn, his former
   commander.*

List of War Correspondents Present at Omdurman . . . . p. 219

Bibliography . . . . p. 221

Directory of Participants . . . . p. 225

I became aware of the Battle of Omdurman in January, 1990. At that time, I was putting together a collection of original works of art which depicted various colonial campaigns, and I acquired a drawing of sick British soldiers being evacuated down the Nile in 1898.

To research the background of this drawing I contacted my friend Peter Harrington at the Anne S. K. Brown Military Collection at Brown University, Providence, Rhode Island. We determined that there was an interesting collecting and research opportunity in recognizing the two important military events of 1898: the Spanish-American War, and the Battle of Omdurman.

It was not easy to acquire original works of art depicting these two events, but we were able to assemble a critical mass illustrating various aspects of the Spanish-American War; from these we developed an exhibition and a publication. In the fall of 1996, an opportunity arose to acquire two important items related to Omdurman: Maud's drawing of Lieutenant Montmorency after the charge of the 21st Lancers; and Hubbard's journal of his own experiences in August and September, 1898.

My own collecting focus had moved in the direction of acquiring manuscript material written by people who were present at important events or in exotic places: the British presence in the Sudan qualified on both accounts! In order to create a meaningful publication dealing with the experience of soldiers traveling down the Nile to the Sudan in 1898, it was important to uncover additional manuscript material.

I reached out to another friend, Glenn Mitchell of Maggs Ltd. in London, and authorized him to act on my behalf in acquiring such material. His skill in discovering important items, and his willingness to assist in the research process needed to illuminate these items, played a key role in making it possible for this volume to become a reality.

In the spring of 1997, I learned that the Museum of Fine Arts in Boston, of which I am a Trustee, was hosting in August, 1998 an important international conference of scholars who specialize in the Sudan. Moreover, Tim Kendall, the distinguished curator at the museum specializing in the Sudan, shared my enthusiasm for collecting and researching the events of 1898. A publication which could be produced in time for this conference would give added impact to our effort.

With the able assistance of Jim Clancey in London, Nancy TenBroeck in Salem, Massachusetts, and Dianne Tine at the Newburyport Press we have succeeded in putting many pieces together. As a collector, a scholar, and a Trustee of a major museum, I know the importance of presenting fresh material to the public. It is my hope that this publication will achieve that objective.

Frederic A. Sharf
June 10, 1998

INTRODUCTION

The events of September 2, 1898 are so familiar to historians of British military history that they do not need repeating here. The sweeping victory of the Anglo-Egyptian force under the leadership of Horatio Kitchener [Sirdar or Commander in Chief of the combined Egyptian and British forces], destroyed in an impressive way the Dervish army of the Khalifa and heralded in a British protectorate over the Sudan which was to last until the country achieved independence in 1956.

In terms of the soldiers who stood on the field of Omdurman, they were a mixture of regular British line regiments and an Egyptian force under General Sir Archibald Hunter. As a volunteer force, the British private soldiers came from the lower classes, many of them escaping the urban squalor which the Industrial revolution had wrought on Britain; and unemployment, always a guarantee to swell army recruitment. In stark contrast were the men who commanded these 'tommies'—officers drawn from the opposite end of the social spectrum, men born to priviledge and financial comfort. For many, they were following in well-trodden footsteps of their patriarchial families. Tradition was paramount for upper middle-class and upper-class families with sons following fathers who in turn followed their fathers into the army—and frequently into the same regiment. An army career brought prestige and power, qualities that served well when ex-officers decided on politics as their new vocation. Others stayed on working their way up through the officer ranks.

The written accounts of the Omdurman campaign and its aftermath published here came from the pens of British officers, ranging from lieutenants to lieutenant-generals; also included are reports written by war correspondents for *Reuters* and *The Daily Graphic*. We have not included accounts by private soldiers, which do exist and have been

INTRODUCTION

published elsewhere. Similarly, the Sudanese participants are not represented—so the impressions of the campaign and battle are biased towards a Victorian British attitude in terms of Empire and colonialism.

While none of the writers question the justification of the campaign, many seeing it as retaliation for the murder of Charles Gordon, they nonetheless admire the bravery of the Khalifa's soldiers and their commitment to religious ideals. They speak with respect and sympathy of the losses borne by the Dervishes. Major Harry Finn of the 21st Lancers stated, "Their losses were terrible...poor beggars," while Lieutenant Hamilton Hodgson of the Lincolnshire Regiment wrote, "I was sorry for these men; they were simply wiped out." Lieutenant Robert Napier Smyth of the 21st Lancers commented on the "horrible sights of dead and dying...men on all fours creeping, finally giving up and lying down to die." "Brave men they are - most certainly! But very misguided," noted Lieutenant Angus McNeill of the Seaforth Highlanders. Even General Sir Archibald Hunter found pity in the situation: "They faced it like men and died shouting out their belief...Poor Devils." Nonetheless, reaction to the mutilation of some of the British dead by the enemy after the battle led at least one of the writers to condemn the Dervishes. Lieutenant Smyth felt that if it had been up to him, "every man we captured on the battlefield should have been shot at once there and then, cold blood or not. If you had seen the condition of our dead you would have said the same."

In terms of the preparations and progress of the expedition to Omdurman, universal praise is given to Kitchener's handling of the operation. For example, Major Alfred Edward Hubbard of the Lincolnshire Regiment commented, "the Sirdar is an absolute marvel....What a reception he will get when he goes home - & he deserves it - and he emerges as the hero in the eyes of the various officers." However several of the writers are critical of certain orders, poor planning and some senior officers. Criticism is occasionally voiced towards orders which seem to display little concern for the soldiers in the ranks. McNeill felt that the march was handled in a deplorable way and hoped that he might "never see such a disgraceful and lamentable exhibition again," while Hamilton Hodgson complained that his commanding officer would not let his men stop for tea.

The writers are unanimous in citing the extreme conditions the expedition had to endure. The burning heat and baking sun, the parched throats and slaking thirst, the ubiquitous sand, the absence of shelter, and the limited supply of water (forcing many, officers included, to seek the muddy waters of the Nile)— all are uppermost in the writers' thoughts. Even though all the officers had their own servants and relative comforts such as 'sparklers', they nonetheless experienced the same discomforts as that of their men and had to eat rations of hard biscuits for days on end.

When it came to the aftermath of Omdurman, the horrible experience of battle showed through. Robert Smyth wrote of the charge of the 21st Lancers, "It was ghastly. The tears streamed down my cheek and I was physically sick. It was terrible." "We had had an awful day (from fatigue and heat)," recorded Alfred Hubbard describing the evening after the battle, "I have seldom been so absolutely 'cooked' - I had a head-ache from the sun and weary from want of food." All the writers spoke of exhaustion and extreme tiredness. Yet on the next day, they busied themselves collecting souvenirs such as banners, swords, spears, Korans and other 'exotica.'

As to the 'gentlemen of the press,' Messrs. Maud and James, they had both experienced warfare before in India and Africa. They represented a breed of Victorian 'specials' who travelled the world looking for the latest scoop. For W. T. Maud, his skill was both as a visual journalist who could sketch the events before him, and as an observer who could compose stories to accompany his sketches. His friend Lionel James was similarly well-endowed as an artist-correspondent, though his skills were mainly evident in the written form. Their views of the Omdurman campaign offer an interesting counterpoint to those of the professional soldiers.

The chapters here represent a composite view of a campaign and battle with vignettes of personal experiences, feelings and attitudes. How organised violence on the scale witnessed at Omdurman is perceived varies from man to man and the memory of events can also vary. Some of the accounts were written as diaries so the day-to-day events are current. Others were written several days after the events when the mind has had time to 'select' points of interest and relevance but where facts may have become blurred. It is for the reader to compare and contrast these accounts in order to achieve an understanding of the men of Omdurman.

CHAPTER ONE:
Preparing for the Campaign
William Theobald Maud

A series of reports published in *The Daily Graphic*,
London, 1898; accompanied by drawings.

INTRODUCTORY NOTES

William T. Maud was born in September 1865. Nothing is known of his childhood or family. He studied art at the Royal Academy School, and in 1893 joined the staff of *The Daily Graphic*. His skillful compositions in pen and ink and his articulate reporting capabilities soon made Maud indispensable to his employer in covering overseas military events.

In 1895, *The Graphic* sent him to Armenia; he travelled overland from the Mediterranean to the Black Sea reporting on massacres. In the following year he went to Cuba to cover the insurgents in their revolt against Spain. In March and April of 1897 he was in Crete to cover the rebellion, and in May he was assigned to cover the Greek army in their losing effort against Turkey.

In July 1897 he was assigned to cover Kitchener's advance up the Nile; he was present on August 7 when Abu Hamed was captured, and at Berber on September 3. This campaign ended with Kitchener's gunboats bombarding Metemma on October 17. He then travelled overland to Suakim, where a telegram awaited him assigning him to cover British military operations on the Northwest Frontier.

He took a boat from Suakim to Calcutta, and a train from Calcutta to Peshawar. Arriving there in December 1897, Maud was able to cover the conclusion of General Lockhart's campaign—the advance into the Bazar Valley and the opening of the Khyber Pass. He remained during January 1898 to cover General Bindon Blood's Buner Field Force in action.

The severe climate difference between the desert heat in the Sudan and the frigid winter of the Northwest Frontier caused a deterioration in Maud's health, and he returned to England early in 1898. He made use of his home leave to get married, traveling to Venice on his honeymoon in April 1898. While returning from Venice, Maud encountered several days of riots and street-fighting in Milan, which he covered for *The Graphic*.

His honeymoon and setting up house in Brighton were short-lived; by early June of 1898 he was on his way back to the Sudan, traveling with Lionel James of Reuters to Cairo, and up the Nile to Atbara. He covered the Omdurman campaign of July and August 1898, and returned to London in September.

In 1899 with war in South Africa looming, *The Graphic* sent Maud in advance of actual hostilities. He sailed on the 29th of September aboard the *Tintagel Castle*, and by the time the ship reached Capetown, war was declared. He travelled at once to Natal, where he managed to get trapped at Ladysmith during the siege of that city. With manpower limited, General Sir Ian Hamilton drafted Maud to serve on his staff. While at Ladysmith he contracted enteric fever.

When the siege ended, Maud resigned from military service and returned to Durban; he was quite ill, and remained there for many months. His wife travelled to Durban to nurse him back to health. They returned to England by the fall of 1900, and in December Maud delivered a sellout lecture on his South African experiences, illustrated with his own drawings which were projected onto a screen.

With his health still precarious, he was given an easy assignment for the summer of 1901, traveling to the West Indies to report on the various British colonial possessions, and returning in late August to England. Upon his return, an American missionary named Miss Stone was kidnapped in Bulgaria, and *The Graphic* decided in December 1901 to send Maud to cover the search for her. He was gone almost three months, once again working in winter conditions, and returned to England in March 1902.

Maud covered the coronation of King Edward VII in August of 1902, and then stood ready for the next crisis in British colonial affairs—the threatening of British interests in Somaliland. On December 16, 1902, the Cabinet finally felt it was time to intervene and authorized the Third Somaliland Expedition. Maud was assigned to accompany the Expedition, and sailed in January 1903 for Aden, from where he could get a boat to Berbera on the Gulf of Aden in the Red Sea, the base for the British Expedition.

Once again, Maud was in a hostile climate, and his fragile health began to deteriorate. On February 14, the British troops marched out of Berbera heading for Bohotle, which was reached early in March; by the end of March the Expedition had gone a further 120 miles to Galadi, at which point Maud was too sick to proceed further. It was not easy or speedy to return to civilization, and it took Maud six weeks to reach Aden. On May 12, 1903, he died there.

His sudden death, at a young age and at the height of his career, was mourned by the members of the London press. His was a unique talent: to communicate in words and in images the events of his time.

THE 1898 CAMPAIGN IN THE SOUDAN
BACK TO THE SOUDAN:
KHARTOUM AND THE COMING CAMPAIGN

[Probably written on June 7th, 1898, on board S.S. Ava, a steamship of the French line Messageries Maritimes de France, en route to Alexandria. Published on July 20th.]

The good ship *Ava* ploughs her way eastwards through the blue waters of the Mediterranean, and she rolls like a porpoise, for no apparent reason. As we near the coast of Africa, the thermometer rises rapidly, and all on board prepare for heat. The captain and officers array themselves in "ducks" of spotless whiteness, and the passengers discard their tweeds and appear in the thinnest of flannel garments. Many of the passengers have their beds brought up on deck and sleep beneath the awnings. The stewards present magnificent silhouettes as they stumble upon the gangway, their heads buried in a huge roll of mattresses, sheets, and blankets. The majority of passengers are British officers returning to their regiments in the Soudan after a brief holiday in England. Everyone is getting back into his place and preparing to play the part in the last act of a great drama which opened in 1884 with the murder of General Gordon.

FRONTIER SPECIALISTS

Some of my traveling companions are old acquaintances, and over the curling smoke of a pipe we recall the memories of past campaigns and discuss the prospects of the present ones. The smoking room of an Eastern liner is the place of all others where a man may gather valuable information upon a vast variety of subjects. Probably half-a-dozen, at least, of his traveling companions are intimately acquainted with one or more of our frontiers. Indeed, one might say that the British officer, with twelve or fifteen years' service, whom one meets abroad, is a specialist in frontiers. His eyes are always fixed upon them, for there lie his ambitions, his hopes of distinguished service, and his best chances of promotion. There are few countries out of Europe where the British soldier is not to be found, but nowhere are the conditions of his advancement so favourable as in Egypt. It has ever been a land of wonders, and it remains so to this day. For instance, where else could a young subaltern be seen landing a whole battalion into action and

15

handling it throughout the fight with marked ability? Yet this occurred last year at Abu Hamed. The railway that runs across the vast deserts between Wady Halfa and Berber has been built by sapper lieutenants, not one of whom can boast of thirty summers. The officer who superintends the traffic on the Kermeh line commanded the *Metammeh* gunboat at Hafir (he was hit five times in ten minutes by bullets and shell without being hurt), and any day might see him back upon the bridge of a battleship.

THE "SPECIALS" HAPPY HUNTING GROUND

From the war correspondents' point of view, what a happy hunting ground the Soudan is. Since the year 1895 a campaign in that country has been an annual affair. Although the Upper Nile cannot be honestly recommended as a summer resort, there are so many solid considerations to be set against the boiling heat, the choking dust, the tinned food, and the fleas and flies, that I have never yet heard of a man who refused the chance of going there. I think we correspondents have an infinitely better time of it than anyone else in the Soudan, because directly one campaign is over, we are hurried off to the northwest frontier of India, Cuba, China, and elsewhere, and we return to the Nile just in time for the next. While we wander through fresh battlefields and countries new, the Egyptian Army grills in the sun upon the ground it has won from the Dervishes, and waits patiently until the river rises and permits it to advance again and conquer fresh territory. But throughout each one of those weary months of waiting for the next fight every officer and man in the force works hard, works patiently, for the ends in view.

A WONDERFUL ARMY

The result of each campaign has been that new provinces fall under the Sirdar's rule and have to be governed—not after the manner of the Dervishes—and above all there is the great railroad to be extended southwards. Vast possibilities hang upon the progress of this work, and to push it forward the rifle is laid aside, and the pick and spade becomes the soldier's weapon. Never before has there been such a wonderful army, such perfect organisation, such mobility. In the summer it fights, ever victoriously, against a savage and warlike foe, and the rest of the year it is busily employed in laying "permanent ways" across the sandy desert, fitting together locomotives and steamboats, building hospitals, barracks, prisons, and resuscitating the trade of a once-flourishing country. Already the strategic railway from Wady Halfa to Kermeh has developed into a going concern, commercially, and the day is not far distant when railway engines will be seen steaming out of Khartoum, dragging behind them tons and tons of valuable freight for the markets of the world. The Sirdar's army has year by year pushed back the savage Dervish rule along the Valley of the Nile, and brought to its suffering inhabitants the blessings of peace and civilization. It has advanced slowly and surely, like an avenging Fate, nearer and nearer to Khartoum. It has chosen its own time; it has struck at the foe only when the conditions were favourable to an attack. Nothing has been left to chance; there has never been a check; never a semblance of a repulse. From every battlefield the routed Dervishes have gone back to their leader with the words "They come! They come!" upon their lips. What must be the feelings of the Khalifa while he sits in Omdurman, and hears from time to time of the Sirdar's irresistible advance? If he were wise he would rise at once and flee into the heart of Africa. But he is an unthinking savage and a fanatic. He trusts in Allah, and the experience of the last four years is thrown away upon him. He cannot see the change that has taken place in his position. There is now no Mahdi beside him to raise hell in the hearts of his subjects, and send them rushing blindly into battle. Now they must be driven like sheep to the slaughter by his own Baggara bodyguard. He has hurled Wad-el-Bisbara and Mahmoud at the Sirdar, with like effect, and now the final struggle is at hand, and these two strong men stand face to face.

KHARTOUM—AND THEN

It is generally anticipated here that the present campaign will be over in four months. The conditions of an advance from the Atbara to Omdurman are so well known to the Egyptian War Office that this estimate may be relied upon. There are some people who go as far as to name the exact date in October when our troops will be in possession of the town. There is quite a lot of betting in the clubs upon the event, the 26th of that month being the "favourite." The day, the hour, or the week is immaterial. The great fact to be kept in mind is that the year 1898 will see the final overthrow of Dervish power in the Soudan. Then will arise a host of great questions, all of which will urgently demand attention. Our continued occupation of Egypt will be the chief among these, and a justification of our position will most assuredly be demanded by one at least of the European Powers. By the end of August we shall have the three British brigades in the country, and when the work in hand is finished what is to be done with them? What, indeed, will become of the Egyptian Army itself! When the whole Valley of the Nile is pacified and a civil government firmly established there will be no need for more than one or two battalions south of Wady Halfa. The Fellaheen troops could not be permanently quartered in the Soudan, and there are not the barracks in Lower Egypt to accommodate them. The finances of the country are not capable of supporting so large a force, and the Soudan could not have been reconquered for many years to come had England not advanced the money necessary to cover the annual deficits upon military expenditure. The interests involved in the Soudan campaign of 1898 are of such vital importance to both countries, and so far outweigh all those which have preceded it, that the end is awaited with an interest unparalleled in the last half of this century.

PREPARING FOR KHARTOUM:
ARTILLERY EXPERIMENTS AT ABASSYEH

[Note: Probably written and posted on Friday, June 10th, 1898. Published Saturday, June 18th, 1898. The first of Maud's reports to be published by The Daily Graphic *from the 1898 Sudan Campaign.]*

A series of most interesting experiments with shrapnel shell have been made at Abassyeh by Major Williams, C.R.A., and Major Stanley Gordon, of the Egyptian Army. Out in the desert behind the barracks at Abassyeh, a stone wall 7 ft. high and 12 ft. thick was built specially for the purpose, and subjected to a heavy cannonading by the 32nd Field Battery (British), and mountain and howitzer guns (Egyptian). Presumably this solid target represented the walls of Khartoum, around which, if Mahmoud's latest declarations are to be believed, there is certain to be some heavy fighting before long. When the time comes for storming that city, our artillery are certain to play an important part, for the place is very strongly fortified. The object of these experiments was to discover what effect shrapnel shell, used as common shell, would have upon walled defences.

It may not be out of place to describe briefly the difference between a shrapnel shell and a common shell. The former is a steel case, and contains about 120 bullets of various sizes. Down the centre of the shell a narrow tube is placed, and this contains the bursting charge, which is ignited by a time fuse. The shell bursts in the air and scatters its contents over an area of about 100 yards by fifteen. A common shell has also a hollow centre containing a bursting charge, but this only ignites when the shell comes in contact with anything that resists progress.

The War Office have wisely decided to issue to the artillery on active service no other kind of ammunition than shrapnel, and the advantages of this change is tremendous. One of the most striking features of the Turko-Greek War was the practically harmless results of very heavy artillery fire when shrapnel was not employed. But when it becomes necessary to breach a wall or a stockade, the shrapnel shell, bursting in the air, is obviously useless for the purpose.

Its character, however, is entirely changed when a percussion fuse is used. This was done on the present occasion, and both Major Williams and Major Gordon were highly satisfied with the results which they obtained, for after thirty-two rounds had been fired the impossible-looking wall was effectively breached for the passage of infantry. Lord Cromer, Sir Francis Grenfell, a large number of officers, and a distinguished company of civilians watched the proceedings, and when the firing was over walked out to the target, 1,100 yards distant, to inspect the breach. The guns of the field battery were each "horsed" with a team of eight mules—also an experiment which is being made by Major Williams.

WILLIAM THEOBALD MAUD

PREPARING FOR KHARTOUM:
THE BRITISH BRIGADE AT CAIRO

[Probably written and posted on Sunday, June 12th, 1898. Published on Wednesday, June 22nd, 1898.]

Sir Francis Grenfell has dispersed the troops which had been assembled under his command for the recent manoeuvres in a camp of exercise at Mena, close to the Great Pyramid. The manoeuvres lasted for a week, and during that time a lot of useful work was done by all the regiments. These consisted of the 21st Lancers, the Royal Irish Fusiliers, the Northumberland Fusiliers, the Lancashire Fusiliers, the 32nd Battery of Field Artillery, and the Mounted Infantry. These troops collectively formed a very fine brigade, and won golden opinions for themselves by the way they manoeuvred in the sand and the broiling sun. This was more particularly so with regard to the Lancers and the "Irish." My sketch represents the 21st returning to Cairo along the beautiful avenue of shady trees which fringe the road and whole of the way to the Pyramids.

The British brigade in Cairo:
The 21st Lancers returning from the manoeuvres.

20

BACK TO THE SOUDAN:
CAVALRY MANOEUVRES AT ABASSYEH

[Written at Assouan on July 12th, but describing an event which started on July 5th, when Maud probably accompanied Lord Cromer's party to Abassyeh. The inspection of the 32nd Royal Artillery took place on July 6th; the Cavalry manoeuvres on the morning of July 7th. Maud probably returned to Cairo that afternoon to start preparations for his trip to Atbara.]

Before leaving Cairo for the Soudan I had the priviledge of witnessing at Abassyeh two most interesting novelties in modern warfare—what one might call specialties for the Dervishes. The first is the horsing of a field battery with mules, and the second is the new form of attack for cavalry. These new departures are the result of experience gained in past encounters with the Dervishes, and have been adapted to the nature of the country in which they must be fought. With regard to the artillery, it was felt that heavier guns would be required when the final attack on the defences of Omdurman begins. But big guns are not easy to move in the desert sand, and the heavy artillery horses which pull them will not live in such a country and climate as the Soudan. However, big guns are wanted there, and the means of getting them up has been found. Major Williams, C.R.A., who is now in Cairo, set himself to overcome this difficulty, and doubtless the experience he has gained in Uganda led him to devise the plan of substituting mules for horses. The experiment was tried with marked success, and the result is that the 32nd Field Battery and a new Howitzer battery are leaving for the front, and will before long be throwing their heavy shells into the Dervish defences.

PROMISING FOR THE DERVISHES

From the commencement Lord Cromer had taken the liveliest interest in the preparations for departure, and on the 5th inst. he went down to Abassyeh to finally inspect the battery and watch some practice at a running target. One saw him down there in the desert not as the ruler of Egypt, but as a major of Royal Artillery, keenly interested in the work of his old corps. The afternoon commenced with shell and shrapnel fire at a moving target 2,500 yards away. The target consisted of a sheet of canvas rigged upon a two-wheeled cart, which was drawn at a gallop by eight mules and a thin wire rope. To a spectator in the battery the mules and their riders at this long range appeared to be dangerously near the target, though in reality the length of the rope was 200 yards. The shooting was remarkably good. The very first shell struck the target, and a long delay was necessary before it could be patched up and set going again. The way in which the shrapnel repeatedly burst and ploughed up the sand around the flying mark promises well for the Dervish cavalry later on. At the conclusion of the practice the guns were limbered up, and Major Williams brought his battery past at a gallop, and in splendid order. Each gun is drawn by a team of eleven mules, which are disposed three abreast in front of the two-wheelers. In order to give the mules more weight for their work, and also to ensure more handiness in the team, the offside mule of each triplet is ridden by a gunner. As the battery galloped by it can be easily imagined that with forty-four hoofs drumming on the sand such a cloud of dust arises that a gun and its limber were practically invisible. To each half-section of the battery is attached an ammunition cart, horsed by four mules, and it carries sixty rounds. The cart is technically known as a "Malta," being lightly built, and running on two wheels. The wheels are detachable and the sides collapsible, the whole being designed for easy transport on rail and river boats. In this fierce sun the warping of gun and limber wheels becomes a serious matter, and for this reason they have all been periodically subjected to sun-baths, and the defects remedied as they developed. The mules that will take the field and the howitzer battery into action have been carefully selected, and they are a splendid set of animals, being very fast and strong. Their average price is £25, and the majority of them come from Syria. Neither time nor trouble has been spared to render the 32nd Field Battery an efficient arm of the great force now concentrating on the Upper Nile, and that it will prove itself to be so no one who knows the officers and men can for a moment doubt.

A NEW CAVALRY MANOEUVRE

And now for a description of the new manoeuvre as I saw it carried out by the 21st Lancers over the same ground the morning after the battery had been inspected. It has been demonstrated time after time that the wily Dervish horsemen will not give or receive a direct attack, but invariably endeavour to execute a flanking movement. I have frequently heard British cavalry officers express their admiration for the manner in which those wild Bagars manoeuvre, at one moment forming up in a dense mass, courting a charge, and the next splitting into small parties, and vanishing into a cloud of dust, only to reappear on the flank or rear. In order to give our cavalry a chance of "getting in" at this slippery foe, a new formation has been devised, and I need not say that "the 21st" is just madly keen to put it into practice. Three squadrons are drawn up in line and charge, while the fourth squadron follows in echelon in the rear. Let us presume that the enemy will refuse the attack and move off to their left. The three squadrons charge straight on while the fourth, which has remained "masked" up to this time, with a half-right turn, dashes out from the rear and meets the inevitable flank attack of the enemy full in the face. As I watched this pretty manoeuvre in the early morning at Abassyeh, the two things that struck me the most were the speed at which it was executed and the dense fog of dust which enveloped the whole regiment. The three squadrons whirled past in a fiery column of cloud, and all one could see was a ghostly horseman or two galloping like mad, and here and there a bright glitter of light on a lance point. Then suddenly out of the heart of the smoke dashed the fourth squadron, "masked" indeed, and any Dervishes bent on flank attack would undoubtedly have been surprised and roughly handled. Half a minute later each squadron trumpeter was heard echoing the colonel's far away, and although the regiment was invisible one knew that the manoeuvre was over. I had seen a rushing whirlwind pass by me, and the next moment, as if by magic, it had turned into the 21st Lancers, with Colonel Martin at its head. The speed, the dust, and the discipline together created an impression of power which I can never hope to reproduce with a pen-and-ink sketch in *The Daily Graphic*.

BACK TO THE SOUDAN:
THE SOUDAN MAIL

[Maud wrote this report from Assouan, after his arrival on July 12th. However, The Daily Graphic *published this piece on August 16th, 1898, weeks after they received it.]*

I once heard of a war correspondent who was sent off from London at such short notice that his only equipment was the frock-coat and tall hat which he happened to be wearing at the time. Such a slender outfit might serve in some countries where a man can pick up things as he goes along, but a campaign in the Soudan is a serious business, and needs a deal of forethought and preparation. Every article of food and every drop of drink has to be taken up from Cairo to the front, and

WILLIAM THEOBALD MAUD

in quantities sufficient to last for three months at the least. Transport for oneself, servants, horses, and stores is also another great difficulty, for with only one line of communication to an army more than 1,200 miles from Cairo, blocks on the way are only to be expected, and when they occur the correspondent's turn comes last. The only thing one can do is to rush on as far and as fast as possible when the conditions are favourable and trust to luck for the rest.

TROUBLE IN THE HORSE TRUCKS

The other day a colleague and myself received permission from the Sirdar to go South, and the following morning we rose early to get our horses and sais, and starting by the first freight train. Besides getting the stud entrained, we had to see that the animals were all provided with seven days' rations. For four horses this amounted to a formidable pile of tibbin sacks, far too big to be crammed into any English horse-box. But in this country the boxes are built differently, and gold letters on the outside of them inform you that they are called "animal trucks." The name is expressive and appropriate. They are not provided with swingbars or partitions of any kind, and the consequence is that the horses get to fighting, unless carefully looked after by the sais. In the present instance it was so, and just before the train started a terrible kicking and squealing arose inside the truck, and my grey horse was up on his hind legs biting viciously at his neighbour, who returned the compliment with his heels. Both sais were hopelessly mixed up in the affair, and they had scarcely succeeded in restoring order when the train moved off. Goodness only knows how many of them will be lame when they arrive at Berber! We followed by the night mail, which was filled with officers going to the front.

HOW THE SOUDAN MAIL GOES OUT

What a striking scene that departure platform presents when the Soudan mail goes out! It is ill-lighted and crowded with people in tarboosh or turban, who apparently have no business there, and perpetually get in one another's way. Uniform-cases, camel-trunks, and portmanteaux are piled together in heaps, and dragged asunder again by gangs of swarthy porters who yell and curse at one another, perspiring dreadfully all the while. The individuals who own the baggage which causes all this commotion appear later on, dressed generally in grey flannel suits and tweed caps, looking very cool and very much like tourists. The tone of the proceedings is restored, however, by the presence of their friends who come to see their comrades off in mess uniforms both British and Egyptian. The final moment is marked by the ringing of bells, the blowing of penny trumpets, and the screech of the engine's whistle. Everyone is cheery as a schoolboy going home, and with many a jest and hearty hand-shake, the travellers clamber on board, and the train crawls out to the desert. How many splendid Englishmen have left Cairo by this night mail for the Soudan never to return! The death roll rises year by year, yet the old Nile still claims its victims, unappeased. Who can tell how many more will make their last bed beneath the palm trees ere the autumn ends, and the river falls again, and the sand-banks reappear? Such thoughts as these no doubt occur to many a man off to the front—but he leaves them behind with his dress clothes in Cairo.

THE JOURNEY TO ASSOUAN

The heat, the dust, and the other discomforts of the journey form a sufficient distraction to most people, for they take a deal of circumventing. As yet there are no Spiers and Pond refreshment-rooms along the railway track, so if a man will slake his thirst with a cool drink he must look carefully after his lump of ice and soda-water bottles. It is really painful to watch the ice melt and form an ever-growing puddle on the carriage floor. How he will want it to-morrow morning when he wakes up literally covered with mud formed of dust and his own perspiration, and his tongue cleaving to the roof of his mouth! As a rule there is nothing new or interesting to be got out of the journey to Assouan, but I was fortunate in having for my traveling companion an officer who was formerly in the police and is now in the Sirdar's army at the front. At Bahana, a village north of Luxor, he pointed out a building in which a band of captured brigands were burned to death with petroleum some years ago. It was one of the dovecotes so common in this part of Egypt. They are square and built of mud and remind one of an Afridi tower. Clouds of pigeons inhabit them, and the yield of guano is very valuable. They are generally isolated buildings surrounded by a high wall, and desperate men could well defend themselves within one of them. Not long since brigandage was quite common in the provinces of Jirgeh and Kenneh, but a greatly improved police organisation has had its effect, and the bands have all been slaughtered, captured, or broken up, though isolated cases occur still from time to time....

WILLIAM THEOBALD MAUD

A NIGHT ON A RAILWAY PLATFORM

Last year, when we came up the Nile, the railway ended at Naghamadi, but now it has been continued right into Assouan, which saves two days of monotony in a steamboat. For reasons of economy the line is a narrow gauge from Luxor on to Assouan, and this necessitates a change of trains. This gave us an opportunity of visiting the temples, but I will say nothing about them, for has it not all been written in the book of Murray? When we arrived there was an old pensioner of the Sirdar wandering among the ruins, minus his right arm and left leg, a pitiable testimony to the savagery of the Khalifa. We slept on the platform of the railway station, in order to be ready for the train which left at five o'clock on the following morning. We should have been better off at the hotel really, because it was very dark, and up to a late hour the porters kept bumping up against our angariebs (native beds) with huge cases on their heads, threatening to crush us to powder. When this nuisance was ended and gentle sleep had closed our eyes, an engine rolled up a few yards away, and when it found that no attention was paid to its whistling it squirted steam out of its side upon us. Staff-Sergeant Kellam, of the 10th Soudanese, happened to be traveling up with us, and he lent me an air-pillow which he picked up in Mahmoud's tent at Atbara. It was quite new, and made in Germany, though how it travelled from the Fatherland to the Dervish camp does not appear.

BACK TO THE SOUDAN:
SHIPBUILDING AT SHALAL

[Written at Shalal on July 17th. Maud had remained at Assouan/Shalal for a 5-day visit, prior to departing from Shalal by steamship on July 18th for Wady Halfa. Published on Wednesday, August 10th.]

Assouan has the reputation of being the hottest station on the Nile, and my own experience certainly confirms it. Last year we correspondents were detained here for some days, and this year also we have been given an opportunity of appreciating the beauties of the place. There are Coptic ruins, tombs, and a native bazaar, but these lie quite beyond my province, because I am not a tourist. There is a huge interest, nevertheless, attaching to Assouan and Shalal, because they form an important link in the huge chain which connects Cairo with the

Atbara. Thousands of tons of provisions have lately passed through here for the troops already at the front, and for those that will shortly be there. Guns, gunboats, railway engines, ammunition, and all kinds of war material have arrived by train and been transferred to the river boats and "gyassehs" with the regularity of clock work. The two men who direct this machinery and keep it in order are Captain Pedley, the Commandant, and Major Drage, D.S.O. Both these officers have been feeding the Egyptian army in the Soudan for many years, and what they do not know about transport and commissariat is not worth knowing.

Shalal is the chief point of interest at the present time, because it is here that the river traffic commences, and every kind of store that passes through has to be transferred from the railway to the steamboats and barges. Shalal is a village of wooden huts and workshops, dumped down in the sand without any order, but exactly where they are wanted. When we arrived the first thing to arrest the attention was a deafening chorus of hammers ringing on the side of an iron barge, propped up on piles by the riverside. The barge was one of a fleet which is being built for the conveyance of "Mr. Atkins" to Omdurman or thereabouts. Each one is built in sections, is fitted with a double lock, and carries 250 men. Speed of construction is the great thing necessary just now, and under Drage Bey's able direction the little shipbuilding yard turns out one boat a week. We saw one launched, and a pretty sight it was. Steel rails, well greased, had been laid from the shop to the water's edge, and one after another the barge came rushing down in pieces, and plunged into the river with a tremendous splash, reminding one of the water chute at Olympia. Directly one section reached the water half-naked men seized it and dragged it to one side to make room for its fellows, and two hours saw the barge bolted together, ready for the voyage to Wady Halfa. The temperature was 124 deg. Fahrenheit in the shade, but everyone worked as if his life depended on it. I watched the performance in the shade, but even then the perspiration dropped like tears upon my sketch-book. From sunrise to sunset this is a condition of life on the Nile in summer time, and no one but a stranger pays any attention to it.

WILLIAM THEOBALD MAUD

BACK TO THE SOUDAN:
FROM HALFA TO ATBARA

[Maud arrived at Atbara Camp late in the evening of Friday, July 22nd, having left Wady Halfa early in the evening of July 20th. His reports were now taking much longer to reach the London offices of The Daily Graphic; *this report was published on Monday, August 22nd, 1898.]*

Atbara Camp, July 23rd

I arrived here late last night, the tedious railway journey from Halfa having taken forty-three hours. General Gatacre and Captain Cox, his A.D.C., were on board the train, and I was fortunate enough to get a place in the saloon carriage. There are at present but two of these saloons in the Soudan, and very comfortable they are. One is always kept at Railhead to bring down any serious cases of sickness, so that the number of carriages available for passengers is limited. Many of the trains which leave the great railway depot at Halfa are not provided with brake-vans, and the traveller has then to content himself with an ordinary open truck. This, for a journey of forty-odd hours across the desert, is not exactly a vehicle to enjoy oneself in, especially when the sun is up. Matting and canvas covers are being made for the trucks, so that when the British Brigade comes up the men will be well under cover from the sun.

TRAVELING BY FREIGHT TRAIN.

At present every train is heavily laden with stores and ammunition, and these covers cannot be used; anyone who travels now must therefore ride on top of the loads, without shelter. The train which I travelled by from Halfa left at one o'clock in the morning, and it was typical of the Soudan military railway. Next to the engines were placed three water trucks for the supply of steam, and for some of the desert stations. There was one of the new iron barges from Shalal, traveling in sections. There were several thousand rounds of ammunition and sacks of corn, biscuit boxes, and field hospital stores. Recruits and details of "Gippy" battalions stowed themselves away in odd corners of the trucks trying to find comfortable sleeping places. Just before leaving the station Lieutenant Blakeney, R.E., the traffic manager, came to tell me that my Soudanese servant Abdul had been caught trying to smuggle

*"The Soudan Advance: Railway Making at Abu Hamed" 1897
Drawn by Amedee Forestier from a sketch by Frederic Villiers.*
Jean S. & Frederic A. Sharf Collection

through a boy, a relation of his, who wanted to go to Berber. The boy was carried off howling by a policeman, and Abdul will receive punishment when we arrive there. Every train has to be most carefully searched for stowaways, and no one is allowed to travel without a pass.

DESERT RAILWAY STATIONS

There are eight railway stations between Halfa and Abu Hamed, and they are unique. They consist merely of a pass-by for trains and a hut built of sleepers, with a telephone wire passing through the roof. Nothing in the world could look more desolate, more forlorn, than these desert stations. By day they appear to be built in the middle of an island and the rails to run north and south straight into a calm blue sea. The ever-changing mirage encircles them; the distant rocks and the telegraph poles dance and swing in the heat waves. A remarkable feature about these desert stations is the little patch of fresh green "dhurrah" (Indian corn) which the signalmen have raised in front of their cabins. The corn grows luxuriantly in the impossible-looking sand, and if only water could be procured in large quantities this ghastly desert could be transformed into a most rich corn country. Between Abu Hamed and Atbara the line follows the river bank for the most part, and passes several villages.

THE LADY, THE ENGINE, AND TWINS

The natives look upon the engine as a sort of god, and stand in great awe of it. The sapper officers who built the line have many amusing yarns to tell about their reception, when first the locomotive came along. At Gennanetti an Arab approached the officer in charge and asked him if his wife might creep under the engine. The reason for this extraordinary request was that the lady was anxious to have a child, so permission was at once given. Not content with crawling under the engine once, she asked if she might do it again, and her husband explained that this would ensure her having twins. A venerable sheikh, watching the railway battalion climb on to the long line of trucks, remonstrated with the officers in charge, saying that it was not fair to make the engine pull so many people.

THE NEW GUNBOATS

At Abadia, which is fifteen miles north of Berber, we dropped one of the iron barges which are being sent up in sections from Shalal. It will be fitted together and sent on to Atbara for the conveyance of the troops. Abadia is quite a busy dockyard, or rather was so, for all the new gunboats have been launched here. Captain Hobbs, R.M., has had charge of this important work, and all the new additions to the Nile squadron have been successfully floated, and they are now busily employed in towing barges filled with supplies up the river. The opinion of the naval officers here is that the new gunboats are failures. The chief drawback to them is that they can accommodate only sixty-five men, whereas boats of the Fatteh class carry 250 comfortably. The most important work of a Nile gunboat is the towing of river boats, and in this respect they are practically useless. Their shallow draught (18 inches) does not permit them to get a sufficient grip of the water, and with a heavy load they can barely steam two miles an hour against the stream. Besides Maxims they carry a 12-lb. quick-firing gun, fore and aft. In this respect, they are better armed than the old boats, and they also draw a foot less of water, but on every other point they compare very unfavourably with the sternwheelers.

BACK TO THE SOUDAN:
LIFE AT ATBARA CAMP

[Written later on the same day as his previous report. Posted to London with the previous report. Published on Tuesday, August 23rd, 1898.]

Atbara Camp, July 23rd

A walk round the camp this morning has shown me what a transformation has taken place since I last saw this place. In lieu of a small fort and a few mud huts dotted along the banks of the Nile and the Atbara, there is now a huge encampment, a railway station, a post-office, a soda-water factory, and rows of well-built houses. Many of these are occupied by the enterprising Greeks who follow the army, and supply it with stores of every description. They are wonderful little cabins, these "Greekie" stores. You can buy anything, from a tinned side of bacon to a reel of cotton. The most remarkable building here is the house now occupied by the Sirdar and his staff. It stands in the

The megaphone on the Nile.

angle of the fortifications, at the junction of the two rivers, and it reminds one of those luxurious cottages one sees on the Surrey hills. It is quite the finest house on the Nile south of Assouan, and it was built by Major Hickman, D.S.O., commanding the 15th Battalion.

UNCOMFORTABLE, BUT HEALTHY

Atbara Camp is the worst station on the Nile that I know. A dust storm rages regularly every morning from dawn to midday—and sometimes longer. There is no escape from it. As long as it lasts life is not worth having. No matter whether you live in a mud hut or a tent, the dust drives in in clouds. It turns the white man black, and the black man white. Every one breathes it, eats it, and drinks it, and yet the health of the troops is exceptionally good. Life in the Soudan may be uncomfortable, but no one can charge it with being unhealthy. At Damali, the percentage of sick in General Gatacre's Brigade is only 4.8. The prophets told us in April that the British troops would die in scores before the advance took place, but fortunately this has not been the case. There have been several cases of enteric fever, a complaint which always makes itself apparent when troops are standing still, but considering that the worst season of the year is past, it is a matter of great congratulation that so few of our men have succumbed. General Gatacre left our train at Damali Station, where he was met by several of his staff officers, and all of those with whom I spoke agreed in saying that the brigade was splendidly fit.

THE SIRDAR "LIKE THE WIND"

Atbara Camp is about ten miles further south, and it was pitch dark when we arrived. Lewis Bey, the commandant, entertained us most hospitably, but it was too late to find quarters or pitch our tents, so we slept on our cases of stores by the river bank. There is never any difficulty about being called early of a morning in this country, because the sun itself does it, and in a most peremptory manner. It begins to make things hot directly it gets above the horizon, and you have to get under cover or put a helmet on. Early as it was, the first white man I saw was the Sirdar, walking down the long street of corn sacks and biscuit boxes on either side of the railway. Unlike the majority of Generals, the Sirdar always goes about alone. He is like the wind. No man knoweth whence he cometh, or whither he goeth, or at what time of day or night he will appear. Nothing escapes his watchful eye or his wonderful memory, and he has the technical details of every branch of the service at his finger's end.

A STUPENDOUS UNDERTAKING

Everyone here is working at high pressure—storing provisions for the British brigade, or loading them on to ghiassehs, ready to be sent on to Shendy. It is a noticeable feature of the journey from Cairo to Atbara, that wherever one sees preparations being made they are always "for the British Brigade." With the exception of a few officers and non-coms, the whole of the work has been done by the Egyptian Army. It has been a stupendous undertaking to so rapidly accumulate at a spot more than 1,500 miles from Cairo a store of ninety days' rations for 25,000 men. In the last five days 900 tons of various kinds of food have been brought here over the desert railway. More than ever one appreciates the vital importance of that single line of rails connecting Wady Halfa and the Atbara. But for it the present campaign would not have been possible; in fact, success alone depends upon it. Though taxed to the utmost, it keeps running perfectly, and no praise is too high for the men who have built it and have charge of it.

CAMPAIGNING MADE EASY

So perfect and complete are the arrangements made for the reception of the new British Brigade that very few men in it will really know what a campaign in the Soudan means. It will travel comfortably by rail and boat the whole way; it will scarcely march fifty miles; it will have a big fight, and then, "Right about turn," and it will be off again to the cool north as quickly as it came.

ON THE WAY TO OMDURMAN:
THE BRITISH BRIGADE AT DAMALI

[The correspondents were living at Atbara Camp, but the army was spread out along the Nile, and the correspondents occupied the weeks of waiting by visiting various camps. Published Saturday, August 27, 1898.]

Atbara Camp, August 2nd

General Gatacre's Brigade is encamped on the Nile bank, ten miles north of the Sirdar's headquarters. The force is divided, and quartered in the villages of Damali and Es-silem, which are about a mile apart. The Seaforths and Camerons are at Damali, with General Gatacre and his staff; the Lincolns and the Warwicks are at Es-silem. As I wrote in a former letter the health of the force is excellent. With the exception of an epidemic of enteric fever, in which the Lincolns lost most heavily, there has been practically no sickness. A certain number of men went down from time to time with ordinary fever, and it was found that the main cause of this was the chills caught by the men after bathing in the river. This practice was stopped, with the result that malaria disappeared. The greatest efforts were made to break the monotony of camp life and supply the men with a certain amount of distraction. The most successful method and the most highly appreciated by the men was a river trip down to Gennetti. Two companies were embarked on barges and towed down by steamer to the head of the cataract, and after a visit of two days returned, the whole trip taking about a week. The squalid little village of Damali has become a great military station, possessing a theatre, a race-course, a railway station, a street of shops and restaurants—at which none but teetotal drinks are obtainable—and an absolutely limitless parade ground.

ON THE WAY TO OMDURMAN:
THE CONCENTRATION AT ATBARA

[Published Monday, August 29, 1898. With the culmination of the campaign about to be known by wire to English readers, the travel time required to get Maud's reports to London will very soon make them irrelevant.]

Atbara Camp, August 9th

The day is fast approaching when the Sirdar will have concentrated his forces on the Nile and delivered the final and crushing blow to Mahdism. The passage of troops through the camp has been continuous since July 20th, when General Lewis left with his brigade for Nasri Island and Wad Habesha, 130 miles south of the camp. A large depot of stores has been formed on the island, protected by two battalions, and Wad Habesha—which is ten miles further on, and only

WILLIAM THEOBALD MAUD

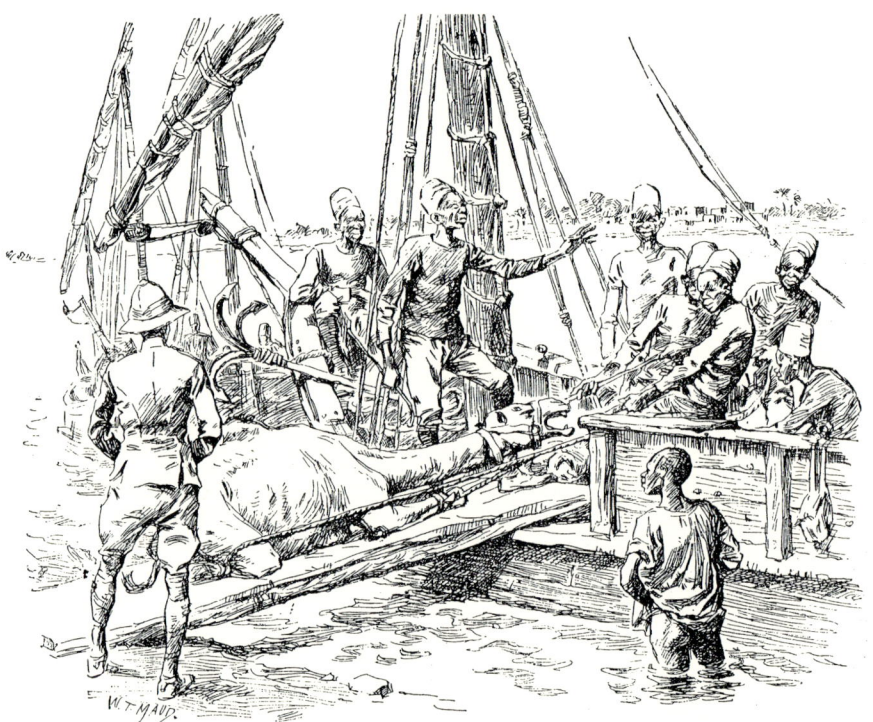

The camel corps for Omdurman: Shipping the "ship of the desert" on the Nile.

On the way to Omdurman: Embarking a 40 pounder on a Nile boat at Cairo.

fifty-eight from Omdurman—is to-day the most advanced post of the Egyptian Army. General MacDonald followed General Lewis with his brigade in boats, the whole of the cavalry, artillery, and camel corps marching at the same time up the left bank. With the exception of two battalions, of General Collinson's brigade, the whole of the Egyptian Army is concentrated at Wad Habesha, and almost within striking distance of the Khalifa. The final advance will commence directly the British troops have been concentrated there, and it is confidently anticipated that seven days later the whole force will be in Omdurman.

THE FEATURE OF THE CAMPAIGN

The Rifle Brigade, the Guards, the 32nd Field Battery, the Howitzer battery, two 40-pounder guns, and the Maxim battery of the Royal Irish Rifles have already arrived here. The remarkable feature of the campaign, so far, is the wonderful way in which the British troops have been brought here from Cairo. They have arrived with a precision and regularity that would be creditable to those responsible for their transport in England, but which in this country is nothing less than wonderful. That the single line or railway connecting Halfa with this camp should be kept running without a hitch of any kind under the heavy strain of traffic, speaks volumes for the watchfulness and forethought of the sappers in charge of it. The British officers arriving by every train are loud in their praises of transport arrangements, and express unfeigned astonishment at the ease with which the long journey has been accomplished. Both men and animals have arrived in splendid condition, and in no way distressed by their ten days of constant traveling. The trucks in which the troops are conveyed are covered by a matchboard roof, which effectually keeps off the sun. In each truck there is also a "zeer," or large earthenware chatty, to clear the water and cool it for drinking purposes.

ARRIVAL OF SIEGE GUNS

General Gatacre, who has moved his headquarters from Damali to this camp, is always to be seen on the platform whenever a train bearing British troops is signalled, no matter if it is at midnight or midday. The scene is always an interesting one, and more especially so when a battery of heavy guns arrives. Strong fatigue parties of Egyptian troops are drawn up on either side of the line, and in an incredibly short space of time the guns are taken out of the train, hauled through the deep sand, and placed in position on the Nile bank, ready to be shipped on the ghiassehs. This morning I witnessed the embarkation of two forty-pounder guns. These monstrous, unwieldy-looking pieces of ordnance were easily moved about by the gunners with a rapidity which was simply astonishing. Each gun weighs over five tons, and it can easily be imagined that to run one through soft sand down a steep bank and on to a river boat is no light task; but twenty minutes sufficed to see it accomplished. These great siege guns looked strangely out of place in this desert camp, their wheels sunk almost to the axles in the sand. They will be transported all the way to Omdurman by boat, and only put on shore and dragged into position when the attack develops.

ON THE WAY TO OMDURMAN:
BRITISH "TOMMIES" ASSEMBLING

[Published on Thursday, September 1, 1898.]

Atbara Camp, August 12th

Day by day the various units composing the new British Brigade continue to arrive, and a week hence the whole force will have assembled, when the general advance will commence. The character of the camp has changed entirely, though it remains the busy, bustling, dusty place it was when I first arrived. The Soudanese and Egyptian battalions have all gone southwards; their places have been taken by British "Tommies," and the English language is predominant. In lieu of the discordant bugles of the Egyptian Army playing their weird march music at nightfall, the rich melodious strains of the "Rifles" brass band or the Guards' drum and fife are wafted to us by the evening breeze while we sit at dinner in the open air.

THE HIGHLANDER AND THE THIEF

...The composition of this letter has just been rudely disturbed by a scuffling close to my tent, and on going out, I discovered a Highlander and a Soudanese engaged in a fisticuff encounter. The black's arms were flying around like the sails of a windmill, and, though getting the worst of it, he took his punishment well. The affair ended in his being marched off to the guard-room charged with theft, the original cause of the row. He will at any rate have the advantage of his antagonist tomorrow morning, for his bruises and black eyes will not show up on his ebony skin. The chief failing of the Soudanese is that they have no

On the way to Omdurman: Fresh arrivals for the British brigade at Atbara Camp.

just appreciation for the terms meum and tuum. They are the most accomplished robbers in the world, and they are no respecters of persons. Even General Gatacre has suffered from their depredations. His little flock of milch goats has been sadly diminished, protected though they were by an upstanding zareba. It was not until an English sentry was placed over them that they ceased to disappear. Neither has the Correspondent's camp escaped, and this morning I found myself minus one valuable case of stores. Fresh milk is a luxury few can afford here, because the Sirdar has most rightly appropriated the scanty local supply for the hospitals, together with eggs and vegetables.

THE "FATHER OF THE MOUSTACHE"

Of fish there is fortunately an abundance, and anyone can buy it in the bazaar. The Nile and Atbara produces many kinds of finny monsters—one can hardly call them fish—and the majority of them are excellent eating. Half-naked fishermen wander about the camp at sunrise, with their night's catch suspended on poles, and they offer them for sale at your tent's door. There is no fixed scale of prices, but one roughly buys the fish at 1s. a foot. The most popular variety is the "Abu Shennem" or "Father of the Moustache," so called for the long tentacles which decorate his jaws.

A MIRAGE JOKE

An amusing tale is going round the camp of a young English "Tommy" who had just arrived. It was mid-day, and he wanted a bucket of drinking water, but the muddy flood of the Nile appalled him. So he returned empty-handed to his mates, who recommended him to try the lake water, and they begged him to bring them some at the same time. All unsuspecting he went into the desert with his comrades' water bottles festooned about his neck, but though he walked far and fast he came no nearer to the lake, and it was not until he chanced to turn and saw water between him and the camp that he understood the meaning of the word "mirage."

HOW THE TROOPS ARRIVE

The arrival of troops by train is an everyday occurrence now, and the scene at the railway station is typical of how things are done in the Soudan. There is no show or ceremony about the Sirdar's arrangements, but they bear the stamp of extreme practicability. Atbara Station can boast a platform, but it was built for the disembarkation of guns, horses, and heavy war material, and not for the convenience of passengers. The trucks bearing troops are shunted into a siding, and the men are ordered to get down. They come swarming out of the train like ants and fall in by companies alongside. Their tents and stores are hoisted onto the backs of camels waiting close by, and half an hour after its arrival the battalion marches away to the camping ground outside the fort, with everything complete. Before moving off, the men are ordered to undo the top button of their tunics, a very necessary precaution, for a suffocating cloud of dust rises immediately they begin to step out. I regret to say that two men belonging to the left half battalion of the "Northumberlands" arrived with sunstroke, and both of them have since died. They were carried from the station on stretchers at the head of the column, and it gave one the impression of troops returning from a battle rather than going to one.

CHAPTER TWO:
Diary

Captain Alfred Edward Hubbard of the Lincolnshire Regiment

13 August to 4 September 1898; Inscribed to his Wife.

[Jean S. and Frederic A. Sharf Collection]

Captain Alfred Edward Hubbard

INTRODUCTORY NOTES

Alfred Edward Hubbard was born in Benares, India on 6 September 1862, the son of Henry Dickenson Hubbard, MA (1823-1913) and Elizabeth Smith (1838-1922). He was educated at Tonbridge School, and excelled at cricket and rugby. He married Mabel Emma Armstrong on 8 August 1894 at Tonbridge Parish Church, Kent. They had two daughters, one born on 4 June 1895, and the other born on 8 August 1900.

Hubbard joined the Lincolnshire Regiment as a Lieutenant on 25 August 1883. He was promoted to Captain on 16 January 1894 and then to Major on 6 October 1904. He retired from the Army in 1912, but came out of retirement during World War I to serve as a Major on the Reserve of Officers. He died on 31 July 1921.

Hubbard arrived in the Sudan in February, 1898, and was a participant in the battles at the Atbara, and at Omdurman. During the final phase of the campaign, Hubbard kept a diary, which was "not intended for public perusal, but is merely written in letter form to my dear wife." He attempted to keep a daily record of events, starting on 13 August and ending on 15 September. However, he found that the actual battle at Omdurman, and his participation in the Gordon Memorial ceremonies at Khartoum, were too overwhelming to record as they occurred.

While traveling from Omdurman to Cairo, Hubbard created a detailed record of events at Omdurman and Khartoum; after reaching Cairo, Hubbard went back into his diary and created a series of footnotes. The resulting document is fascinating, reflecting one man's attempt to come to terms with a great event in history in which he participated.

CAPTAIN ALFRED EDWARD HUBBARD

13th August 1898
On board *S.S. Nassir* (En route for Khartoum)

We are off at last after awaiting the steamer for the last three days with everything packed - Times have been fairly peaceful once we got things packed & away off our hands - a European morning most days - only the worry of wondering when the Steamer would arrive, as our orders were to embark at any hour of the day or night the Steamer might put in an appearance - Personally, I thought we should go yesterday, the 12th August - but no - At 7 a.m. to-day arrived a telegram, saying, our Steamer had left Dakhila at 6.45 & the battalion was to be ready to embark at 7.45 - We stood by ready - having despatched all Small Kit to the river bank - & eventually our Steamer arrived about 11 a.m. - she couldn't have left Dakhila at 6.45 - I suppose it was one of Gatacre's ideas of a pleasant surprise - He by the way, arrived on board the *Nassir* in person accompanied by his "glittering staff".

The Embarkation, loading up etc., etc. passed off quite quietly & pleasantly - No cursing, swearing or stentorian abuse! So different from the times of good old T. E. V. Everyone commented on the difference - We got all our mess stores safely on board - & now, at 3.10 p.m. we are well away, past Darmali (where we took on a little extra stuff), & steaming about 2 1/4 miles an hour for Wad Habshi. We expect to reach W. in about 3 1/2 to 4 days & to be there for about a fortnight before concentration & a general advance - We lunched frugally off sardines & pilsner beer - worse luck - we only have 1 case of the latter on board - I had an awful row with Simpson at dinner last night - He left the table, ignomoniously routed, as one of my remarks (wh. by the way was absolutely true) got him between wind & water - He left the table, refusing to say "good night" to me & arraigned me before the C. O. [Lowth] at orderly room this morning - Result - a very mild & half hearted wigging from the C. O. who, I think had a bias in my favour - having been present at the discussion over-night - Simpson expressed himself as disatisfied with the up-shot of the interview - I was quite satisfied.

We are, on board, 15 of our own officers, the parson Watson & doctor Cummings 6 companies with Hd. quarters - we have two barges filled with men & two gyassas ditto. The other two companies of the battalion (G & H) under Simpson follow when their Steamer is pleased to put in an appearance - We left them on the bank - I only took 1 photo of the Embarkation *viz*. the barge of which my own company occupies the lower deck - I took 2 or 3 at the mess this morning as a kind of farewell memento.

Thank goodness we are off at last - I feel better already - The hanging about was sickening - we are almost within measurable distance of the finish of this campaign & then - my sweetheart - we shall be together again.

[Sunday,] 14 August

Sunday & a very warm one too - no church service as accomodation is too limited - unless the parson stood on the top deck & shouted his exhortations to the swarming decks beneath him - We are making very fair progress - somewhere between 3 & 4 miles an hour I shd. guess - We had to have a great clearance of our small deck-space last night to allow of everyone getting sleeping room but it was managed at last - We tied up all night for some reason best known to the naval officer - in consequence it was frightfully hot all night - They tell that a small hurricane blew in the night, but I perceived it not - it blew two or three helmets overboard so must have been fairly powerful.

[Monday,] 15 August

I had to end somewhat abruptly yesterday as the heat was too sickening - my hand literally clove to the paper - today has been equally hot - we landed about 2 o'clock for about 2 hours in the midst of the heat as we had to take on wood for the engine fires - We are making excellent progress & are now (6.30 p.m) close on Shendy - A storm appears to be brewing in the East - so we shall probably get a ducking - hope not as there's no means of getting shelter on this open deck - We have flown our regimental flag at the mizzan (by permission of the Captain) and this afternoon the band played from 5 till 6 - so it was quite festive - I played 'nap' with Jim (Woodcock) most of the morning - Last night at dinner there was a terrible 'splosion' & Mainwaring's 'sparklet' bottle 'sploded' with a great report - no one injured - it was an old pattern one without a safety valve - The country on each side is very dense with scrub mimosa jungle - We are all thankful we havent, to march through it - I must try & get a letter back to Dakhila on this boat - Our pilsner has run out & as Hollins & my 'sparklets' are not yet arrived I have to drink whiskey & water or limejuice & water.

CAPTAIN ALFRED EDWARD HUBBARD

[Thursday,] 18th August
(Camp. South end of Shabluka Cateract)

We arrived here early *yesterday* morning after a very pleasant voyage - I think everyone rather regretted leaving the 'Nassir' though glad to get to our journey's end - The river & river scenery all along this reach are lovely - There are little green islands dotted about, with green trees growing right down to the water's edge - & there are any number of wild geese, ducks, plover & other water birds always on the wing - but of course no shooting is permitted - We passed a barge with the 2 big 40 pounders on board moored to the bank a little below us here - & I saw old Waymouth on the bank & had a chat with him - We had a very busy day after landing - all the miscellaneous stores, tents etc., etc. with which steamer & barges were crammed had to be unloaded & then carried to our camp-ground, which is about 1/4 mile from the river - The first view of our camp ground gave one the idea of a hay-field run to seed (if that's possible) long rank grass knee-deep & small shrubs & a few trees - of course this had to be cleared & then tents pitched - We had most of the tents up by 1 o'clock, but there was no chance of anything to eat in the mess before 2 o'clock - & as we had had a very light & hurried breakfast before 7 o'clock we were fairly famished - I got a whiskey & soda & some biscuits off Hood on the gun-boat about 11 o'clock & shall feel for ever grateful to him - We were parched with thirst & had a difficulty at first, in getting our filters going - & the Nile water is as brown as coffee & full of mud & sand - I am in a mountain service tent with Greatwood - We have 2 E. P. tents for the mess & are now quite comfortable - We have been on fatigue work - all the morning - getting the tents into proper dressing - enlarging the zareba & cleaning company lines.

Hollins has just arrived & brings my 'sparklets' - thanks to the forethought of my darling wife - I have had lunch today with Gamble & the 13th Soudanese - a bottle of pilsner & a whiskey & Rosbach-nipping - went over with Bob Maxwell - Gamble sent 2 ponies for us to ride over & sent us back on ponies - Our last joined sub (Dyke) arrived with Hollins this morning - have only caught a short glimpse of him so cant judge what he is like - some of the Camerons have just arrived, so our 1st (or Atbara) brigade is nearly complete - We are in Zareba, with an outlying picquet on some rocks just in front & each company has to find a double sentry by night & keep 1 section armed & accoutred through the night - There is also an officer's patrol all night, so that there should be no danger of a surprise - Also, we all (officers) sleep fully dressed behind our companies with our arms beside us...

Khartoum is about 45* miles distant - & once we are all concentrated we shant be long getting there. If we were to march there we could get there in 5 days easy. *[*I measured this by the map - but when we came to march to Omdurman, the maps turned out to be all wrong - we must here have been about 70 miles off (Notation made in Cairo on Sept. 20th)]*

Camp Shabluka. [Saturday], 20 August

G & H companies (under Simpson) joined us early yesterday morning - They reported very warlike times on board - under the régime Simpson - an officer on watch day & night - armed guards on each barge & general arrangements for meeting a Dervish attack at any moment - We had a very lazy day in camp yesterday - though it was quite the hottest day we've had in this camp - Yesterday's rumours in camp were, thusly:- (a) The entire Army Corps moves south from here on the 24th August - (b) Omdurman is to fall into our hands between the 4th & 8th September (c) The Khalifa with his black troops has withdrawn inside his inner citadel which is surrounded by a high & thick loop-holed wall & means to fight to the death, having posted his scallywag retainers in the outer environs of the town - (I mention these rumours for the purpose of being able to verify their accuracy (?) later).

From the plans of Omdurman which are being circulated, I should judge, that there will be some bloodshed if the Khalifa stands his ground - as it will be a case of house to house & hand-to-hand fighting - Let us hope that the artillery do some considerable execution (which I rather doubt).

We had a mild 'alarm' last night - I think a sudden wind squall upset some empty biscuit tins which clattered loudly - This sudden noise at dead of night was sufficient to put the whole brigade on the 'qui vive' but matters quieted speedily & a chorus of snores again resounded around the Zareba - I did not wake myself till it was nearly over & then found 'Spider' standing beside my bed - I thought reveille must have sounded when I heard the subdued rustle of moving men - but he told me it was an 'alarm' - but didn't know the cause - I looked over to my company & saw them settling down to slumber once more - so followed suit - but was shortly awakened again by Cumberland who borrowed (?) a drink out of my water bottle - thence oblivion till reveille sounded at 4.45 a.m. (Moral - when in Zareba, unless on patrol duty, always sleep heavily till awakened by force.)

I am on patrol duty tonight - I hear, on excellent authority, that

CAPTAIN ALFRED EDWARD HUBBARD

Mahomet Fir Ali has come up the river with Villiers, the 'Graphic' artist at a salary of £5 *per mensa*. The reason he wouldnt return with me (I am told by Tatchell's servant) is because of the kicking I gave him, for impertinence at Ras-el-Hadi - I dont really mind as for this kind of work, Gomah is a far superior servant - Fir Ali's temper was too impossible.

Sunday, 21 Aug.

Last night after dinner a sudden squall came on, followed by torrents of rain - out we dashed, from the mess tent & brought our companies back from the Zereba into their tents - As luck would have it I was on night patrol duty & had to tramp up & down from 11 p.m. till 1 a.m. in the rain - It was my first experience of this duty - The night was so black that it was impossible to see more than about a yard in front of one & I blundered about for 2 solid hours through the wet grass with the responsibility of the safety of the battalion on my shoulders - It looks like another storm tonight, but as I am not on patrol I dont mind. The XXth Regt (Lanc. Fusiliers) arrived this morning & the 'Guards' are now disembarking - with the former came Lyall, Rennie & Earle - all looking fairly fit - I got all the Lincoln news off Lyall - We expect to move south from here next Wednesday (the 24th) Let us hope it will be so - a days march nearer Khartoum is also a days march nearer home & nearer to my darling ones.

Tuesday, 23 Aug.

Yesterday morning saw the arrival of the 5th Fusiliers, with whom came also Gen. Gatacre & staff - (They had got a rumour at Dakhila that the troops *here* were to move at once, so, Gatacre being afraid of arriving too late for the fall of Khartoum, had his things bundled on to the first boat he cd. catch & came up here). Everybody who had nothing else to do went down to see the Vth arrive - I got hold of George Ray and asked him to bring in any of their fellows he cd. get, to refresh in our own mess - At 6 o'clock yesterday morning I thought I would go & see how the corps d'élite of the British Army *viz*: H. M.'s Grenadier Guards, were getting on as they had arrived late the afternoon before - I was sorry I hadnt brought my camera, when I got there, as their camp was truly a fearful & wonderful sight to behold - most of their tents had been blown down in the night & the ones that were still standing were perched in the long grass in the most broken-backed fashion...

"The Soudan Advance: A Sick Convoy from Berber Embarking at Shalal" 1898.
Drawn by H.M. Paget from a sketch by W.T. Maud.
Jean S. & Frederic A. Sharf Collection

CAPTAIN ALFRED EDWARD HUBBARD

A very draggled & dilapidated sentry stood on guard before a row of piled rifles, looking with weary eyes into a bush just in front of him - several of the officers fully armed were to be seen stalking through the rank grass aimlessly. It was hard to recognize the smart Guards-men of Pall Mall in the unshaven khaki clad warriors of the desert - The 20th Regt. (Lanc. Fusiliers) who had arrived the previous morning, also appeared extremely uncomfortable though their tents were up - somehow - One of their officers who was wondering about in tussore silk pyjamas at about 6.30 a.m. seemed quite at his ease - I wonder what would have happened had Gatacre come upon him in this attire - considering we all sleep fully dressed & armed & are only supposed to doff our clothes once a day hurriedly for purposes of ablution.

Yesterday afternoon we practiced camel loads - Had to pack all our things & put them out to see if the camels could carry them - I went around to see the 'Maxims' & had tea with them - Every staff officer in Cairo seems to have come up here on some pretence or other - Col. Hope's title is somewhat ludicrous - He is "the disembarking officer at Omdurman." It's a lovely title, especially as Omdurman at present belongs to the Khalifa - & may continue to do so for some years as far as we know (in that case what does the disembarking officer at Omdurman do?) Is he attached to the Khalifa's staff? or what? I believe they cd. think of nothing else to call him.

I saw Mahomet Fir Ali yesterday - His present master (Villiers) has, I hear, brought up a bicycle!!! This morning the whole *army* paraded for inspection in the desert - We arose from our slumbers at 3.45 a.m. & got back to breakfast about 9 a.m. fairly weary in mind & body - When all the brigades were in line, I believe, they covered about 3 miles of ground - We sat about in the desert for most of our time out, as a force so large takes some little time to put in motion - The horses & donkeys have just arrived - & among them Achmet Ibrahim on 'Shendy' - both looking very fit & well - I'm very glad they have got here safe, as 'Shendy' will be most useful for the move.

I had to send Bilal (the cook's mate) to get a flogging to day - He was most unsubordinated & refused to do his work - so the provost-sergeant & a policeman led him forth to the place of execution - Bilal returned with a chastened mien, having received 20 stripes with a 'Korbash' on a tender part of his person.

Thursday, 25 Aug.

Been too busy to write much lately - We leave here to march south at 4.30 p.m. this afternoon - The night of the 23rd was a beast - High wind, dust & then sheets of rain - we all got soaked through standing ready dressed for parade behind the zareba before the order came to get into tents - the darkest & foulest night I can remember - Yesterday, I got away all our surplus mess stores down to the river for transport up by boat - We have got 3 Camel loads of mess stores to accompany us on the march - That sounds a lot but is not much for 30 officers - Yesterday, too, arrived our long deferred mail - Two letters from sweetheart & one from my mother - also a consignment of papers (wh. are most welcome) - The 2nd British brigade consisting of 5th 20th Rifle Brigade & Guards left here this morning - we follow them this afternoon - Shant get into Camp much before 10 or 11 p.m. I fear - I hear it is very rough going though only about 10 miles - 'Shendy' has got a beastly sore back - I hope he will last the march out all night - I was on patrol duty last night, so didnt get much of a night - Earle is sick again - I believe they contemplate sending him back to Dakhila - wh. is the only place for a sick man - I & my two subalterns are keeping well & fit up to date - lets hope we get no wet weather, now we are losing our tents, as the damp & wet will send me up sooner than anything else - I didnt feel very fit after my writing on the night of the 23rd - The latest rumour is that we shall take Omdurman by the 3rd Sept - Hurrah! that will mean a speedy return to Cairo & also a speedy meeting with my darling wife - if I only come safe through the assault - I suppose some of us must go down - however, its no good thinking of that now - "sufficient for the day, etc." It's no good being too 'previous' - We strike camp at 1 p.m. to day - Lunch at 1 p.m. & then nothing else to eat till 10 or 11 p.m. tonight except what we can carry on us.

Friday, 26 Aug.

We marched away from Wad Hamed at 5 p.m. yesterday & halted for the night in the desert at about 8 p.m. It was a short march but appeared to try the men very much as numbers fell out - more from other regts than from us - Only 1 man in my company fell out & he came in this morning - Gomah took 'Shendy' down to the river & lost him - He came back in great excitement - but I ordered him out to search & not return til found - He found him in about an hour - Luckily there was a faint moon, otherwise we should have all been in hopeless confusion - We slept in 'square' formation - with sentries out -Unfortunately, the camels with the cooking-pots got astray on the march, so we could get no tea or coffee last night, but there was lots of water & we had 'sparklets' & some whiskey, so had nothing to complain of in a supper of sardines, bully beef & biscuits.

I had a most refreshing sleep - Reveille sounded at 4.30 - We got something to eat - Goma [sic] made me some tea & we marched on at 6 a.m. & arrived here about 8.30 a.m. (name of this camp unknown) - Our Camp ground is a mass of mimosa bushes & low scrub - we are packed fairly close up regiments all round us - The whole British Division, under Gatacre, is now concentrated here, except the 21st Lancers who are following in 2 days when their horses are rested after the march from Dakhila.

I feel very fit & in excellent spirits - in fact I feel so well, that it makes me think something must be going to happen - we march on at 5 p.m. this evening & halt in the desert far from the Nile - We go on early next morning & reach the river - We shall then be getting somewhat approximate - In other words we shall not then be long.

Saturday, 27 Aug.

Camp Royan - We marched here at 8 a.m. this morning having left last night's camp at 5 a.m. - When I say last night's Camp I mean our last night's desert halt - There was 20 Camps - we merely halted in the open desert, formed some kind of enormous divisional square & lay down in ranks as we were - We were some distance from the river so had to rely entirely on the water from our Camel tanks - The allowance was fairly liberal - viz. 2 Camel tanks to each company, wh. allowed every man nearly a quart - besides the water for making tea - The marches though short have been excessively trying - numbers of men have fallen out - considerably more than on the forced marches to Berber in February - I think this is because this summer in the Soudan has tried everyone's health - & the men are not nearly so fit as they were then - Our marches now are seldom more than 6 or 7 miles - we march in the early morning - halt for the heat of the day - then march again in the evening - so we get over about 10 or 12 miles a day - The going is bad, mostly loose rocks or else heavy sand - in the latter case the dust raised by so large a force is simply stifling - hence an unquenchable thirst - fearful parch in the throat, sore eyes etc., etc. - All this is particularly trying - I am quite off my feed - cant eat at all - by a.m. always thirsty - My servant Gomah is kept fairly busy with my filter - my water-bottle being no sooner filled than I can empty it almost at a draught - we are more than a mile from the river here, but there is a 'khor' (or 'nullah') filled with water 400 yards - From this we may get drinking water - but have to go to the Nile to bathe - a somewhat long walk in the middle of the day - The men are kept busy with fatigues almost all day - The general (Gatacre) never gives anyone a rest - no sooner is off a trying march than out everyone has to go, some to make a Zereba, some to cut wood for cooking, some to dig trenches - some to fetch water, besides having each man to cut sticks & rig his own blanket shelter - All this is very hard work in this sun at any time - but coming on top of a weary march - strains their endurance & spirits to a very high pitch - I believe we are to halt here for a day or two - but we never know anything for certain - It is never a certainty whether you can count on a 1/2 hour to get your boots off - Just as your boots are off comes an order to move your company somewhere, because the general thinks there is better shelter there - tho' why he couldnt think of that before settling you down in a place I can't imagine - The men, who possibly have just come in off a 'fatigue' & are lying down under the shelters having a smoke have to be turned out, get dressed, pull down their shelters which they have taken an hour to construct - carry their blankets, rifles & all their odds & ends some 1/2 mile to the right or left - This is so unnecessary & harassing to men that it makes them sulky & almost insubordinate - Ruins their tempers & makes them generally sick of life - It has a somewhat similar effect, though less marked on some officers - No, as Smith said the other day "I never want to go on active service again".

Sunday, 28 Aug.

We leave here this afternoon - We are still it appears 40 miles from Omdurman - We march 8 miles a day - that brings us to Omdurman on Thursday, the 1st September & I presume we shall assault on Friday the 2nd Sept - We had a stirring sermon from Mr. Watson this morning - His text was "Fear not him who can destroy the body, but fear him who can destroy both body & soul" (is the quotation *quite* correct?) - He said that a soldier's death on the field of battle, fighting under his national flag was the grandest death possible & not to be feared by anyone - Regtal. colours, he said, are consecrated, & so may be taken to be banners blessed by God - the Union Jack, too, being composed of the Crosses of St. George, St. Andrew & St. Patrick, is essentially a holy flag - This too (the present Soudan campaign) is a crusade - & so blessed by God - It is a campaign to avenge (not revenge) the murder of one of the finest Englishmen that has lived (Gordon), who was murdered because he would not forsake his trust & those who looked to him for guidance.

It was a very fine sermon - Then uprose Gen. Gatacre & made a long & sarcastic speech on the hardships of the present Campaign - He said that a soldier was entitled to 5 days fighting every year - so far we (the 1st Brigade) had had one - so we were due 4 more - the 2nd Brigade having had none yet had a day to make up - He made some very direct hits at the Guards - he said, that this was our last Sunday before the Capture of Omdurman & also, for some of us, our last Sunday on Earth, which was decidedly cheery hearing at 6 a.m. - He said, we had 5 days of real hard work before us - then would come our reward, 2 days good fighting - He knew that officers & men would do their duty, but he expected everybody to do at least *five* times as much as their duty.

After church I took my company down to the river to bathe - It was a long walk, about 3 miles (there & back) but well worth it - I havent enjoyed anything so much as that bathe since leaving Cairo - beautifully refreshing & invigorating - Poor Spider is being left behind here, as he is sick - He is very upset about it, but he really isnt fit to do heavy work in his present state - We (the regt) are also leaving behind 68 cripples & sick whom it is useless to drag further - Of these 11 are from my Company - which reduces my strength sadly - I shall go into action at Omdurman with only about 76 rifles at my back, instead of 106 as I had at the Atbara - The heat & general discomfort yesterday were intolerable - I dont know when I have had such a miserable day - Everyone was fairly knocked up by dinner time - but we had a really good dinner wh. bucked us up considerably - & we wanted it badly - Poor Maxwell was very seedy yesterday.

Tuesday, 30 Aug.

Sunday afternoon's march was a particularly beastly one - dust, dust, dust, & a frightful thirst all the way - We got in about 9 o'clock fairly weary - & then, I had two hours patrolling, which was rather trying coming straight on the march, so it was 11 p.m. before I got anything to eat - Monday it blew a strong wind all day & the dust flew thick - we were covered with dust & had a miserable day - I hardly had the energy to wash - in fact washing was useless, as you got absolutely black & dusty the next moment - I felt rather seedy all day & put in some sleep - On Monday night it came on to rain about 2 a.m. - with a thunderstorm - I woke up & found my self swimming in a bath of water.

The rain stopped at 4 a.m. when we got up, but began again directly after, & we got wet through before starting marching at 5 a.m. - I felt wet, draggled, miserable & cold, got a cup of tea & started off - It was a cool morning, but a long weary march & we did not get in here till 12.30 - As I had nothing to eat since dinner over-night I felt somewhat weary, though some of dear Missis' savoury lozenges were sucked assiduously. We must have marched about 12 miles & on absolutely empty stomachs. I have just lunched heavily off sardines & onions & veal patté - I ate like a pig I was so famished - The 21st Lancers & the 'Gyppy' Cavalry are out in front & are, I believe, engaged with the Dervish Cavalry - We are now within about 18 miles of Omdurman & things are getting exciting - The general expects a night attack tonight, for some reason best known to himself & we are now making a strong Zereba - The whole Army Corps is packed & wedged in close - A night alarm tonight would not be exactly a joyous performance - We may get a small fight at Kerreri tomorrow, if we go on in the morning - If only the Khalifa will send his myrmidons out to fight in the open it will be grand for us - Last evening, arrived an unexpected mail - most refreshing - one letter from my darling & one envelope containing a silk handkerchief; & also a letter from my mother - The silk 'handky' I put around my neck there & then & I believe it saved me from a cold in the rain of last night - The whole immense camp is absolutely humming with business - like a swarm of bees - & I think we must be getting very near a climax at least - I can see two of the gunboats on the river alongside us now - How the Khalifa can sit calmly & await such a great show of power as we are now developing beats me - I suppose he has nowhere to fly to - so the sooner we can lay hands on him the better - why, this day next week we may be on our way back to Cairo. I shall be getting near to meeting my darling one - 'Roll on Khartoum' say I speedily.

Wednesday, 31st Aug.

We rose at 4.30 a.m. this morning & marched out of Zereba at 5.30 - It was a fairly exciting march as we could see the cavalry ahead of us having a very busy time - There seemd always a chance of coming on some of the Enemy's force - but we had no luck & found no one - after going about 5 miles we halted for about an hour & got some water for the men - The cavalry scouts reported (from the top of a high hill near us) that they could see a Dervish camp about 10 miles ahead & that there were clouds of dust rising over Omdurman, which seemed to intimate that the Dervishes were moving out towards us - we marched on again & came on to this place about another 6 miles - made a Zereba at once & threw out outposts - It is a time of bustle & excitement, as there is no doubt the Enemy is in force within some 8 or 10 miles of us - The Sirdar was himself standing at the signal station for some time with his glasses fixed to his eyes - We did not get in here much before 12 noon - very thirsty & travel worn - We had been boring our way through dense scrub jungle most of the time & it was very tiring marching - I had been told by the Colonel it was only a 5 mile march, so expected to be in by 8 a.m. & only took 1/2 a biscuit in my haversack & 1/2 a water-bottle - It was about 1.30 p.m. before we got anything to eat or drink - however we are near the end of it now - & if we can get a decent fight in the next day or two nobody will mind the fatigue & discomfort - We have no shade in our camp to day & I am now sitting, writing this, under a low mimosa bush with a blanket thrown over it for shade - The gunboats have been shelling the Dervishes on about 5 miles ahead & the sound of their guns has been very irritating, as if they shell too vigorously, the Enemy will have cleared before we arrive - The latest 'shave' is that the Khalifa is sallying forth with his myrmidons to wipe us out - only wish he would come on - it would save us a lot of trouble - I told Gomah to-day that we should fight tomorrow - so he said "I hope we win, Sir" - It was quite a new aspect of the case to me - as the mere idea of not wiping out the Khalifa's hordes, has, I shd. fancy, seemed to no one in our force - our only anxiety has been as to whether he will stay to fight us - I heard one of our men to-day on the march, say, as he was forcing his weary way through a particularly thorny mimosa bush "Oh Khalifa! you have a deal to answer for! Wait till I get a-hold of you." We are all simply praying for an early fight & an early finish - The general discomfort & fatigue of this Campaign have been a good deal worse than I, or anyone else, ever anticipated.

The two most trying things are the sun & the dust - the accompaniment of which is a terrible & un-slakeable thirst - when you get your food you eat it ravenously like a beast - I manage to get a shave most days, but often dont get my boots off at all, all day - A bath, you may snatch time for once in 3 or 4 days - I saw Mahomet to-day wheeling a blue bicycle behind us - It looked very out of place in the desert - *I got a cold whiskey & Rosbach this afternoon from Hamilton of the 14th Soudanese* - we have to man the Zereba at 5.30 p.m. now & remain at our arms all night - though I dont think there is the ghost of a chance of an attack - dont know yet when we move on again - Probably the small hours of tomorrow morn. I think we shall fight on Friday the 2nd Sept.

I lost my watch yesterday - sickening - it must have dropped out of my haversack on the march.

DIARY

Monday, 5th September
CAMP OMDURMAN.

I resume my diary after some important & very busy days - The big battle is over - Omdurman is in our hands & we are on the eve of returning to Cairo.

To resume where I left off last Wednesday - Wednesday night was a sickener - It rained nearly the whole night heavily & what was worse, continued raining when we got up (off the ground) & "stood to arms" at 4 a.m. on Thursday morning (the 1st Sept) - For two solid hours (from 4 till 6 a.m.) we stood, in pitch darkness with the rain coming down & a damp wind blowing - I have seldom felt so miserable & cold & wet - At 6 a.m. the welcome order to move on south came & off we went - We marched out of Zereba with the cavalry & horse artillery ahead of us - The rain ceased about 7 a.m. & our spirits rose - We marched through a deserted & burning village - apparently only recently evacuated - with beds, cooking pots & household goods left broadcast everywhere - When we approached the ridge of hills by Kerreri, we could hear the distant fire of heavy guns - It was surprising what an effect it had - The columns of men, which had been dragging their way somewhat wearily through dense scrub - heavy sand & rocky wastes & were showing signs of fatigue, at once became re-animated & stepped out briskly to see what was going on in front - When at last we gained the ridge line we got a view right up the river - Far ahead of us - some 5 or 6 miles up the river we could see a long line of gunboats (I counted nine, through my glasses) standing along the bank & apparently shelling the Omdurman forts - They were too far off for us to see much - but the outskirts of Omdurman were now in sight & we all knew we were nearing our journey's end - At about 12 noon we halted in a village on Kerreri Plain - 'Zerebad' ourselves & were preparing to get some much needed food (and drink) as we had been up since 4 a.m. & marched on a cup of tea & a biscuit - when orders came to be ready to move at 1/2 an hour's notice - It then became known that a large Dervish force had been seen by the cavalry vedettes from a hill in front of us - This force was leaving Omdurman & marching towards us - It was reported to be an enormous army - This news appeared too good to be true, as I dont think anyone thought the Dervishes would give up their Stronghold at O. & come & fight us in the open - We had time for a hasty meal, & then the "fall in" sounded & off we moved again - We did not go far, only about 800 yards into the desert & then formed up in a long semi-circle covering the river &

CAPTAIN ALFRED EDWARD HUBBARD

facing west - here we formed line & halted.

It appeared a somewhat thin line, but no one had any fear of the thin red line of British bayonets being pierced by any rush, however strong, of the enemy - though had the black or Egyptian line been pierced, it would have been equally bad for us, as we should have been outflanked - It appeared to me a too extended position, though offering a great field of fire - The perimeter of the arc on which we were extended, from the left of the 2nd British Brigade to the right of the extreme Soudanese Brigade, must have been 2 miles - We waited patiently for the Enemy, till 4 p.m. - then 'piled' arms & returned to the village & dragged out our Zereba - We also got tea out & finally had everything brought out, mess stuff, our own baggage &c. & had it placed behind our line - We had dinner at 7 p.m. - & lights were extinguished at 8.15 p.m. A night attack was expected by some people - Luckily, it was a bright moonlight night, & our sentries had a view over a flat sandy plain, covered here & there with low scrubby bushes, so it was impossible to be taken absolutely by surprise - (Had the Enemy attacked by night - in the enormous numbers that attacked us next morning, no doubt we should have had a very bad time, as we couldn't have opened effective fire on them before they got to 300 yards range). I lay down in the moonlight just behind my company & was almost immediately fast asleep - & so sound asleep too that I heard nothing, though it appears the Enemy were firing guns & rifles from the top of a hill about a mile in front of us - I slept till midnight, when the Colonel awoke me, & gave me an order to have the "magazines of my men's rifles changed" as, so he said, information had arrived, that an attack would take place about 3.30 a.m. I obeyed the order - & again lay down & slept soundly til reveille sounded at 4 a.m. (so apparently there was no attack at 3.30 - or anyhow I slept through it). I had thought that on the eve of a battle, I shd. be too excited to sleep - but both at the Atbara & here, I slept, if possible sounder than usual - I think this was probably due to the excessive fatigue we had undergone & want of sleep - I have found no difficulty in sleeping, but a great difficulty in keeping awake ever since active operations commenced - We "stood to arms" at 4 a.m. & watched anxiously for the Enemy - Personally, I was still sceptical of their coming to attack, but at about 5.40 a.m. my doubts were set at rest - Against the far range of hills, straight in front of us & about 3 miles off, could be seen (through the glasses) lines of high banners; they appeared to be everywhere - Far as the eye could see, were banners & behind them moving masses of men.

(Read here account of the Battle of Omdurman, page 67)

It looked as if the entire world was coming on against us - The spectacle of these advancing armies, the whole armed strength of the Khalifa (as afterwards turned out to be the case) - a kind of gigantic & final effort of Mahommedan fanaticism - an attempt to crush us by sheer weight of numbers, - this spectacle was the most magnificent & imposing I have ever seen (or am likely to see) - Anything like these moving hordes, over every hill & valley within sight, was a spectacle such as I had never conceived.

My description of the battle must wait till I have more leisure, going down stream - as there are so many other things to be put in, which I may forget - The battle I am not likely to forget - so I omit the battle to chronicle our entry into Omdurman on the evening of the 2nd Sept & my visit to KHARTOUM (yesterday).

Well, we marched into Omdurman on about 7 p.m., frightfully tired & done up - Halted in a fairly open square & threw ourselves down - dead beat - I was too tired to care whether I had anything to eat or not & almost too stiff & tired to sleep - but Mainwaring gave me a cup of hot beef tea with a dash of whiskey in it & this revived me somewhat - We had had an awful day (for fatigue & heat) as you will see when you read the account of the battle & our subsequent movements - We couldnt see much of Omdurman as we marched in, - but it appeared merely a long straggling mud village with flat roofed houses, & endless lines of mud walls - Reveille sounded at 5 a.m. on Sept. 3rd & we woke & looked around us - We were in a court-yard - & about a mile ahead of us rose the sadly shattered "Tomb of the Mahdi" - It had been shelled by the Howitzer battery the previous day & looked very sorry for itself - We breakfasted at 8 a.m. & at 9 a.m. fell in & marched back, out of the town again & took up our present position in bivouac on the river bank - The whole British division is here, under blanket shelters & thank goodness we are right on the river, & water can be got easily - On the afternoon of the 3rd were a series of funerals - those who had died of wounds since the battle - We most of us went out of respect for poor Caldicott (of the Warwicks) whom we all knew well.

On Sunday morning, the 4th Sept. there was held a memorial service at Khartoum - Only a limited number of officers & men from each regiment were allowed to go - I was, luckily, of the number - It took us about 2 hours in a gun-boat to get there - We passed all along the river front of Omdurman & got a very good view of the town - the shattered tomb of the Mahdi - & the breaches made for us by the Howitzers in the big wall of Omdurman - These breaches were made for the infantry (that's us) to rush through & storm the Khalifa's stronghold - (I'm glad we had not to do this, as they were poor breaches - not half wide enough - We might have scrambled in 4 a-breast).

We reached Khartoum about 11 a.m. & disembarked.

(*An account of Khartoum will follow later, page 71)

The spectacle must have been very imposing, as seen from the gun-boats - but as for us, taking part in it, we could see nothing - We could hear the "Dead March" being played, the gun-boats firing a salute, while we presented arms - Then followed a rather plaintive Xmas Carol - beautifully rendered & sounding very mournful - though a Xmas Carol hardly seems appropriate to a funeral. *[I saw in a paper account (afterwards) that Gordon's favourite hymn "Abide with me" was played - I dont recollect hearing it - Can I have mistaken it for a Xmas hymn? Possibly - but not probable.]*

I believe the Presbyterian minister was reading the funeral service, but we couldnt hear it. Then the Highland pipers played a "Lament". The British & Khedivial flags were hoisted on Gordon's house *simultaneously* & a guard of honour of Soudanese was mounted - *[This makes my bet with Cottingham a drawn one - Just as well as you cant procure a bottle of 'fizz' here - I bet Cottingham a bottle of Champagne that the British flag would go up before or above the Khedive's flag.]*

Exactly in front of where *we* stood for the ceremony, was the ruined stair-way on which Gordon was massacred - We were allowed about 1/2 an hour for sight-seeing & I took a dozen photographs.

Then embarked for return to Omdurman - I was very tired when I got back at 1 p.m. & after a light lunch (no appetite) slept for a couple of hours - In fact I was hopelessly weary - from the heat & worry & probably the reaction from the fatigues of the past two or three weeks - This morning, at 5.30 a.m. the whole British Division paraded for a formal march through Omdurman - We marched to the Mahdi's tomb & round a part of the big wall - The walk was fairly interesting, though the sights & smells were appaling - We got a good idea of the power of "Lyddite" as an explosive - Those Howitzer shells were most destructive - I took a few snap-shots with the Small Camera - but it was impossible to see, or do much on the march - I think the march was merely intended as a display of power for the benefit of the inhabitants - Omdurman stinks of dead donkeys! Some of the Warwicks have already embarked for Cairo & they say that we are the next to go - whether we go to-night or tomorrow depends on the movements of the gun-boats - I am feeling very fit & strong again to-day, after a most refreshing night's sleep - It hardly seems worth while posting a letter now, if we start for Cairo at once.

Gordon Memorial Service at Khartoum.

Having brought this diary up to date, I conclude for the present, somewhat weary with much writing.

By the way, I ate my plum-pudding last night - It came all the way from Cairo to be eaten here, so has fulfilled its destiny - & it was a very good plum pudding too! This plum pudding left Cairo on Jan. 29th.

Wednesday, 7 Sept.

(On board a gyassa.) We got away north yesterday morning - that's to say we embarked in the morning but did not sail till 1 p.m. - They have crowded us up awfully - In this gyassa, there are the whole of D Company (my company) with 2 officers & 3 native servants - We have come down stream in the most happy-go-lucky way turning round & round, & drifting, sometime head-on, but usually broad side or tail-end on - We have collided with other barges many times & have narrowly escaped being sunk & having to swim for it - Last night, we had to tie-up early, as a tremendous squall came on & the river got just like a rough sea - with small choppy waves - We tied up & remained stationary till 12 midnight when the moon rose - We had some slight rain & got very damp - We got some hot tea & Greatwood & I dined off a tin of sardines & some biscuits - The spot where we halted was very low lying, damp & feverish & I took some quinine as a precaution - slept for an hour & woke up feeling very damp & miserable - We drifted down by moonlight, in a rather precarious state & finally reached Royan Island about 10 a.m. We stayed there two hours & got some breakfast cooked (bacon, biscuits & tea) picked up a mail (*four* letters from sweetheart) & started away about noon - I found time to go & see 'Spider' in hospital - He still looks very seedy & pulled down & is most disappointed at missing the battle - We have just come through the Shabluka pass.

It has been a most dangerous passage, as the boatmen appear to have absolutely no control over the boat - I forgot to say, the battalion is packed in 12 'gyassas' or sailing barges - & these have drifted with the current - in the most hopelessly random fashion & collisions have been the order of the day.

*[*I have heard now (Sept. 20th) that 3 gyassas containing Guardsmen upset here - no lives were lost - but all their rifles, equipment - loot & baggage was lost - They then had to march 12 miles over the rocks to their next halt - So we really were very fortunate.]*

How we have all come through the rapids safe is more than I can say - Shabluka pass is a couple of high hills with a rapid river flowing through & endless eddies & currents.

We expect to get to Nasri Island this afternoon & (with luck) Dakhila tomorrow evening - but - I have my doubts. It is impossible to sit with comfort on this boat, so tightly packed in is she - 89 men on board not counting the crew & a lie down or back rest is impossible - However, we are on our way to Cairo - & I, to my dear sweetheart, so what matter.

Thursday, 8 Sept.

We did not reach Nasri Island yesterday afternoon after all but sailed on with various fortune till dark set in (about 7.15 p.m.) Then the welcome sound of the "assurance" from the C.O.'s boat, which was leading the van, announced a halt for the night - It rained slightly as we started dinner, but then stopped - Greatwood & I got a dry bed on top of an old disused gangway planking - We got a good night's rest & started again at 5 a.m. this morning - reached Nasri Island about 8.30. Had breakfast there & got some more stores & drink out of one of the mess cases - Also had a much needed shower & wash & then on board once more - All the battalions great-coats wh. were sent to Nasri Island have apparently been lost - also a sock containing some odds & ends of mine - nothing valuable or even particularly useful either - I had to speak rather severely to our head boat-man to-day - He has no more idea of sailing a boat than a cat & is perpetually getting hung up in an island or fouling another boat - I told that if we were the last boat in tonight I shd. beat him - so he offered to jump over board & leave the boat - but an offer on my part, in that event, to shoot him, made him change his mind - We are running fairly well now before a strong breeze & ought to reach Atbara Camp tomorrow evening, with luck.

Friday, 9 Sept.

To-day has been a terrible day - all day drifting, drifting, drifting, at rather a slower rate than the stream itself - Anything like the dreary monotony I have never experienced - not a breath of wind, millions of persistent flies & a terrible hot stifling day - No halt for a run ashore to stretch one's legs even - We were nearly wrecked last night when we made for the bank to tie up as our boat-man with sails set & a strong current went stem-on for a palm tree on the bank & ran us straight into it 10 miles an hour - The crash was awful & nearly threw us all overboard - We landed in pitch dark, from a slippery gangway - Then the C.O. sounded the officer's call some miles off in the darkness - I've never had such a walk - through thorn bushes - breast high - tumbling about in the dark - arrived - we all received a severe wigging for not keeping the 12 boats together - a physical impossibility - I fear we shant reach Dakhila tonight - got some sausages cooked in the little galley at end of barge - These & some tea have been our sole refreshment today - Hope to get a little dinner when we halt for the night.

Cairo [Thursday,] 15 Sept.

We reached here this morning & got under canvas at the Polygon Camp - Shant write up my back diary - The gyassa voyage I have touched on at great length - The rest of the journey, by rail & steam-boat was prosaic in comparison - We are safe & sound in Cairo - & I suppose there will be an onslaught on the canteen beer by thirsty souls who have been looking forward to their first go at it for some nine months.

• • • • •

DIARY

The Battle of Omdurman
fought on Friday, Sept. 2nd 1898

This battle, is, I shd. imagine one of the most difficult to write an account of - partly because of the numbers engaged on both sides, & partly because of the nature of the ground, wh. made it impossible to see what was going on except in your own immediate front - The difficulty of writing an accurate account is proved, to anyone present at the battle, by reading the newspaper accounts, which are in every case, full of gross mistakes & inaccuracies - I propose merely to say what I saw myself, - so that my account will deal entirely of the part taken by my own regiment, & the 1st British brigade.

To resume where I left off in my diary account - *We* sighted the Khalifa's Army at about 5.40 a.m. - though of course the cavalry must have seen them considerably earlier - In the rough sketch on the opposite page [not included] I have shown the British lines with the Nile behind them - The arrow heads, to the front & flanks show the advance of the Dervishes - When we first saw the long lines of Dervish banners they must have been 2 miles away - The entire length of front occupied by the advancing force must have been 3 to 3 1/2 miles - As they came on there was a murmur like the sound of the sea, which was, I presume their battle cry - In the sketch A marks the 2nd British brigade - B marks our's, the 1st British brigade - C marks the position of the Lincoln Regt - on the extreme right of the British troops - D & E show the line extended by the Black & Egyptian brigades.

With long range volleys at 1400 yards - The firing all along our line was now continuous & rapid & the ground in front began to get dotted with white clad corpses - The Dervish rifle men began to fire before they were properly within the range - but soon, as they crept up, the well remembered sounds, heard at the Atbara, began - the faint whistle of bullets, & the spurts of sand which flew up as they struck the earth - Two or three men of my regiment were quickly down & being carried by the stretcher-bearers to the rear - others too, were quickly hit (six men in my own Company).

The first man hit in my company had a bullet smack into his haversack - the bullet finally burying itself in his prayer-book - from which I extracted it myself - still warm.

One bullet (which I have got) passed under my foot, grazing the sole & buried itself in the sand - I picked it up still warm & put it in my pocket - & we saw that nearly all these losses were caused by a group of Dervish riflemen lying down in a little sandy hollow, about 700 yards

CAPTAIN ALFRED EDWARD HUBBARD

off, & quietly popping at us - Fire was brought to bear on them from our rifles & also some Maxims & after a short time their fire ceased - There was a great fusilade for a few minutes from a party who had come round "Signal hill" & were advancing on the Warwicks & Grenadier Guards - a tremendous fire was opened on them & they quickly were silenced & very few got back round the hill again - I could see lines upon lines of white figures stretched out dead or dying & I also saw dead & wounded being carried away by their retiring comrades - A small body (about 200 men) of Baggara horsemen with desperate gallantry endeavoured to charge the whole British Brigade. It was a splendid sight to see them coming along - & we all rather hoped (or I did) that some would reach our bayonets, but they simply withered under the terrible fire of our rifles & the small handful remaining wheeled at about 600 yards from our line, & endeavoured to retire - I saw men rolling out of their saddles & riderless horses everywhere - and I dont believe six of the whole lot got back again - The pluck & bravery shown by the Dervishes, under an absolutely appaling hail of bullets, was most marked throughout the day - To our extreme right - where the Camel Corps & an Egyptian battery had taken up their position, on Kerreri Ridge - was developed a Dervish flank attack (marked in sketch) - so great were their numbers that the Camel Corps & artillery had to retire, the artillery losing a gun or two - Guns were recovered later in the day - as the teams were all shot, & now, in place of our own men, was seen a Dervish host, led by a Green standard, coming over the ridge & threatening our right - as they came round the ridge, however, they came under the fire of one of our gun-boats (the *Malik* I think) & so accurate was the shell-fire from the gun-boat that this green-standard led host, could not stick it, but retired slowly & in perfect order back round the hill with shot & shell dropping thick among them - *[There were counted on this ridge alone 1185 dead bodies by Burrowes (of ours) two days after the battle - This same green flag lot took part in the 2nd & subsequent attack on MacDonald's & Maxwell's brigades.]*

The first phase of the battle was now over - Nothing was in front of us except dead & dying & some small scattered fugitive parties - The attack was beaten off all along the line - We now began to count up our losses - load up ammunition mules & prepare to move forward.

One of the chief incidents of the first phase was the behaviour of a small party of Dervishes, headed by a white banner - I suppose that banner had, at one time led an army - but when I particularly noticed it, there were about a dozen men round it only & they came slowly &

deliberately on straight for us - As one man dropped another took on the banner - until only 3 were left - still on they came & then only 1 man was left - & he staggered slowly on, spear in one hand & banner in the other - no one could hit him though thousands of bullets were directed at him - At last he dropped, about 500 yards from our line, but as he fell, he planted his white standard in the ground & there it remained until we moved on later.

[This standard we have got - It was presented to us by the 10th Soudanese for coming to their assistance later in the day - They picked it up when we advanced out of the Zereba - We had no time for looting on the field.]

Well, the first phase being over, we got orders to advance on Omdurman - The Sirdar's intention being to block the road to Omdurman & then march on & get there before the routed Enemy could get there - The 2nd British brigade led & we followed in attack formation - The wounded Dervishes scattered around began 'sniping' at us & there were some very ominous whistles of bullets over & through our ranks, but I dont think anyone was hit - We disregarded this & marched on round the shoulder of "Signal hill" (see sketch) - We had gone about 1 1/4 miles when the solitary sniping shots gave place to quick & incessant firing & our brigade was halted - We then heard that a fresh & untouched Dervish Army had nipped round Kerreri Hill & fallen upon McDonald's & Maxwell's brigades who were doing rear guard - An excited staff officer came riding furiously to Gen. Wauchope & we got orders to go back to assist the black troops - Back we started - It was now about 10 o'clock & getting very hot - Faster & faster grew the pace, as we were urged on & we broke into double time as messages reached us that the blacks were being hard pushed - We could see nothing at first for the blinding sand, but the noise of firing now became tremendous - Such a din I've never heard. The first part was child's play to it - Every gun & maxim & rifle seemed to have gone mad with excitement. Up "Signal hill" we could see the Soudanese scrambling - firing as they went & faster & faster roared the guns - At last, we rounded the shoulder & got a peep into the valley - The other three regiments of our brigade were swung to the left & my regiment was sent on (at the 'double') to prolong the Soudanese line to the right - We now came under fire again - & about 1/2 a dozen men in E Company, alongside mine, went down in about 3 minutes - At last we reached our place & found ourselves shoulder to shoulder with our old comrades the 10th Soudanese - They cheered us as we came up, as their ammunition was nearly done & the Dervish spearmen were getting perilous close - We opened fire as soon as were were in our places & in about 10 minutes, there were no Enemy left.

[The Soudanese are most indifferent rifle-shots - They blaze away merrily but seldom hit anything except by accident.]

The Soudanese now began "charging" & away on our left, where there was a confused mass of standards, charging cavalry & cheering Soudanese, we could hear the lively strains of the 'Charge' - The Colonel now rode out in front to lead us in a charge over the demoralized enemy & we had just started when up came our Brigade Major, very excited, & said "Stop sir! Stop! General's orders no British troops to charge!" Why couldnt the beast let us alone? So we perforce, halted sulkily & watched the Soudanese going away from us - & joining that confused mob away, far away, to our left - Gradually the firing died down - & we sat down where we were & (I regret to say) indulged in a little bad language - We thought we were losing the final & culminating bout - but as it turned out, we were the only British regiment that got a 'look in' at all, that second phase - We halted about 1/2 an hour in the midst of dead & dying Dervishes - (Grand fellows they were too - far finer men than I saw at the Atbara.) Rifles & spears were lying about everywhere - I picked up a very neat & unhealthy looking spear, of the fish pattern & a very business-like dagger - We then had to rejoin our brigade which we could see a long way to our left - The brigade then started marching again for Omdurman, only this time round the *far* side of "Signal hill" - We were all getting a bit weary by now - but on we went & we knew we had a good six miles in front of us to Omdurman - When we had gone about 2 miles, it was discovered that some stretcher-bearers belonging to my regiment who had carried some wounded back had not rejoined - The general was in an awful rage & ordered us to halt where we were till they were found - so down we plumped in the sand while the rest of the brigade went on - Past us too, by turns came Soudanese & Egyptian brigades & hundreds & hundreds of captive Dervishes - *[We must have sat in that pitiless sun in the open desert, miles from the river, for about 4 hours! from noon till 4 p.m. - How any general in his senses could do this I cant understand - Two men to my knowledge got sun-stroke - one of them died next day].*

We were tired, hungry & parched with thirst & the sun fairly blistered us - a Soudanese regiment sent us some camel-tanks containing lukewarm Nile water - otherwise we should have died - (I drank pints of the nauseous stuff) at last a staff officer galloped out & told us to march on - gladly enough we rose & resumed our weary march - *[Our missing men had done what any man of sense would have guessed they had done -*

Finding they were separated from us, they made for the river, got on a gun-boat & steamed up to Omdurman - (I told the C.O. they had probably done this) (The General (Wauchope) was put out about something when he gave us this absurd order.]

We reached our halting place about 5 o'clock & as the jaded men threw off their accoutrements - we were told to be ready to move on again in 1/2 an hour - (The other regiments had been here 2 hours) We just had time to fill our water bottles & get a bite of bully-beef - when we had to start again - We were now on the outskirts of Omdurman - As we marched in the 10th Soudanese halted ahead of us & presented us with the White Standard I have alluded to - They cheered us frantically too & struck up "The Lincolnshire Poacher" - It was quite refreshing after the toils of the day & so to the strains of our regimental march & with the White Standard flying side by side with our own regimental flag, in front of us, the battalion stepped along gaily once more & the toils of the day were forgotten (for the time). We did not know quite what had happened in Omdurman - though we heard the Khalifa with 10,000 of his black body-guard was inside his big wall - (This turned out to be false) - but on we marched right into the centre of the city - we could hear desultory shots & an occasional big gun ahead of us, which seemed to say all was not yet over - At last, just as it was dark, must have been about 6.30, came the welcome halt - & we halted (we did really) piled arms & threw ourselves on the ground - I have seldom been so absolutely 'cooked' - I had a head-ache from the sun & was weary from want of food - (My diary now takes up the story).

Khartoum

I attended the Gordon memorial service (as mentioned in my diary) on Sunday Sept. 4th - I have described the service, so will merely give a short description of the Residency - The Palace (or Residency) stands facing the river & is built on a stone platform with landing steps down to the water - The building stands about 10 yards back from the water - It is a long, stone built building, with big windows - & in the centre is a court yard with an empty tank in its centre - The roof is completely gone & the steps leading to the roof on the north side, where Gordon used to stand to look for the British aid that never came, is a mass of crumbling ruins - On this side, we found a small cannon, I presume one of Gordon's - Opening up from the central Court yard, on the south side was a lovely garden - very much over-grown & neglected of course - but so cool & refreshing & green to look at - after the glare & sand of the

CAPTAIN ALFRED EDWARD HUBBARD

desert - There was a smell of oranges & pomegranate blossoms - There were fig trees & tamarinds & bananas - There was also a vegetable garden - The outhouses, for servants I suppose, were round the north & west sides of the quadrangle & outside - The whole place was terribly tumble-down & dilapidated - There were numerous other ruins - of inferior house - & among the palm trees about 1/4 a mile from the house, what looked like a ruined Church - We had only about 20 minutes or so to look round us.

Final remarks on the Campaign

Taken from start to finish, I do not suppose that a better organized campaign has ever been known in the history of warfare - Everything was carefully thought out & every plan laid with the greatest prudence & forethought & with consummate skill - There was never the slightest approach to a hitch anywhere - The gun-boats moved up parallel & in touch with the land forces - When we slept in Zereba at night, the search-lights of the gun-boats lit up the surrounding darkeness for us (They only did this the last night or two before the battle - but that's all we wanted).

The search-lights were indifferent of their kind - The whole final advance could only be likened to the precise & methodical movement of some enormous machine, which approached gradually, silently & remorselessly, lessening the distance daily till near enough to strike a paralyzing blow - (If I had been the Khalifa, the mere sight of the relentless & Nemesis-like steady advance, would have been too much for my nerves long before Sept. 2nd) - We were never short of food & provisions - The men had extra delicacies, such as ham & bacon & issues of Rum continually - & the baggage convoy was always up with the column.

These things speak for themselves - It is not for me to praise the Sirdar, but I suppose, in the world, there are few men gifted with such tireless energy, unflinching determination & inflexible purpose, combined with a marvellous memory & tremendous brain power - I think every man who has followed his flag in this last campaign would be proud & eager to follow him blindly across the breadth of Africa, if necessity arose - (which by the way, I hope it wont.)

All this sound rather 'bunkum' - but to put it tersely, the Sirdar is an absolute marvel - He knows & goes into every little detail of all the work carried on by his subordinates - His ADC told me the S. never makes a note of & never forgets anything - When we started for the final advance - there was no question in anyone's mind of the ultimate issue - it was a mere question of time.

What a reception he will get when he goes home - & he deserves it.

"BUS"
FINISH.

CHAPTER THREE:
The Omdurman Campaign

Lieutenant Hamilton Hodgson
of the Lincolnshire Regiment

Letter to his Father.

[Jean S. and Frederic A. Sharf Collection]

INTRODUCTORY NOTES

Hamilton Hodgson was born on 6 July, 1874 and was comissioned into the Lincolnshire Regiment on 20 February, 1895. He served with the regiment in the Sudanese Campaign in 1898 and was present at the battle of Omdurman. He was promoted Captain in 1904 and went on half-pay in 1909. He served in the Egyptian Army from October 1899 until around 1910, achieving the rank of Bimbashi. He volunteered for service in World War I and was killed at Achi Baba, Gallipoli on 6 May, 1915 while attached to the Hampshire Regiment.

His account of Omdurman appears in a letter sent by him to his father, Joseph Hamilton Hodgson, who was at the time a Lieutenant-Colonel in the British Army. J. H. Hodgson had at least one typed copy prepared, of which this may be the only copy, or there may well have been a carbon of this copy. At the top of this copy, he wrote:

"True Copy of What H. Hodgson Wrote. J. H. Hodgson"

Since this account was published in 1898 by several provincial newspapers[1], it is likely that this typed account was the source for those publications. The fact that this letter shows signs of having been folded and re-folded a number of times, might confirm this.

At some point, this letter came into the possession of Ernest J. Martin, and it is likely that he made the manuscript corrections on the typed copy. He then published his edited version in the *Journal of the Society for Army Historical Research* Volume XXI, Summer 1942, No. 82, pages 70-82. There are a few places where Martin inaccurately transcribed the typed copy, and other places where he altered words slightly so that it became more readable. These inaccuracies have been corrected in the current transcription.

[1] *The Grantham Journal*, 1 October, 1898; *The Reading Mercury* 15 October, 1898, and on the same date in the *Oxford Gazette*, Newbury *Herald*, and *Berks County Paper*. We are grateful to Professor Edward Spiers for this information.

Oh first, we have passed the Dervish forts on the river here, built to stop the gun boats.

If they had stuck to them and made a defence here I don't think it would have done them any good. For as far as I could see, they were badly planned, same as those at Omdurman; and I can't imagine a Dervish in defence, they were utterly fearless advancing under fire but quite useless when they tried to defend a khor against our last advance.

August 25th. -

We left Wad Hamed at 4.30 on 25th August. Did about seven miles or so over very sandy ground, and after dark made a sudden turn towards the river, with the result that our camels and the Warwicks—at least the part of them carrying the camp kettles—got lost, went on past us and struck the river about five miles ahead where we found them next morning. The men had no tea that night or next morning.

August 26th. -

Next march we came across camp kettles; they had tea ready for us, but the General would not let us stop, as he had arranged for tea to be served in our camp two miles on where we joined the 2nd Brigade again. Very good shady camp; arrived about 9.30 breakfast and sleep until 2, bath, lunch at 2.30, and parade at 3.30 p.m. The best camp we had, I think.

The whole division paraded, and that combined with the fact that the going was very bad—rising ground with loose stones, and constantly passing dry water-courses, with tussocks of rough grass and stunted mimosa and other thorny bushes, the intervening part being sometimes a mile, sometimes a few hundred yards, of loose shingle—made the march very trying and tiring; also we had that night to depend on the water carried in camel tanks, so most of us were carrying extra by way of a water bottle. After the 3rd halt some one shouted out it was all down hill the rest of the way which was cheering, and the drums came across some better ground and started playing; in fact played us into camp. I don't think I ever appreciated drums more, they got a very long step, and soon the whole brigade were going to the step. After each tune they were applauded and cheered vociferously. Dr. Hill our show drummer, who prides himself on having a black mark the size of a penny on the centre of the vellum, got his chance occasionally with a side drum solo. Poor chap, his drumming days are over, as he is wounded in his wrist—bullet came through drum first.

Well, our bivouac was a level piece of hard sand about a mile square, and about a mile from the hills lining the river (Shabluka pass).

These hills are dark red rock and piled up most fantastically—volcanic origin, I should say. I was caught for fatigue that night, only got off about 10 for dinner, and then found myself on patrol from 1 to 3.

Reveille at 3.45—began to find me thinking myself hardly used. We were due to go about 4 miles nominally, and started at 4.30; but once we got off our bivouac the sand was very heavy and we certainly went four miles before reaching the blacks' camp, when we had to go about another 1 1/2 miles to our camp which the native troops had partially put zareeba round for us - I must own I was fairly done. This was camp Jebel Royan.

August 28th. - Sunday.

A most extraordinary conical hill here on the right bank just at the head of the cataract, which is Jebel Royan—Jebel means hill or desert indiscriminately as far as I can see. We had service for whole division, and Watson gave us a most excellent sermon. Gatacre also got on his legs and addressed us; but as he turned himself entirely to the Guards and what was heard was twaddle, no one was sorry when he finished.

I don't know much about that compass. I slept fairly solid till we paraded at four, the blacks had marched that morning.

Level going, very dusty. The drums got cheered again for their playing. We got in at 8 where we were packed rather closely in columns of double companies half a mile from the river. We did not Zareeba that night, but did so first thing on Monday.

A dust storm started at dawn and continued till about 2 p.m., when it got very hot and promised rain, and sure enough we got about two hours steady down-pour between 2 and 4 Tuesday morning.

August 30th. - Tuesday.

Marched at five. I don't know how the camels were loaded, the blankets must have been very wet and over-weight. We marched ourselves dry; it kept very dull and overcast and was cool. About 8 o'clock we had another shower, and after that they decided to prolong the march, as it was such a favourable day. Any way, we went on until we passed a village which was still burning. The gun-boats shelled it or may have been set on fire by the Dervishes themselves. Everything in confusion. Angareebs (beds) thrown down and a few dead animals. The Lancers caught a couple of men. We were rather a long time settling at the next camp, but finally got fairly comfortable.

Cavalry report Dervishes in another village near Kerreri. A big fire about six miles away, at night.

Wednesday, [Aug. 31] March uneventful.

Thursday, [Sept.] 1st. We fully expected to start partridge shooting, as the saying goes—the Lancers did come across some of their patrols, and cavalry, and had a rather good day. Rained at 2 a.m. so the month started wet.

It continued so until after we moved, about 6.30; it was dark and rather uncomfortable. There was a deep khor to pass which had a little water in it from rain, which delayed the march frightfully. At 10 we passed a village where some Dervishes had been the previous night, and we heard the gun-boats firing in the distance, but all our view was blocked by the ridge, and the 2nd Brigade.

At last we got on the ridge and saw river and some mud forts along it on our left, and a village with chief houses Zareebaed to our left front, most awfully disappointing after all we heard of Kerreri we quite expected to see some Dervishes. The gun-boats had gone some miles further.

We got to village, and at once started making a Zareeba, being in very close order.

The Native Brigades or Rifles and 2nd near river; this was about 11 or 12. I had gone to river with party to fill bottles and on returning found everything on the move; at 1 o'clock we fell in and took up a line about half a mile to the front; we were all rather disgusted, as we had just settled and finished transferring Zareeba from round huts to where it was required. The blacks were trenching as there was no wood. We had no idea why we moved and lay out in the sun until 3.30 or so; then we were told to leave one company under arms, pile the rest, and drag out Zareeba and replace in our new line, and bring out men's tea, etc.

Tatchell went sick, completely knocked up; he had had very hard work with mules last few days, and had, I believe, been suffering from diahaerrea [sic] for some time past. Plunkett took Tatchell's job; glad I did not, as it turned out he was stuck in rear of battle.

We knew absolutely nothing of what was going on. In fact, I was seriously thinking of sending up bed with kit to the new pitch, my servant managed to get bed from village, in fact several times he looted me one and got it carried into camp. But finding Fitz-Cox busy signalling I got news from him at a slack time. He had post established out on high point in front and he said he had barely got his men there about 12 o'clock when they sent news that men were swarming out of Omdurman and forming up.

At this, Sirdar did not budge, but sat and ate his lunch and told Fitz to find out what Cavalry and gun boats were doing. Fitz said he was in a mortal funk lest the sun should go out and stop the helio. It did not! The last news he got before retreat was, that there were two huge armies in front with cavalry. And just as light was dying we saw a skirmish between these and the last of the Lancers; so that is how we finished the 1st.

All inside Zareeba. I was not on patrol and had a fair rest. There was a good moon.

[Friday,] September 2nd. -

3.30. Word was passed to stand to arms.

4 Reveille sounded.

5 o'clock dawn, some cavalry sent out along the river and we heard gun-boats firing on far side of ridge.

6.15. Dervish army got in view, their main body was two miles away with Standards, Colours and horsemen and cavalry galloping about the front and whole lot coming on shouting and firing in the air.

6.30. A body appeared over ridge at our left front, our Cavalry got in to Zareeba on our left. The field guns had the range and slated them most fearfully, so that many sheered off into a hollow to our right. This main body was advancing more to our right and a huge mass were right over the hills behind them again.

6.45. We opened fire with rifles just then, the Kalifa's black flag and a mass appeared round the cliff side just in front of us.

We blazed away into the brown of them at long ranges for about 20 minutes, when fire slackened, as they were awfully decimated and scattered.

One tribe of these bearing a yellow flag, got it down within 300 yards of our Zareeba just opposite to C.

I was watching them occasionally with my glasses. I never could have imagined anything so cool and brave as those men were, especially one, the last but one to fall; he had been wounded in his arm and limped, yet his ambition was to get the flag, and he got it and carried it some 50 yards at a sort of slow trot, when he was shot, and as he fell his companion took it and came on a few yards only, when he fell, with the flag. I was sorry for these men; they were simply wiped out.

7.15. Fire had ceased on our front.

Nothing could live under the fire, so the Dervishes gradually broke up and scattered towards our right. I dont suppose the majority ever got within 1,000 yards except the lot who came to die. Meanwhile a mass of Dervishes had worked round and appeared on the extreme right, but they got so slated by the gun-boats and guns in the Zareeba that they never came within rifle range.

7.45 to 8.15 we fired very little, personally was watching fire of guns on a point to our extreme right. We checked ammunition and refilled pouches up to 100 per man. In my company we had fired between 12 and 13 hundred rounds or about 400 per sec. of 20. Sergt. Sanderson of A was wounded by a random bullet.

The Camerons lost more men than we did, chiefly because they kept standing all the time; whereas we ordered ours to kneel between each volley. Zareba our only protection from view. One of our men got a bullet caught in the roll of his shirt sleeve above the elbow - he had his shirt sleeve rolled up under his tunic, luck for him.

Another got a bullet in his haversack and stuck in his prayer book; one that Mr. Watson gave away to us all—red bound, with "Nile Expedition 1898" on the outside. I think R.C. would make a kind of miracle of it. One bayonet broken in the Company, bar that, got off scot free I am glad to say. C & D in reserve seemed to suffer as much as any.

About 8.15 Dervishes rallied and came on again, and for about a quarter of an hour we were firing hard again, then we sat tight till near 10, I think. We formed line to support two black brigades, Macdonald's, which were being attacked, but as our fire was not doing much we were ordered to move in fours in rear of blacks to their right. As soon as A company got clear of Soudanese right, they left formed and opened fire so our order of Co's was changed, H. being on right.

I could not note much of what was going on now, as the last part was done at the double and I had all I could do to see after the men, who, I must say, were awfully willing, and did their level best. We were next to the 10th. Soudanese now, and they were glad to see us, as they were running short of ammunition, they afterwards told us. The Dervishes broke and went—a quarter of an hour we formed up. A company tell some yarns how near the Dervishes got to the Soudanese line, but I did not see much, being away off on the right where we were and some rifle-men in a khor kept us busy. Then, they, these riflemen, fled back to hills, cavalry went out on our right and drove them right across our front to the left. Blacks advanced, we followed in echelon to black brigade, they gradually wheeled to the left and we conformed and went across most of the battlefield with A company out seizing rifles and ammunition; breaking the former and scattering latter, and so on across plain, behind where the Kalifa and his crowd first appeared where there was a gun which the General took—Some Egyptian Regts. afterwards joined here—and we joined our Brigade somewhere here. Shortly after we halted for about two hours or more, while a man was buried, and 16 stretcher bearers who had strayed were found, and camels were got to bring in wounded. We had some water served out from camel tanks. 3 o'clock—the rest of the brigade went on and we finally joined them about 2 1/2 miles on, where we found some tea had been prepared for us by transport men in charge of Plunkett, we only had half an hour's rest and fell in again.

That halt in the desert from 8.15 to 10 was very trying, as we just sat as we were expecting to move at any time. I luckily had a lot of biscuits (ration) and got down most of it by soaking in water, and this, with the remains of a box of Brands lozenges, kept me going.

We halted again just outside Omdurman, and as soon as we started got among houses, and almost immediately crossed a water-course, about up to the middle of calf in water. The Quarter Master of the Warwicks' horses lay down with him to everyone's amusement.

About two miles on the Soudanese Brigade caught us up, the 10th leading, playing away at their bugles hard. I was on the other side of the Company not paying much attention when I heard a man say "Why, its the 10th" and almost simultaneously they struck up the "Poachers." We were rear company (D). And by jove there was a howl when the old tune started, and we got in step and tried to keep pace, but the Companies and Regiments in front blocked us.

The Soudanese were going half as fast again and as they caught up each company, we howled, and they howled and shook their rifles in the air; great excitement.

About half an hour later they had been blocked and halted, and we passed them, our drums playing - they gave us a captured standard to carry ahead; more howls.

6.30 it was getting dark, sun set, we were going very slowly along a sort of street, at last halted, and we formed up in a quarter column in a kind of square. Word came round that there was no necessity for patrols or sentries only a sort of watch to keep natives out of lines. My servant looted me an angareeb and a basin and I got my boots off for the first time for 48 hours, and had a wash, and generally got comfortable. There was firing and noise going on till very late. We were about 3/4 mile from the Mosque.

[Saturday] September 3rd. - We all spent a very quiet day. I did not feel like worrying after anything. Very annoyed with Dowhard, as the Batt. paraded at 9 o'clock and I left at 8.30 to go to the hospital to fetch our sick and carry them on stretchers to our new camp. I got in about 10.30, the Batt. had been in about three quarters of an hour and fellows were getting their blanket shelter up and comfortable, but no Dowhard appeared till after 12. Then he turned up laden with a great collection of things with a Skallywag black carrying a lot also. These antiques or Anteeka as he called them being his sole excuse.

However, he lost a basin, a sort of carved wooden one (which was a luxury I appreciated and had meant to keep) which he had got me the night before, also the bed.

However, he assured me that he could get much better of each and was very contrite, and as I had been lying in the Doctor's tukal most of the time and had my shelter rigged up by a Tommy, I forgave him.

His (Dowhard's) idea seemed rather to have run on Korans as he brought five printed ones, and one hand-written.

At least one of the printed books was different and rather more used than the others, so I kept that and another printed Koran, and of course the hand-written one.

He said he had paid 21/- for the six, but I have my doubts, anyhow he got rid of the other three at about 6/- each to others.

All day there was bargaining for guns and swords and spears and jibbas and anteeka of every sort. I won't tell you what I have. I hardly know, and it may not arrive.

We all told our servants that as we had brought them up they must get us something; most of them played up well, but tried to make all they could out of other people's masters, as I found when I bought a jibba from Hubbard's servant.

Dowhard got a pair of bracelets and a necklace which he says are for Madame at Halfa and were supposed to cost 2 1/2 guineas. The bracelets are large napkin rings, to look at evidently taken straight from the tusk, roughly carved and burnt on the outside. The necklaces were long shaped beads of onyx or agate, not bad either.

[Sunday] Sept. 4th. - We had church and then nearly all the officers and about 50 men from each regiment went over to Khartoum by about 11. We drew up by Regiments. Union Jack and Khedive flag went up side by side. Fired Royal salute, presented arms, cheered, etc. etc. Of this all the papers will give you better account than I can, as I could not see all. We then fell out and wandered round the ruin and gardens of the Palace.

The garden must have been a paradise at one time. Now all a tangle, but there were a lot of oranges, the green kind. I cut a swagger stick, but I fear have lost it.

I saw a correspondent carrying off enough bricks to tile a hearth.

The Guards and Generals nearly fought for a small gun which the Sirdar eventually gave to the Gunners.

As Gordon was an R. E. I think it might have gone to Chatham. Altogether, it was a most enjoyable trip.

Burrows [sic] that day went off to the battle-field with a party on mules to count the Dervish slain; each regiment sent similar parties. They counted 10,700 I believe in a radius of three miles of the Zareeba; so what with wounded estimated at 30,000 and 2,000 supposed to have gone with the Kalifa, I should think we had 70,000 or more against us.

I don't think I told you about our going to present a Colour to the 10th Soudanese, they seem pleased at the idea—with this last battle they will have 8 Honours to put on.

They have no facings, but their distinguishing badge is black. The Soudanese wore the tarboosh or fez with khaki cover all over it rolled puttee fashion, with their badge of distinction on either side with brass Arabic numeral on it; they are very proud of these pompoms.

The 11th have some pipers, these chaps fancy themselves awfully, their swagger is too killing.

[Monday] Sept. 5th. - We marched triumphantly round the Mahdi's tomb. We only saw it from over a wall, as it was considered dangerous to march too near with all the troops. The best part of the dome was shattered, I believe the gunner ranged it exactly with the third shot and made a hole through the dome 3,000 yards off. They then turned their attention elsewhere, leaving final smash up as a kind of *bonne bouche* just before Sirdar entered; unfortunately he was too quick, and signalled cease fire, and was in Omdurman before they carried out the project.

There were crowds of natives, the womankind shewed a certain amount of excitement, by yelling, but mostly the crowd drew back to wall and watched sullenly; the men seemed very stolid poor brutes, they have had such a bad time lately they are indifferent and callous to everything. They vary in colour into every shade from quite light copper yellow to negro black. There were some intellectual looking men of the Arab type.

We saw Neufeld looking very well I thought for a prisoner, he was sitting on a donkey with a small crowd of followers when he met us. I believe latterly he has been well treated, but asked to be put into chains on day of battle and was found there by Slatin Pasha. He means to stay in Khartoum now as there is money to be made by a man in his position with a level commercial head on his shoulders.

All kinds of shaves as to going north.

[Tuesday] Sept. 6th. - We really did get off after many delays.

Lionel James

CHAPTER FOUR:
The Omdurman Campaign

Lionel James,
Reuters correspondent

Handwritten Telegrams on Reuters Letterheads,
as sent to its London office.

[Jean S. and Frederic A. Sharf Collection]

On the way to Omdurman: How the "Daily Graphic" sketches were sent down the Nile during the march to Wad Habesha.

INTRODUCTORY NOTES

Lionel James was born in England in 1871, and was educated at the Cranleigh School. He was the fourth son of Lt. Colonel L. H. S. James of the Royal Artillery.

In 1888, James was sent to visit India, where his father had served, with the expectation that he would return to England and join the army. However, he loved horses and hunting, and decided that he would have more time to pursue such activities if he became an indigo planter at Behar, approximately 350 miles distant from Calcutta. He began to write for Indian newspapers, using his extra income to race and trade polo ponies.

James spent seven years at Behar, investing heavily during these years in a horse-racing stable; but by early 1895 his stable was in financial difficulty, and he had lost all his money. Not wishing to return to the isolation of Behar, James accepted an offer from a Calcutta newspaper to serve as their correspondent with the Chitral Relief Expedition. He spent three months on this assignment, and his dispatches were also used by Reuters.

Returning to Calcutta, James found that his bankrupt racing stable had finally produced a winner, thus restoring his finances and enabling him to return to England to visit his family. Meanwhile, he had established a working relationship with *The Daily Graphic* of London, to which he submitted articles about life in India that were accompanied by his own illustrations.

Back in India in 1896, James resumed a life which combined agriculture, racing, and journalism. He traveled within India to produce articles for The Calcutta Englishman. With trouble again looming on the Northwest Frontier in 1897, James was eager to be involved: he failed to convince The *Allahabad Pioneer* to send him as their special correspondent, but was delighted to receive a telegram from Reuters, the British news service, offering him this assignment.

Arriving in Peshawar in September 1897, James found that most of the correspondents were serving soldiers, who had signed on as "specials" to see some action. However, at the end of that month two well-known professional war correspondents arrived—Melton Prior and Rene Bull—and James felt honored to spend time with them learning the trade. A contemporary description of James at that time characterized him as "versatile, smart, and excellent company, and able...to undergo any kind of hardship, (and) privation..."

James covered the campaign in the Tirah Valley until it ended in mid-December. He sent written reports to several Indian newspapers, plus Reuters. He sent sketches to *The Daily Graphic*, where professional studio-based artists worked them up into finished artwork which was published. All of his employers complimented him on his work.

Early in January, 1898, Reuters asked James to return to Peshawar in anticipation of the resumption of the campaign. Traveling through the Khyber Pass to Landi Kotal, James met Winston Churchill and resumed his friendship with William T. Maud, who had arrived at the very end of the Tirah Campaign and who also remained on in the expectation of covering the next campaign.

In March, when it became obvious that no serious campaign was contemplated, James left the front and traveled to Calcutta, and briefly to his home at Behar, before returning in April to England. Meanwhile, he was working on an account of the Tirah Campaign, which was published in London in 1898 under the title *The Indian Frontier War, 1897*. *The Graphic* permitted him to use the artwork which they had developed from his on-site sketches.

With war on the horizon between the United States and Spain, and with Kitchener planning to return to the Sudan, James felt there was an opportunity to sell himself to the *Times* covering one of these events. He was turned down, and was preparing to settle down in England training polo ponies when Reuters asked him to leave immediately to be their "special" in the Sudan. Knowing that his friend Maud was also under orders to proceed at once, they set off together for Cairo.

They journeyed from London to Marseilles by train, and from there to Alexandria by boat. When they reached Cairo, they discovered that Kitchener would not permit correspondents to travel to Atbara; so they remained at the Continental Hotel in Cairo, covering the army training exercises.

James and Maud remained in Cairo for at least 30 days before taking the train for Assouan, which was then the end point of the railroad. They then made a brief overland trip to Shalal, from where they traveled by steamship to Wady Halfa; from Wady Halfa they traveled 43 hours on the desert railroad (which Kitchner had built specifically for this campaign) to Atbara, arriving there late at night on July 22nd. They were the first two correspondents to reach Atbara.

By the end of the month other correspondents arrived. James and Maud were joined by Frank Scudamore and George Steevens, forming one mess unit. Winston Churchill was a frequent dinner guest. Finally, on August 14th, the correspondents were permitted to leave Atbara; they crossed the Nile to the west bank, and marched overland with the army and the cavalry to the field of battle.

After the battle of Omdurman, James returned to England. While Reuters had been very pleased with his work in the Sudan, they were unwilling to hire him on a permanent basis, and so he decided, reluctantly, to return to India. Having booked his passage, James was quite suddenly offered a staff position on the *Times*, which he accepted. He remained with the *Times* from 1899 until he retired from journalism in 1913.

In September 1899, James was sent by the *Times* to South Africa, arriving prior to the declaration of war. He was in Ladysmith during the siege, and then with Roberts on his march to Pretoria. Arriving in Pretoria in June, 1900, James received insructions from the *Times* to proceed to Capetown and board one of the British naval vessels heading for China, where the Boxers were threatening the western settlements. However, 24 hours prior to sailing for China, James was notified that the *Times* had made other arrangements in China, and was ordered back to London.

By late 1900, the war in South Africa evolved into a series of Boer guerilla attacks, and the *Times* decided to send James back to cover this aspect of the hostilities. James returned to South Africa in January 1901. He traveled to De Aar in order to cover the British campaign against De Wet, and found himself recruited into the army for a ten-week stint as Intelligence Officer with Bethune's Commando. By the spring of 1901 he had resumed coverage of the war for the *Times*, and in August, 1901, he was ordered back to London.

During the fall of 1901, James was assigned to assist in the preparation of *The Times History of the War in South Africa*, and much of volumes II and III represent his efforts. At the same time, his military experience under General Bethune in South Africa lead James to become one of the founding members of a new regiment, named "The King's Colonials"; James was present on February 11, 1902 at the first muster of this regiment.

He spent the summer of 1903 in the United States, covering the American Army as well as the use of wireless telegraphy in reporting an international yacht race. Returning to London, full of enthusiasm for the potential of wireless telegraphy, James was immediately sent to the Balkans where trouble was brewing between Bulgaria and Turkey. He returned to London in December 1903, but within a few weeks was sailing on board the S.S. *Majestic* bound for New York City; reaching New York on December 31, he went by train westward to San Francisco and then by S.S. *Siberia* onwards to Japan. Once again, he arrived prior to the actual declaration of war between Japan and Russia.

James had traveled to Japan with the well-known American writer, Jack London. In Tokyo, they found that numerous war correspondents were assembling in order to be on site when the inevitable war broke out between Japan and Russia. While most of these men simply languished in Tokyo, where they awaited permission from the Japanese military to go to the front, James had a separate agenda.

The *Times* had authorized James to establish a wireless telegraphy base at Wei-Hai-Wei, and to hire a boat with appropriate crew to report the action directly from the scene of battle. He completed the necessary planning by March 3rd, 1904, departing from Yokohama for Nagasaki and onwards to Korea. He was successful at observing the naval actions of March and April 1904 at first hand.

In June 1904, James returned to Tokyo in order to obtain the necessary permits to proceed to Manchuria, where the major land battles of the war were taking place. Once again James had his own agenda, and at the battle of Liao-yang in September 1904, he was able to escape from the Japanese censors, observe the battle by hiding in millet fields, and travel to Shanhaikwan to wire an uncensored report to the *Times*. He returned to England in October, 1904.

While the years from 1905 to 1914 were not years of major military confrontations, James was kept busy by the *Times* covering numerous foreign assignments. In 1907, he was sent back to India; and in 1908 he reported again from the Northwest Frontier before returning by way of Persia and Turkey. In 1909, he was in the Balkans, then covered the Spanish army in Morocco. In 1910, James was with the Turkish army in Albania. In 1911, he joined the French army on their march to Fez, and in September of 1911 went to Tripoli to cover the Italian army as it went to war with the Turks over Libya.

James was back in the Balkans again in 1912. He arrived at Constantinople on October 7, 1912 to cover the Turks in their war with Bulgaria; he remained for about six weeks until cholera broke out in the Turkish camp, and all correspondents returned to London. He was back in 1913, this time to cover the Bulgarian army in action. James retired from the *Times* in 1913.

When World War I broke out in the summer of 1914, James held the rank of Major in a cavalry regiment which he had been instrumental in establishing in February, 1902. Originally known as "The King's Colonials," it changed its name to "King Edward's Horse." James commanded this regiment in action, both in Italy and France, from 1915 to 1918. His bravery in combat earned him the Distinguished Service Order.

THE OMDURMAN CAMPAIGN

James retired from service in the summer of 1918 with the rank of Lieutenant-Colonel. He settled in Newbury, where he managed a racing stable, and raised polo ponies. He also continued to write books.

Omdurman: A lull in the fighting.
Photo by Rene Bull.

Omdurman: General Gatacre calling "Cease Fire!"
Photo by Rene Bull.

Directing the Battle.
Photo by Rene Bull.

Via Reuter's Telegram Company, Limited

Wad Hamed - Tuesday, August 23rd (evening):
Twenty thousand men are now encamped on the grassy banks of the Nile, waiting to cover the few short marches which separate us and retribution. The camp is full of stories from Omdurman. Many of the reports current, especially that of the Nile being sown with mines and torpedoes, must be received with incredulity.

At the moment the whole available forces by land and water are concentrated here, none are further south.

Wad Hamed - Wednesday, August 24th:
I went with a camel-corps picket two miles outside the camp. From a rocky eminence I saw the prospect of the whole country to Shabluka at my feet, while the camel corps reclined in the shade afforded by the black boulders, cleaning their rifles after last night's rain. To the south stretched the expanse of the Nile valley, fed by the luxuriant flood. The country, which twelve months ago was green and cultivated is now a luxuriant jungle, abruptly ending to the west in desert shingle. With my glasses I could trace General Hunter's column trailing forward having left at 4 o'clock this morning in the rain. To the north rises Gebel-royan, a rocky range through which the Shabluka cataract forces its way.

Amongst the riverside growth, the outlook discovered a party of Omdurman refugees, adding to the daily detail of deserters. They came with goats and camels, shewing signs of distress and of a hasty flight. Looking north past three miles of teeming camp with the white tents of the British and the brown grass shelters of the native troops, the scene is the usual bustle of an active camp, backed with the stretch of blue river, the white gunboats rising stately above the forest of masts of the chartered Nile boats.

Wad Hamed - Thursday, August 25th (1):
The gunboats have seized Gebel Royan, and rapidly all stores are being pushed up by water to make it an advanced depôt.

General Hunter's advance brigade, which marched yesterday, should reach Hegair, on the bank opposite to Gebel Royan today.

The 2nd British Brigade marched out here this morning at 2 o'clock.

Major Stuart-Wortley is organising on the right bank the remnant of the Jaalin warriors and other friendlies, chiefly of the Menelemieh, Shukerieh and Batakin tribes. This cohort will march on the right bank, parallel with our advance on the left.

LIONEL JAMES

Amusing stories come in from Omdurman. During a review of his whole force, Ali Wad Helu, the Khalifa's second in command, while heading a charge meant as a rehearsal of the overthrow of the infidel invaders, fell heavily from his horse. His arm was fractured, and he sustained other injuries.

Wad Hamed - Thursday, August 25th, evening (2):
The 1st British Brigade followed the 2nd en route for the front this evening. The veterans of the Atbara with the Rifle Brigade and Royal Artillery Maxim Battery formed up in lines of column "H" route, and to the music of the bagpipes the two Highland regiments stepped out to make the first march, which is to culminate in retribution for fifteen years' bloodshed. The men march absolutely light.

Wad Hamed - Friday, August 26th:
As our advance guard is almost within touch of the Dervish outposts, a description of Omdurman may help our readers when the situation develops.

Lying on the left bank of the Nile, the city roughly represents an isosceles triangle, the base of which is towards our advance. The sides are about six miles long and the base three. Its area can thus be appreciated and it is closely built over. Only the inner portion, a comparatively small area, is walled in. Opposite the city, the Nile varies from 500 to 1000 yards in width, along this left front being at least fifteen forts and some blockhouses. Judging from Metemmeh, these are probably most serviceable earthworks. Just this side of the city, impeding our advance, are the three arms of the Nile, which at this season may be formidable, and one at least is entrenched.

The cohort of friendly Arabs leaves today, marching down the right bank.

A small party of Dervish horsemen has been seen on the right bank, and another party has been reported some miles south of Gebel-royan camp. The wire has reached Gebel-royan. The correspondents move on to the wire-head this evening with part of the Headquarters.

Gebel Royan - Sunday, August 28th (1):
[From Camp Hegair, opposite Nile Island, Gebel Royan.]
From the summit of Gebel Royan hill can be seen the first view of our objective. In the clear evening, away to the south appeared a dull dark streak with a splash of white. It was Omdurman, and the splash of white is the Mahdi's tomb. The nephew of General Gordon was the first to see the streak on the horizon which means so much to us. It is now

but a matter of thirty - odd miles, and General Hunter's patrols are constantly in sight of Dervish parties, which invariably fall back before our advance, but yesterday they illuminated the skyline with signal fires. The Khalifa, according to latest information, has concentrated his force, intending a bitter resistance.

Gebel Royan - Sunday, August 28th (2):
All the troops had a trying march from Wad Hamed here, over the Shabluka rock and ankle-deep in sand. General Hunter's division, which had arrived first, turned out to help the British into camp, and the massed bands played each British regiment in. Here we are almost in view of the enemy, and last night was the first on which the real strain of war has been felt. I went round the camp in the moonlight, and it was an impressive scene, the men lying prepared, at a moment's notice to stand to their arms. Tents are but few and far between, the men simply rolling themselves in blankets. The Sirdar and staff arrived from Wad Hamed yesterday and this morning has seen the advance continue, General Hunter having taken a part of his division to camp 8 miles south. It is impossible to adequately describe the enthusiasm of the force now almost within striking distance of the goal which we have taken 13 years to reach.

Gebel Royan - Sunday, August 28th (3)
There has been an accident resulting in the loss of the gunboat *Zafir*. She arrived ten miles off Shendy, when she sprung a leak. Owing to the coal in the hold and the small draught, it was impossible to rectify before a list set in. She was run for the shore, but unfortunately sank within a fathom of it in comparatively deep water. Only the funnel and crosstrees are above water. The gunboat sank in three minutes. Luckily they noticed some native barges, which were cut adrift, and General Rundle, Commander Keppel and Prince Christian were able to make the shore. No life was lost, and the sunken boat has been secured by a hawser. The wrecked passengers had an unhappy time on a swampy bank till picked up by the *Tahrea* and brought on. Luckily the boiler did not explode, but it is a most serious loss.

General Rundle rejoined the Sirdar's staff, and Commander Keppel has hoisted his pennant on the *Sultan*.

I hear today that the messages which I sent 50 miles down stream by rafts arrived safely.

LIONEL JAMES

Sogal - Tuesday, August 30th (1):
The daily glimpses of a phantom enemy were turned into reality today. The cavalry screen, both British and Egyptian, constantly put up the jibbah-clad enemy, who galloped before them into the bush.

Working on information supplied by the water-flotilla, the 21st Lancers succeeded in locating a position which is presumed to be an outpost of Kerreri. Here the enemy lay in considerable numbers showing a determined front and a disposition to fight, by beating war-drums and displaying battle flags. Captain Montmorency's troop came into actual contact with one party of the enemy, and emptied a few of the Dervish saddles.

News by water: On the troops marching the *Sultan*, flagship, followed by the *Melek*, *El Fateh*, and the *Naser*, steamed up stream and soon got in front of the troops. They located the town and entrenchments of Kerreri, but the latter being, as usual with the Dervishes, in a hollow, they could not ascertain its strength.

Later. After orders had been received from the Sirdar, the gunboats shelled the enemy's position, after the British patrols had fallen back. The enemy's loss is uncertain. On the right bank considerable moving bodies could be seen, and are presumed to be Major Stuart-Wortley's levies.

Sogal - Tuesday, August 30th (2):
The army marched this afternoon and through a miserably wet night, in double line of Brigades, General Lewis' Egyptian Brigade taking the desert side, and General Wauchope's British Brigade the river side, while the advance of the gunboats covered the left, and the cavalry and artillery the left. Viewed from a knoll it was a most impressive sight, the cavalry lost from view in the dust and scrub, and 15,000 infantry in line of column of companies, prepared to deploy in battle array in a moment, while the gunboats kept pace on the flank and the British cavalry and camel corps were on ahead. The army halted after ten miles but the British cavalry pushed on and took the eminence of Sheik-el-Taib, which had been occupied by the enemy as a post of observation. From here there is a splendid view of the margins of Khartoum and Omdurman on the Nile reach; it is even possible with glasses to make out the silvery reach where the White Nile and Blue Nile join. It was too cloudy to clearly discern Omdurman, but though nothing of the Dervishes was seen but fleeting horsemen, a pillar of moving smoke against the skyline showed the Khalifa's outposts were alert, and the signal fires on the Kerreri eminence stood defined. Throughout the day's march in the distance a haze prevented the distances from being carefully reckoned.

Camp Agaiga - Thursday, September 1st. (1):

[Telegraph lines did not extend beyond Nasri Island. Correspondents sent their dispatches down to Nasri by boat, and from there they were telegraphed to Alexandria. Since such communication to the outside world was uncertain, James prepared multiple reports, which he sent whenever there was a boat departing.]

The cavalry division made a most complete reconnaissance of the actual city of Omdurman this morning, first from Kerreri hill. The whole of the Nile basin lay stretched at our feet, and the dome of the Mahdi's tomb stood out a landmark in a hundred square miles of plain which actually surround Omdurman. Of Khartoum we could only see the green of the palms which grow in the river-angle. Omdurman is even bigger in its straggling area than the dimensions already given, and when the Egyptian cavalry swept round to a hill which commanded a view of it five miles to the west, it appeared infinite. It will be a terrible place if well held—must end, as the boat is starting.

Camp Agaiga - Thursday, September 1st. (2):

The cavalry division this morning, leaving the last camp at daybreak, reconnoitered up to Kerreri and found the Dervish outpost evacuated. The Egyptian Cavalry and Camel Corps then made a grand detour to a hill five miles west of Omdurman city, and made a full reconnaissance. The 21st Lancers, hugging the riverbank also reconnoitered up within five miles, the gunboats pressing up the river to engage the forts both sides of the Nile, and succeeded in landing the Howitzer battery, which itself came into action against Omdurman. But the main feature of the day lay with the Egyptian cavalry, for the enemy, having once seen them, debouched from every alley in the seven miles of front which the city presents, and formed up in battle array on the plain to the west of the city—five phalanxes in full array with all insignia of war, & drums & banners. Nor was it a mere show, for they began to advance steadily on the cavalry, a solid fine advance at least 20,000 strong, and moved so rapidly that they almost came into serious action with the rearguard in retirement, in fact a few shots were fired. The Lancers, whose outposts came into actual contact, had one casualty. The enemy followed so determinedly that the infantry in camp prepared to receive an attack, which was not made.

LIONEL JAMES

Omdurman - Friday, Sept. 2nd. (1):

> *[Once again James sent multiple reports by boat to Nasri Island. These reports reflect his increasing knowledge of the various aspects of the battle, as well as his desire to scoop the other correspondents.]*

The Dervishes left us undisturbed last night. This morning we received a determined attack and drove them back after an hour's fighting. At 8.50 a.m. the Sirdar began to advance on Omdurman and was once again heavily attacked on the right flank. The Dervishes were driven off with heavy loss, and the army, under the personal command of the Khalifa, was completely dispersed by noon. At 2 p.m., the Sirdar advanced and occupied Omdurman. During the afternoon the Khalifa fled, and is being hotly pursued by the cavalry. The Sirdar is unable to give a complete list of the casualties. The British loss is probably 100. Charles Neufeld is rescued.

Omdurman - Friday, Sept. 2nd. (2):

The cavalry patrolling towards Omdurman found the enemy advancing in battle-array to attack, with a front 3 or 4 miles long. There were infantry and cavalry with countless banners, all chanting war-songs. Our infantry formed up outside Camp Agaiga. On the left was the Rifle Brigade, then the Lancashire Fusiliers, the Northumberland Fusiliers, the Grenadier Guards, the Maxims of the Royal Irish Fusiliers, the Royal Warwickshire Regiment, the Cameron Highlanders, the Seaforth Highlanders, the Lincolnshire Regiment, the Maxims of the Royal Artillery, Colonel Maxwell's and Col. MacDonald's Soudanese fighting line, with General Lewis's and Col. Collinson's reserve guns on both flanks. At 7.20, the enemy crowded on the ridges above the camp steadily advanced in enveloping formation. At 6.40, our artillery had opened fire, answered by the enemy's riflemen. This attack developed on our left, the enemy sweeping down from the ridges, but their design of rushing us was absolutely crushed by the fire they received from all arms in 15 minutes, and they swept to the centre, where another attack formulated. Their horsemen trying to face the fire of the Camerons, the Lincolns and the Sudanese battalions were swept away, and their whole force drew off, leaving the field strewn with bodies. Our casualties are not ascertained yet. The bravery of their attack cannot be overrated. Their flagbearers struggled on within a few hundred yards of us, and the mounted Emirs absolutely threw their lives away. Firing has now slackened, maybe they are now recouping for further attack.

Since the above was written, the day developed a decisive action. Our force advanced and destroyed thousands of the Dervishes, and is at the gates of Omdurman. The casualties included Lieutenant Grenfell, of the 12th Lancers, Captain Caldecott of the Warwicks, and the wounded. The Khalifa has escaped, Omdurman is taken. Neufeld has been released.

Omdurman - Friday, Sept. 2nd. (3):
Colonel Rhodes, Correspondent of the *Times*, was wounded. When the enemy drew off behind the ridge, the Sirdar detailed General Lewis's and Colonel Collinson's Brigades to watch the attempt which the Dervishes made on our left. Tins filled, our whole force left camp in echelons of battalions for Omdurman. Just as the British brigade had made the crest adjoining the Nile on the right of the Egyptian battalions marching out, the camp became engaged, and it was found that the Dervishes had reformed under cover of the rocky eminence 2 miles from camp, and had massed under the Black Standard of the Khalifa to make a supreme effort. A mass 15,000 strong was already bearing down on the 2 Egyptian battalions on the right, who, aided by the Maxim, succeeded in forming up steadily to face the attack. The Sirdar swung round the centre and left, leaving the 1st British Brigade with the transport. Colonel Maxwell's Soudanese seized the rocky eminence, the rest of Colonel MacDonald's Brigade joined the firing-line, and in ten minutes, long before they could drive their attack home, the flower of the Khalifa's army were caught in a depression and came under the withering cross-fire of 3 Brigades and their attendant artillery. The devoted Mahdists manfully strove to make headway, but their rushes were swept away, and their main body mown through and through. Defiantly they planted their standards and died by them. It was more than human nerve can bear, and after masses had melted into companies, and companies to mere driblets, they broke and fled, leaving the field white with jibbahed corpses, like a meadow of snowdrift.

Omdurman - Friday, Sept. 2nd. (4):
But there had been sidelights in the battle scene. The 21st Lancers, charging some of the detached enemy found swordsmen "en masse" behind them, and were forced to charge home against appalling odds. They hacked through the mass, rallied, and kept the horde at bay by carbine magazine fires—but lost 1 officer killed, had 4 officers wounded, and about 40 men killed and wounded. The Egyptian cavalry on the right have been strenuously engaged all day with Baggara horsemen, and for a short period a gun remained in the

enemy's hands, but it was brilliantly recaptured. One could not but be moved at the heroic bravery displayed by the enemy; time after time dispersed and broken masses were re-formed and hurled against the line until they melted into units, and then ceased to exist. The Emirs would dash forward spurning death to encourage their following, some almost reaching the line before they sank before the leaden stream, and wounded even turned in their death agony to fire a parting shot. At 11.15 a.m., the Sirdar sounded the advance, and the whole force in line drove the scattered remnants of the foe into the desert, while the cavalry cut off their retreat to Omdurman. At 12.15, columns preceded by the Sirdar with the Khalifa's Black Standard headed for Omdurman, and I sit writing this in a suburb of that city, waiting to see if the final occupation takes place today. Roughly our losses are nearly 200; the Dervishes lost thousands, & Mahdism has received a blow from which it can never recover.

Omdurman - Saturday, September 3rd, (1):

> *[James now devotes an entire dispatch to what was regarded as "the incident" of the battle: the charge of the 21st Lancers. Since it is unlikely that he observed this event, he drew his material from participants.]*

There has been such a press of daily work that the incident of the fight has been forgotten by now, *viz.*, the charge of the 21st Lancers against enormous odds. Colonel Martin's orders were to prevent the broken enemy from remaking Omdurman, distant from the battlefield five miles. They unexpectedly came upon the enemy's reserves, two thousand strong, but the exact amount was hidden by the lay of the ground. The cavalry then, in column of troops, deployed into line attack and charged; when within 30 yards they found the enemy ensconced in a nullah and a depression of ground, wild with excitement and courting attack. There was no moment for hesitation; the Lancers charged home, the brunt of the work falling on No. 2 squadron. They absolutely had to hack their way through the enemy twenty deep, while exposed to a withering infantry fire. They struggled though, but every man that fell was immediately hacked to pieces by the frenzied swordsmen. The cavalry rolled on bleeding and blown to the far side of the lanes which they cut for themselves in the enemy's ranks, and with fortitude the men re-formed as on parade. The corporal, covered with blood and reeling in his saddle, when ordered to 'fall out,' shouted waving his bent lance, "Never. Form up, Number Two" (i.e., the squadron). Then it was that young Grenfell was missed, and Lieut. de

Montmorency with Corporal Swarback dashed out to effect the rescue of the body. Captain Kenna joined and with revolver fire the two officers kept the enemy forty yards away, and would have secured the body, if the horse had not shied with his burden. Then seeing a second charge, they dismounted ten men and with magazine carbine fire drove the enemy steadily back into the zone of the infantry fire, having accomplished their object of covering the enemy's line of retirement. The Lancers' maiden charge was a most brilliant affair.

Omdurman - Saturday, September 3rd, (2):
[James devotes a brief mention to the funeral of his colleague Hubert Howard, an event in which James participated. He then resumes a lengthy series of descriptions on various aspects of the battle.]

I have just returned from the funeral of the Hon. Hubert Howard, 2nd correspondent of the *Times*. He was carried to the grave by the representatives of the *Standard,* Reuter's Agency, the *Daily News*, the *Graphic*, and the *Daily Mail*. Generals Rundle and Hunter were present.

After the battle, the Sirdar halted his force at midday at Creek Sambat in suburbs of Omdurman. At 4 o'clock, taking the Sudanese brigades and heading the force with his staff, the Sirdar marched upon Omdurman. When the outskirts of the city proper were reached, the Sheikhs of that part showed under a flag of truce. When the populace perceived that truce was accepted, they left their shelter in hundreds, men, women and children, with shrill cries of exultation, and received the victors, a most impressive demonstration, shewing the absolute overthrow of Mahdism. Following the principal street leading to the Khalifa's walled citadel, the demonstration increased as they passed through the poorer part of the city, and dense crowds of black women singing, and when they recognised their fathers, husbands and sons marching by in the battalions many touching scenes were witnessed. As we neared the citadel, the buildings improved in architecture, and then suddenly we came upon the great Citadel wall, behind which they believed the Khalifa to be in hiding. It is a magnificent stone wall, 10 x 24. Detachments were sent to surround it, then shots from the interior raised our hopes that the news that the Khalifa would die in the Mahdi's tomb were true. Taking 32nd Field Battery, the Sirdar followed the wall to where it joined the Nile where the Howitzers had breached it and the gateway.

Here they were met by a wonderful sight. The populace anticipating the Khalifa's downthrow had already in masses commenced to loot the Beit el Mal, the treasury and store. The scene was a regular pandemonium. Down by the water we made an entry by the breaches, three gunboats supporting us, and desultory street fighting was taking place at this period within the walls.

As the Sudanese gained an entrance they found three walled partitions to the enclosure, and forced an entry, when the residue of the Dervishes surrendered there. The Sirdar, when he arrived at the Mahdi's tomb found it much damaged by shell-fire. The interior itself is completely gutted by falling portions of the minarets and dome. In comparison with the rest of the city, it is a fine building, with its domed square, rudely ornamented. In the interior of the wooden tomb is the Mausoleum with glass panels and palled standards, enclosed by a rail from the church. After [he] visited the tomb, though it was nearly dark, the Sirdar, being satisfied that the Khalifa has escaped, went to the prison and released Neufeld and others. The Italian sisters found have since married and settled. Neufeld was dressed in a jibbah and was heavily chained. The city teems with gruesome scenes and evidences of the bombardment. In one place lay 2 mounted men and two footmen, evidently mangled by one concussion. The army camped outside the city, and this morning is moving further away for sanitary reasons. Our casualties total over 400.

The features of yesterday's fighting were the splendid handling and discipline of Col. MacDonald's Sudanese Brigade, when the forces changed front twice and caught a flank fire in order to prevent being enveloped by a mass of the fresh enemy, here a thousand strong—and the brilliant charge of the 21st Lancers against a mass six times their strength, & over deceitful ground.

I will describe the former. The attack on the Agaiga zereba being beaten off, the Sirdar ordered the force to advance in echelon brigade to the British left. Colonel Macdonald, when 1500 yards from camp found himself in a plain face to face with two masses of the enemy. On his left was the whole of the original attacking force reformed into battle array, but masked by the eminence which they held and by the nature of the ground. On the right rear he was suddenly menaced by 10,000 of the enemy, of all arms, who had attempted the left attack on the Zereeba and then retired. Colonel Maxwell's brigade gallantly turned the enemy out of the rocky eminence and somewhat relieved Col. MacDonald's troops by flank covering fire; but to prevent being enveloped by the mass on their rear and stop them from cutting off Colonel Collinson's brigade with the transport, Col. MacDonald was forced to change front under heavy fire and receive them, a critical manoeuvre beautifully executed. The situation was so critical at this juncture that General Hunter sent for aid from the right, General Wauchope's brigade being moved to his support, but not arriving till Col. Macdonald had changed front again; so that eventually when the enemy had been driven off, the whole line of divisions advanced and drove the remnants into the desert, Colonel MacDonald wheeled completely to come back into line.

Omdurman - Sunday, September 4th:

[James reports on an event which was both a celebration of the British victory and a funeral service for General Gordon, whose death in 1889 was now avenged.]

The Union Jack and the Crescent have both been left to wave in the desert breeze above the ruins of Khartoum Residency, half a dozen paces from the spot where General Gordon died. The Sirdar, with all the generals of the Staff and detachments from the whole force steamed up the Blue Nile to the ruins of Khartoum this morning, and landed at the masonry water-stage opposite the Residence. The latter, though gutted, still maintains its foundation in completeness. On the summit of the dismantled walls two flagstaffs were placed, and detachments, with the band of the 11th Sudanese, the drums and fifes of the Grenadier Guards and the bagpipes of the Highland regiments, formed up reverently round the historic spot. The gunboat *Melek* made fast to the quay behind. In the centre was the Sirdar with his Staff, and the complete {———} Staffs; on the left were the officers of the Sappers, Gordon's old corps, with palm, acacia and lemon trees behind. At 10 o'clock, the Sirdar gave the signal, and amid the crash of the first salute and of the national anthem, Captain Watson, A.D.C. and Lieutenant Stavely unfurled the Union Jack, and Bimbashi Badr Effendi, A.D.C., and Major Mitford unfurled the Crescent—and the 15 years cry for vengeance had ceased. Amid the booming of the 21-gun salute, and the bars of the British and Khedivial anthems, could be heard the shrill cries of the crowds of natives and slaves, now exulting in their emancipation from serfdom. Then the music changed to a dirge and a Dead March was played in memory of Khartoum and Gordon, and of the present hour. The Chaplain of the Force read appropriate prayers. Fifteen minute-guns were fired. Then the Sirdar called for three cheers for Her Majesty and for the Khedive.

Omdurman - Monday, September 5th (1):

Amongst the incidents of Friday's fight one of the most impressive was the final effort of the fighting members of the Khalifa's own family to retrieve the day. Seeing the white flags bearing down the front of Colonel MacDonald's Brigade, and spurning the crossfire from Colonel Lewis's troops, these valiant Arabs, foot and horse, surged forward round the Black Banner, and gathered an impetus which, if it had not been for the opportune arrival of the Lincolnshire Regiment in support, would have carried them on to the very bayonets of our black troops. As it was, decimated at every yard, they faltered on till a mere handful of dismounted men remained to plant the banner in the sand and die round it. It may be said that round this banner Mahdism died. The handling of Colonel Young's galloping battery shews how severely the Egyptian right was pressed. He had so many of his horses hit, & the team were so fatigued, that at one period he had no alternative but to dismantle 2 guns and leave them to be recovered when the right was secured.

The battlefield today was a miserable spectacle: for miles it is a march of death, and it is not an overestimation to say that 10,000 bodies are staining the yellow sand while at least 1,000 of the wounded, aided by the women of Omdurman, have dragged their mangled limbs to the Nile edge. The numbers that perished after our fighting line drove them into the desert it is impossible to say.

Omdurman - Monday, September 5th (2):
Little is known of the naval action as the majority of the fighting boats proceeded up the Nile. But, viewing the earthworks which at intervals defend the waterway of the city, their fire must have been most destructive and so accurate that not a single embrasure remains intact. I have only heard of the return fire hitting one boat, *viz.*, Lieutenant Beatty's, which had its fore-armour pierced. The boats have gone up the White Nile, one in pursuit of the Khalifa, one returned, the others due today after having gone 60 miles. That returned reports seeing fleeing horsemen, about 1,000 strong, also the beginning of a dense forest on both banks....

Later. Dervishes are surrendering at every turn, and hostilities are now absolutely over. Every labyrinth and maze of this mushroom city is practically clear of the skulking fanatics who were responsible for many casualties in the first 48 hours.

Omdurman - Monday, September 5th (3):
The British Division, with all military display, marched round the city of Omdurman today. It was an impressive scene. All is quiet, and no further complications seem imminent. 1,000 camels, which the Khalifa sent to meet him on the west bank, have been captured by the friendly levies.

CHAPTER FIVE:
The Omdurman Campaign and the Charge of the 21st Lancers
Major Harry Finn

A series of letters written to his wife.

[Jean S. and Frederic A. Sharf Collection]

THE OMDURMAN CAMPAIGN AND THE CHARGE OF THE 21ST LANCERS

INTRODUCTORY NOTES

Born on 6 December, 1852, Harry Finn was the youngest son of Samuel Finn of Tenterden, Kent. Educated at the local school, he enlisted in the 9th Lancers in 1871.

He saw action with the Lancers in the Second Afghan War, 1878-1880. In the following year, Finn was a 2nd Lieutenant in the 21st Hussars; he was promoted Captain in 1887 and Major in 1894. From 1893 to 1898 he served in Madras but in his last year he joined the 21st Lancers, assembling in Cairo in July for the Sudan expedition. He returned to Cairo in the following September.

By 1900, Finn was Lt. Colonel in the 21st Lancers, and was assigned to command military forces in Queensland, Australia for a year. In 1902, he transferred to the same position in New South Wales where he stayed until 1904. He was Inspector General (with the local rank of Major-General) for all His Majesty's forces in Australia for 1905-1906.

Finn was promoted Colonel in 1907 followed by elevation to Brigadier-General in 1912. Retirement followed and he lived out his final years in Sydney, Australia, dying there on 24 June, 1924.

Finn's first letter describes the journey down the Nile and the problems he encountered. His account of the Battle of Omdurman is contained in a second, 32–page letter written to his wife.

Having left Omdurman on Tuesday, September 6, 1898, Finn reached Camp Royan, south end of Shabluka, the 6th Cataract on the Nile, on Thursday, 8th September, and it was here that he commenced his letter which was not finished until Thursday, 15 September. On the following day, it was sent by boat to Atbara, and probably reached England during the last week of the month. This was the first communication from Finn in over a month.

Finn tells his wife that he did not keep a diary on a day-to-day basis, and therefore this letter is his only record of the events of Omdurman campaign. In addition, Finn tells his wife in diary format how his return trip is unfolding and his thoughts as he travels back to Atbara—in particular, the news that the 21st Lancers would not be returning to England but would remain in Egypt for one more year. In another account, Finn described his journey back to Sudan in 1899.

There are two references to Winston Churchill, who served under Finn: one in the context of Churchill's accuracy in his reports back to England; and the other relating to a joint assignment on September 1.

MAJOR HARRY FINN

The entire letter has a 'stream of consciousness' aspect to it, as Finn moves from the present to the past, and from the past to events further in the past. Recalling one event leads him logically to recall yet an earlier event, as he does when recording what he observed on September 4, and then moved backwards in time to recount September 1. Hence, there is no logical sequence to this letter.

I will number the letters while away like this, so that you may know if you get them all, this is *No. 2*.

Stern-wheeler *Amokeh,* Wed., 10 August, 1898

My darling,

The Assouan-Shellal change was a great strain on all, a bottle of ginger ale was all I could manage to get between 1 pm and 9 pm. Tiffin had been at 1 oc, but as it was evident we should be at Assouan by 2 oc instead of 6 or 7 we decided to feed everybody while there was a chance. The Staff Officers at Assouan headed by Capt. Pedley & those at Shellal by Capt. Sargent proved a good level-headed lot & altho' our unexpected early arrival was upsetting & caught all the barges & gyassas unready for the horses, they fizzed away & got all rigged up a little before dark; most of the horses embarked well; a couple fell into the river but were soon fished out. 23 Officers' chargers on one gyassa gave no end of trouble, screamed, fought, & kicked like demons making a veritable pandemonium. Pedley had a lot of coolies & prisoners to help unload the barges at Assouan & load the train, leaving most of the men free for the horses; after examining each & to our relief finding all fit I sent them off by road to Shellal under Eadon, with Friend, a good R. E. Major, as a guide. A block on the line delayed us 1/2 hour at Assouan; at last Shellal was reached—the baggage, stores, forage &c. unloaded, sorted & put on the 2 Steamers & 6 barges & gyassas; most of it had to go into the hold under where the horses stand & as we do not stop between Shellal & Halfa, stores had to be correctly placed. Everything was aboard at 8.10 [pm] and then along came Major MacNeece R.A.M.C. mad keen to go with us; so I consented but the poor man had to leave his horse behind, the syce was wandering about in the dark & got lost till just as we were moving off, & could not stop any longer. You may guess what it was having to split up the men & horses among 1/2 doz. boats carrying various numbers, some without accommodation for men; sent Eadon & 5 officers with 40 men & 85 horses to the *Toski* rationed for 3 days, while I have 11 Officers, the balance of the men, 115 & 94 horses with the *Amokeh*; instead of being towed the barges are lashed to the sides of the steamers. We left Shellal at 8:30 pm Monday. I had to haul in shore about 6:30 next morning to investigate case of a horse dying on Eadon's boat. Proved to have inflammation of the intestines & he had to go overboard. Very bad luck & I was glad our Vet was present. The current was terribly strong at places yesterday; brought the whole to a standstill occasionally & once took us right into the bank broadside on; nothing serious, only delaying; later in the day the roof of one of Eadon's 6 barges fell in, knocking Clerk's syce overboard; they soon got him; at best lost a couple of nosebags, very precious things now. We ought to have made Korosko at 9 am but can't get there before noon, probably later. I hope to be able to post this there. We are due at Halfa tomorrow evening, but unless there is a good chance of getting in well before dark I shall see that we don't arrive till daylight Friday. There are some who want us to disembark & entrain at once; the men & horses play up well, but it is well nigh impossible to prevent loss of various small things when doing all this in the dark. We have had two stiff nights' work. That which I have written is only a very small part of all there has been to do & think of; the Officers have done *well* & stand to me in every way, still most of them are inexperienced and naturally turn to the Squadron commander to decide many things. The horse with the sprained shoulder recovered enough to march across to Shellal; *these* Arabs are little wonders. I have not had much time or inclination to study the scenery; indeed there is nothing startling in that way, but rather a sameness.

We heard at Shellal that Gen. Hunter with 2 Infantry Brigades & 6 Squadrons Cavalry was going forward at once to seize Shabluka & possibly to reconnoitre towards Omdurman.

6 pm. We have had bad luck today, a very heavy flood is running down, making progress slow. We were a big hour going full speed & only just holding our own & thus was near the bank where the river was fully 1/2 mile wide; at last by tacking across to the other side, easier water was found & we managed to creep along; the consequence is we are not yet in sight of Korosko.

I wonder how you and the dear chicks are; they told me at Assouan our letters would be at Halfa. I do hope to get one there; it seems ages since your last came; three arrived at Cairo the night of the day we left & probably another is there tonight. The silk stocking *is a blessing* little wife. I am thankful to have it. The days are scorching but the nights are cool. We sleep up on the roof; cabins are much too stuffy. I have one to myself; the others are doubled up.

This boat is not so good nearly as the *Cleopatra*; very old engines; still she is sound & will surely get us to Halfa by Friday morning early, which will be better than late tomorrow night. My kit is quite all right. Clerk & I have a mule trunk each for the camel we are to share; this is judiciously packed, the valise Abdool made has my blanket, etc., etc.— the donkey saddle-bags carry the things I require every day.

Buscton, my soldier servant, has a daily washing; both chargers were very fit when I saw them last at Shellal; the syce and small syce have come along very well & up to this have not lost anything of importance. The house-wife has had considerable use already, dear.

1 am. Korosko. Just arrived! 16 hours late!! Now have to coal & clean tubes of boiler or something of the sort, hope an hour will do for this & then on again. I am finishing this on the steps of a hut adjoining the letter box. Postmaster lives in the town, but telegraph man says letters will go this morning so I must trust this. God bless you wife darling, do hope all is well with you & the chicks. Fondest love dearest, many Kisses, ever your loving husband.

Harry.

Camp Royan
South end of Shabluka the 6th Cataract
Thursday 8th Sept/98.

My own darling,

Your dear letters of 9th & 16th August with a couple of papers and a letter from Fred Solest & one from V. C. Hill (who sent a special message to you) reached me last evening. *How* glad I was you can imagine, ages had seemed to have elapsed since I last had had news of you. It was a bit of luck getting them, we had bivouacked (no tents since leaving Cairo) down by the river at no special place & the postboat bound South came in to see who we were. Such a sorting of mail &c. I am delighted to know you are all well & happy and things running well at "the sea." (Hurrah! a loaf of bread each tomorrow—a luxury after many days of hard biscuits.) How I would like to see you & the family on the sands. Surely the few weeks will build up the youngsters & make them strong to fight against the cold winter—dear little beggers how thoroughly they must be enjoying the whole thing. I hope too, darling, it will do you a lot of good—try not to let expenses worry you—please God we shall always have enough to get on with in a quiet way when I leave the service and we can make a home somewhere. I often wonder where that "somewhere" will be. Taking all things into consideration our funds at Cox's are keeping up well, the next two years must be heavy ones but we shall pull thro'.

The latest rumour is that the 21st are to remain another year in Egypt. I did hope the Regt. would have got home after this, but things point against it, no one can give a good reason; 'twould be such a good thing for the Regt. to get home at once—it has done well up here and it is more likely by getting to England *now*, the powers that be would be more ready to help those of us who want it than if we remain at a distance.

Everybody at Khartoum was loud in praise and hearty in congratulation; the Sirdar made a short (long for him) & highly complimentary speech to the Regt. when we paraded to march away on Tuesday [6th September, 1898]. Among other things he said that "that charge would ever be remembered with pride by the whole British Cavalry"—attacking 1500 to 2000 unbroken dervishes with a Regt. about 350 strong will probably lead to criticism, but the Sirdar's written order at 8.30 am was to "annoy the enemy as much as possible and head them off from Omdurman" this was after the guns had played havoc with them, we came across this lot about 9 o'c or soon after & went for them.

You will have read all about this in the papers dear, but you will I know like to hear what I saw of it. The only correspondent the Hon. Hubert Howard who went thru' the charge with us—was killed the same night in Omdurman near the Mahdi's tomb, so all the accounts are hearsay—except young Churchill's letters to the *Morning Post* (I think that is the paper)—he was leading the 3rd troop in my Squadron which was on the right of the Regt in the charge. My squadron was the first to turn out that morning & was sent out of the Zereba at 5.30 oc to ascertain whether a ridge & high rock in front was occupied; we were the last to leave that ridge the evening before. I sent in Smyth & his troop who soon gained the ridge, quickly sending back a report of the enemy advancing in thousands. I passed this on to the Sirdar & galloped forward to verify it. It was a grand sight seeing them coming on, beating drums & shouting, and waving their banners (I have two taken that day). We remained in observation till they got within a few hundred yards & nothing more was to be gained beyond unnecessary probable loss from the fire they directed at us. We then rejoined the Regt. which meanwhile had come out to our support—and the whole were ordered to the left flank so as not mask the fire from the Zereba. The left of the Zereba rested on the river & the ground fell gradually towards it from the ridge. I've mentioned which was about 2 miles distant. The dervishes 20 to 30 thousand strong came steadily on firing their rifles in the air!, shouting &c.; our artillery soon opened on them and their losses were terrible; they were mown down; as soon as it was certain none of them were coming round the hill & along by the river the 21st were ordered back to the Zereba while the artillery fire continued & later was added to by infantry fire.

It was probably about 8 o'c when we were sent out again with orders given personally by Gen. Gatacre to see what the enemy had on & about the hill, poor beggers had few men left in those parts but dead & wounded; we opened fire on the remainder just to clear them away & got a few shots in return, nothing much; one man in an (to us) inaccessible place got our range at last & dropped a bullet or two among us. Soon after this we received the Sirdar's order & proceeded to carry it out going away into the plain beyond & to our left of the hill; Omdurman was a few miles to our left front & we drove back to our right all we could of those who were making for the town.

While thus engaged we came across the big body of dervishes; the Regt. had been in various formations, troops & small parties having been detached for work & all rejoined & we had got into column of troops—when the dervishes were both seen & reported in considerable strengths on our right, smart rifle fire opened on us at about 250 yards distance; "A" was the rear squadron of the column so was on the right when the Regt. wheeled into line & galloped to the attack. The 4 Squadrons were thus in line : (1) "A"; (2) the made up one under Eaden; (3) "B" under Fowle; (4) "C" under Doyne. The Colonel led in front of "B"—Wyndham was away on my right; the two centre squadrons got a *very* hot fire & our reception on the right was not cool, the left squadron suffered least; there was a small nullah in which the dervishes were 3 to 6 deep & before reaching this there was some loss, poor young Grenfell fell before reaching the nullah.

(must stop now dear good night, Eadon wants the lantern precious few lanterns left now).

Opposite Nasri Island, Saturday, 10th September, 1898

Very stiff march yesterday—not a chance of adding line, today's was shorter but as we have to march slowly on account of many of the men & horses being much run down, we did not get in very early; the heat from about 9 or 10 till 4 or 5 is rather trying, only prickly mimosa bushes at this place affording little or no shade, blankets are rigged up to make as much shade as possible & everybody tries to get an hour's sleep. We have been getting up every morning at 3 or 1/2 past - but make it 4 oc now marching at 5. 30 when it is getting light. We halt here tomorrow making arrangements to send back all camels but our private ones, transferring surplus baggage to the gyassa supplied for that purpose—there will be 3 others to take 11 days forage & rations, field Hospital sick horses &c; if this small flotilla manages to hit us off at the end of each day's march we shall be very lucky.

Sunday 11th. 1 pm. We are awaiting Sirdar's reply to a wire calling to retain some of the camels, hope he agrees; the river is so variable now that it is impossible to say whether or not we shall be able to get to it at the end of each march so we must take at least a day's forage & ration with the Regt.; the horses are not fit to carry any extra weight so we ought to have that much transport. Tremendous hurricane blew early this morning, accompanied by enough rain to wet us thro'—I had my "angareeb" (charpoy) moved to the top of a hill about 300 yds away to get the full benefit of the storm. The waterproof sheet & Jaeger sheet kept much of the rain off & then there was the boom blanket I was lying on to roll up in afterward. We generally turn in dressed but did not last night on account of not marching today & as the country now is pretty safe. The cooler morning compensated for the night's disturbance so far as we are individually concerned—but one gyassa broke loose & sank while another had its mast carried away; very few horses got loose, the poor beggers were too tired. Two of my Squadron go on the barge today—one from laminitis and another from exhaustion.

To continue about our fight. Mine being in flank Squadron I inclined it to the right a little while galloping forward, then brought up the right flank so as not to make an enveloping attack, not a dervish was left out —indeed a few could have been conveniently spared; the men rode straight & well, a couple of horses were shot dead before the squadron reached the dervishes, they were thicker opposite the centre squadrons but the "A" lost 6 killed & 8 or 9 wounded—my trumpeter riding on my left dropped back with two sword cuts & S. Maj. English who was a guardian on my right got a slight wound on his foot & his horse very badly wounded still it carried him for some little time afterward. I intended, if we did get a charge, to have my sword blade between the forefinger & thumb of my bridlehand for ready use when the revolver was empty, but the charge came so quickly that I did not have time to draw it when I thought of it; this probably led to my shooting being steadier as a shot could not be thrown away, no chance of drawing a sword in such a crowd. The six rounds got me thro' & four of them got home. There was little time for thinking but I did think of my darling & the dear little chicks as we rode into the enemy & that was a "steadier."

The Regt. was much broken up, but rallied very quickly; after getting the squadron together I considered it was not good enough to ride back thro' the enemy, they were very thick, we must have lost a good many men, so I wheeled to the left & joined the other Squadron getting between the dervishes & Omdurman & then attacked them with dismounted fire, they returned fire & came towards us for a bit, not for long as the men were firing very steadily (magazine fire). I was rather glad when they turned, they fight well & so greatly out-numbered us.

Our dead were collected & left to be buried that afternoon by troops coming up, the wounded were sent to the Zereba. "Khartoum" carried me like a bird, never put a foot wrong & went perfectly straight. He never liked revolver practice from his back & I always had to hold him to it when firing galloping down 1/2 doz. targets placed one behind the other and a doz. yards apart. Probably he recognized the danger from the dervishes as they boldly met our attack with their very murderous looking swords & spears. I am bringing a few of each picked up on the 1st, 2nd & 3rd Septr: with a few other trophies all from Khartoum and Omdurman—the Dad will be able to make his selection and he shall be the first. I have a couple of their standards taken on the 2nd if I can be lucky enough to get them to Cairo without being stolen, they are in great request & we have numerous charges to make, one is white on a 12 ft pole the other was torn off its pole probably because it is one of the black ones, said to be used only by the Khalifa's own troops or by his family and therefore had to be secreted to get away.

Our horses had no water that day between the early morning and latter part of the afternoon when we got near a flooded Khor (nullah); did not stay there long but went off miles away to the South side of Omdurman while the Sirdar & the Infantry marched thro' the town to the Mahdi's tomb; we were left without orders for hours—the Egyptian Cav. & Horse Artillery & ourselves were together discussing the situation, keen to get away after the Khalifa if a clue to his line of retreat could be given & found & food & water could be obtained. Several big fellows, reputed Emirs, joined us with various stories (the biggest swell of the lot gave me his string of wooden beads, a sort of rosary)—all were more or less untrue. No orders coming we made our way in the dark a couple of miles or so across the plain to Omdurman, hoping to find food at least if not water; we dropped across the Guards in the 2nd Bgde. & picketted near them — frightfully hard ground & rough from sun-baked footprints in originally soft soil, so a drop of water & but barley for the horses — the men had a few biscuits; so had some of us also meat tabloids [sic] (those you sent with the new socks reached me dear & were awfully useful), the fellows were soon down by the horses & asleep. Soon after 9 I went outside the Guards' picquet to see whether there were signs of our baggage [—] some coming in—not a sign but hearing it had been seen in the big square near the Mahdi's tomb, I strapped on my revolver & trudged off to find it; after a walk of 1 1/2 miles thru' rather a pimpy part I found the whole of baggage with

MAJOR HARRY FINN

its Guard picketted down awaiting us. Someone had blundered, Warrington soon got some tinned stuff & a couple of camels, with water while I got a lot of the tea (already made) for the troopers put into water tanks & packed on mules — 'twas close on 11.30 when we got back but no one grumbled at being woke up. The Egyptian Cav. spent that night & next day looking for the Khalifa but got no distance.

[3rd September 1898] We were out at 5 & went right away clear of Omdurman to keep watch on the enemy who had retreated in that direction; we got to a good watering place at about 7.15, you can guess how anybody drank gallons of muddy Nile water, my squadron went a mile or two further into the desert & disarmed all those who were returning to Omdurman, hundreds of them, we were relieved by another squadron at 12 & glad of a rest before returning at 4 p.m. to the North side of the city (it is about 7 miles long) for the night.

Next day, Sunday 4th [September, 1898] a few Offrs & men from each Regt went across the river to Khartoum to assist in the great ceremonial there, this was most impressive, we assembled round the front of the ruins of the Palace which is close to the river, when all was ready the Sirdar standing in front with his Staff gave the word & up went the Union Jack next the Egyptian Flag—our old Flag of course was *loudly* cheered & the Khedive's got a good share—then came 3 cheers for the Queen followed by 3 more for the Khedive—then the Guards drums played the "Dead March in Saul" in memory of Gen. Gordon, this was followed by a Funeral Hymn (can't recollect it) by a good band of one of E. A. Regts. Next the C. of E. Presbyt & R. C. Padres each gave a short prayer standing alone back to the palace facing the troops—then the Pipes & Drums of the Camerons & Seaforths played what people called the (or a) Scottish Lament, I've heard it but can't put a name to it—after this the E. A. band played "Sun of my Soul"—congratulations to the Sirdar ended one of the most impressive ceremonies I have ever witnessed, a gunboat alongside fired guns the whole time, live shell too as there were not any blank I expect. Teck was the first fellow I shook hand with after the ceremony—he came up looking very thin. We dispersed and wandered about the grounds, garden, &c. A few of us were shown round by Slatin who pointed out all the interesting places, including the part of the palace where poor Gordon met his death—the stair-case is in ruins now.

It was well that Omdurman and Khartoum were not held by the Khalifa, had he awaited our attack in either or in both of these places, the business would have lasted much longer & our losses would have been far & away greater. It was nothing short of Providential the Khalifa not attacking our Zereba on the night of the 1st and not even seizing & holding the ridge I have mentioned. Mine was the central Squadron on the 1st when the Regt. went forward to reconnoitre, I sent Smyth & Churchill ahead with their troops when we left our bivouac, they found the Kerreri position unoccupied & from the top of one of the heights Smyth was the first to see Omdurman, we pushed on and gaining *the* ridge some miles further on discovered the enemy in force 2 or 3 miles ahead, and the Egyptian Cavalry & Horse Art. with the Camel Corps away on our left separated from us by very boggy ground (we had had rain)—a few dervish horsemen who started in our direction were driven back & a couple "bagged," later the enormous army in front of us increased, commenced deploying & advancing, compelling us to retire towards the ridge; of course full info. had been sent to the Sirdar who had his army ready drawn up for the fight which, altho 'twas 2 oc or later, threatened to take place. However, for some reason the Khalifa's force halted again & nothing happened that day. We remained on the ridge till the last then to the bivouac in the Zereba—'Twas wonderful their not attacking that night or early in the morning; everybody turned in ready for a fight any moment; the Sirdar, we are sure, was most anxious but the night passed peacefully & most of us slept like tops—the work of the 2nd I have already written. I can never forget the sight of those thousands marshalled in really good order on the afternoon of the 1st and again when they came on the 2nd under the terrific fire from our many guns. I've not been able to keep a diary so write from memory only.

Camp El Hobegi Monday 12th September 1898
The Camels turned up last night so we were off at 5.30 a.m., a very wearisome march of 18 or 19 miles principally over stony ground, could only move at foot pace & many walked a good bit of the way, got in here at 12 noon the last two hours very hot; the Nile is still "up" we can't get within a mile of the bank owing to the flood, luckily we have food & forage till tomorrow night—we hope to make Metemmeh by then & to find communication with the gyassas possible there. It has been a scorching hot afternoon, my squadron had a few mimosa bushes, the rest of the Regt. & we Offrs. had nothing beyond that improvised with blankets; a mess camel with two men was given 1/2 hour's start & the line to go on - it is now 6.30 p.m. & they have not shown up! the men are right enough for food - hope they will have sense enough to give their horses a feed of biscuits. I had to put 1/2 doz. men of my squadron on the gyassas this morning - not fit for this day's march; this business has been more trying for them than for us, we all

are on the same rations but of course we can supplement ours in a way it is impossible to add to theirs, one does all one can for them & they have played up *well*. Both my lanterns have gone march & I am now writing by the uncertain light of a candle without a globe & bothered with many "janwars"—these latter will soon make writing impossible. This tinned Australian beef & mutton better suits me, so do the biscuits only it takes me a long time to eat them. Thanks to having started with a good supply of stores, eked out by purchases from Greek merchants & others, we are able to get a bottle of pilsner or whisky & water for dinner. I do *not* despise pilsner now dear, & am only too glad to the half of a second bottle when an extra one is available. Owing to its rise the Nile water is very muddy but we drink it unfiltered very often, I should say we *have* done so - as now there is less to do, we find time to filter it thru' canvas bags, the leg of a pair of Khaki drill trousers does splendidly; this sounds much more than it really is. It is easy when one gets in & all are picketed down to train a little water & make some bovril - those you sent me stood to me right well. Dinner is called - good night wife dear.

"Maghawir" Thursday 15th September 1898

Going strong this far dear, though yesterday's was [...] long hot march with 300 yards of water *above* the horses girths to ford before we could get in here to the river. The Colonel talked of staying two days here, just now he has decided to leave tomorrow—I have written 4 1/2 sheets to Dad today & a similar letter to George Westwood, thinking of writing to Eliza & you tomorrow but now I must close this & write a few lines to [...] tonight & send them by Eadon who leaves in a Gyassa early tomorrow for Atbara, where he should arrive in the afternoon, this should get to you in a mail earlier than if posted after we get down; I'm so sorry wife dear to end so hurriedly and please tell the chicks how glad I was to get their letters & that I shall write to them when there is time. I'm *very* pleased indeed with Kathleen's report, it is really most creditable to the dear old girl. I shall recollect to drink her health on Saturday night at dinner & wish her many happy returns of the day. I will send Eliza a cheque for £50/- which will carry her on for a while & until we see how things sort themselves. There are sure to be several things I've left unwritten dear - forgive me for this sudden closing is upsetting. Do hope this will reach you all right & that you will not have

much to pay on it. God bless you & keep you & the dear chicks quite safely—many kisses to them & fondest to my darling—
Her very loving husband

Harry

Love to Nate Heath & the boys. Be sure to tell the chicks how much I liked their letters dear.

Omdurman: In sight at last.
Drawn by Lt. Angus McNeill.

CHAPTER SIX:
The Battle of Omdurman and the Charge of the 21st Lancers

Lieutenant Robert Napier Smyth

Written to his sister, dated 4 September 1898.

[Jean S. and Frederic A. Sharf Collection]

*Lieutenant the Hon. W. DeMontmorency and his wounded Sergeant-Major
after the charge of the 21st Lancers before Omdurman.*

Drawn by W. T. Maud.

Jean S. & Frederic A. Sharf Collection.

BATTLE OF OMDURMAN AND THE CHARGE OF THE 21ST LANCERS

INTRODUCTORY NOTES

Robert Napier Smyth was born on 26 June, 1868, the son of General J. H. Smyth, C.B. of Primhurst. He was educated at Wellington School, and entered the army in 1890. He was promoted to Captain in 1899, Major in 1905, Lieut.-Colonel in 1910 and Colonel in 1914. He died on 14 October, 1947.

He served with the 21st Lancers in the Soudanese Campaign in 1898 and was present at the battle of Omdurman. During the South African War, he was D.A.A.G. Intelligence, and served with the 13th Hussars (mentioned in despatches). In the Great War, he was a General Staff Officer, 2nd Grade, 1915, and a Brigade Commander, 1915.

Smyth was an avid correspondent, writing frequently from various campaign sites to his three sisters: Elinor (known as Nelly), Alice and Ethel. Whichever sister received the original handwritten letter would then prepare a typed copy to be circulated among the others. In some cases, this typed copy would be marked "True Copy"; it was normally typed on a long, plain, heavy piece of paper, which was embossed at the top left corner with a coat of arms.

His account of Omdurman was written to Alice; she then prepared the typed copy and sent it on to her sisters. The copy used in this publication shows signs of having been folded and unfolded on many occasions; it finally ended up in the hands of Nelly, who was married to Hugh Eastwood, another army officer. The letter descended in the Eastwood family, and was acquired at auction as part of a lot which included a number of Boer War letters from Smyth to Nelly.

OMDURMAN
4/9/98

My Dear Alice,

Herewith a full account of my experiences during the last few days. You will have read the whole account by now in the papers, so I will confine myself to what I saw and did.

I am rather handicapped as owing to my servant having been wounded (in 5 places) my kit has been in charge of chance servants who would help, and one of my most important bags containing my diary and holdall has been lost, which is more than annoying.

I will write in diary form and that makes it easier to quote one's facts.

29th August. Final concentration of whole force. Arrived in bivouac after 22 miles march, about 6.30. Pouring rain all night. Horses, men and saddlery wet through.

30th August. Reveille 3 a.m. Still Raining. Saddled in the dark. Started 5 a.m. I went out with my troop as right advance patrol. Saw no enemy though 2 prisoners were captured on my left. Halted at 1 p.m. Was sent on 2 miles with troop as advance picket. Remained out till 6 p.m. The bush in front of my picket was full of Dervish Horsemen. I counted about 100. They did not come nearer than 12 to 15 hundred yards of me. Eventually about 5.30 they lit a series of bonfires and retired. It was a sign the days work was over. Returned to Zereba with rest of Regiment. Had peaceful night's rest.

31st August. My Squadron in reserve saw nothing, but had a long tiring day; 14 hours in the saddle. Montmorency and Pirie went forward alone to reconoitre the camp and Kerreri. Only saw 30 horsemen who almost cut them off. They escaped with difficulty. It was a foolhardy thing to allow but was very plucky.

1st September. Sent out as Officers Patrol at 5 a.m. to see if same camp was occupied. Found that it was not, so sent back to that effect, after which I was recalled, and we advanced in force to range of hills further off. This Range was the scene of everything. I shall always refer to it as *the Range.* From there we had a grand panoramic view of Omdurman and the Mahdi's Tomb. In front was there [sic] first army of 30,000 strong drawn up in battle array just like they are formed on Laffans Plain for a *feu de joie.* We made two demonstrations to try and make them advance but they did not. We held this Range till 2 when we returned to the Zereba. During the night there was some desultory firing, but you will see no damage. Having been 16 hours in the saddle so to speak I slept soundly through it all. More rain.

2nd September. My Squadron first out of Zereba 5.30 a.m. I am sent out again to the Range as Officers Patrol. Saw the whole first Dervish army in two long lines with about 10,000 troops in reserve on the right. Sent in my information. First line about 1,200 yards from me. Recalled temporarily about 7 but sent out again to watch any change of front. Found their centre halted about 600 yards from me. My patrol concealed behind rocks. I advanced with one man to hold my horse and find the whole of the right swinging round. I sent in to that effect. While writing, a correspondent rides up and remains mounted. Riflemen in centre see this and fire 2 volleys. Bullets whistling and splashing on rocks very close. The Colonel hearing this sends for me to retire at once. Both he and Pirie much excited and annoyed and very fussy, saying I was unnecessarily exposing myself. It was the Correspondent's fault, and after all it was only one Private and myself —no great loss if we had been hit. However we got away without being so. My Squadron Leader leaves for orders. I take charge of Squadron and retire them to rejoin Regiment behind Zereba. Half way there (about one mile) guns on both sides opened fire. Enemy have occupied the Range with their right. The whole hord advances howling. Have to trot my Squadron past not to mask fire front. The whole Regiment halt in rear Zereba. Artillery duel goes on. Having good view of it all. Frightful slaughter of enemy, not much damage to Zereba. Colonel Rhodes wounded inside it and a few privates of Infantry. Maxim and Infantry fires very steady and deadly. Enemy gets within 300 - 400 yards of position. Break up and fly. We are ordered to high ground right of the Range to wait orders to pursue. Good view of battlefield. Horrible sights of dead and dying. Wounded horses and men trying to get away. Men on all fours creeping, finally giving up and lying down to die. Horses lame and galloping aimlessly. Regular inferno. Retreating enemy cross the Range, and no longer under fire, begin to try and reform. We are ordered to stop them, and clear plain on Omdurman side of Range of any formed or forming body. We mount and go down at sharp trot to plain, in line of squadron columns. See formed body of about 200, 600 yards to our left. Front troops "Left Wheel." Immediately met by volleys fairly accurately aimed. My right hand man drops, his horse shot under him. Bullets seem to be whistling and splashing all round. "Right Shoulders." Manoeuvre well carried out and I am left troops leader. Looking round see nullah (ditch) 8 feet wide, four feet deep in front. Every side a compact mass of white robed men, apparently countless, still firing and waving swords. Find myself at nullah. Man bolts out leaving 2 donkeys in my way, catch hold of horse hard by head. Knowing to fall would be fatal. He blunders against donkey, recovers and scrambles out. Am met by swordsman on foot. Cuts at my right front. I guard it with sword. Next, man with fat face, all in white having fired, missed me, throws up both hands. I cut him across the face. He drops. Large bearded man in blue, with two edged sword and two hands cuts at me. Think this time I must be done for but pace tells and my guard carries it off. Duck my head to spear thrown which just misses me. Another cut at my horse, miss guard, but luckily cut is too far away and only cuts through my breastplate and gives my horse a small flesh wound on neck and shoulder. Then I remember no more till I find myself outside with four or five of my troop. See Major Wyndham running. Gallop to help him. I am just too late. Kenna has seized him and he takes him out, not me. Rally my troop as well as I can. Horrible sights. Everyone seems to be bleeding, including my own horse. I dont know even if he is badly hurt or not. It seems to be blood, blood, blood everywhere. Horses and men smothered with either their own or other peoples, wounded men being carried off by others as one sees in pictures. Horses dropping down and running away. See Nesham led away with left hand hanging down. Words are passed on, "Poor Grenfell killed." "2,000 men." "Brinton shot" and "Poor little Smyth killed" etc. (The Colonel, Montmorency, and Dauncey at first mistook Grenfell for me.) He was so horribly mutilated.

We reform, take up their position, and use dismounted fire. Men fire steadily, the break up is complete. The one formed band is dispersed. Our charge has been successful. We are left in possession of the ground, and the whole plain is ours. Some say we did right; others wrong, but the fact remains that we achieved our object, and did what we were told to do. 300 Cavalry had dispersed 1,500 to 2,000 riflemen who stood their ground. They may say that the charge was *pour la gloire*, but it was not only a brave feat, but a successful one. The casualties were big for these times. 1 Officer killed, 4 wounded, 20 N.C.Os and men killed and 40 - 50 wounded. More than 20%, not counting the horses. In my troop, only 18 men, 1 lost one killed, 3 wounded, and 4 horses. After we saw complete success of work, we revisited the scene of the charge. I was told off to get 6 men of my troop and collect our dead. The less said or written about that the better. It was ghastly. The tears streamed down my cheeks and I was physically sick. It was terrible. At this present moment I dont wish the morn repeated. It cost too dear. I have always wanted to be in a charge and have got my desire and am satisfied. We then proceeded to collect and disarm stragglers - an easy object as none of them showed fight. This lasted 2 hours, while the Infantry battle with the second army was going on at our right. They had gone straight for the Camel Corps, Egyptian Cavalry and Horse Batteries. They were practically cut off and had to gallop. The ground was heavy and 3 guns had to be left, but only temporarily, as when the Soudanese came up the second army were driven back again. After this the Colonel was ordered to see if Omdurman was occupied. He sent me on with 4 men. I got into the Camp and found that completely deserted, but the buildings were occupied, and as I could get no cover we had to retire about 1,000 yards, as they were firing rather straight at us. However I discovered all that was wanted, and think I am entitled to say "I was first in Omdurman" as the camp was part of it. We then went back to water and found our horses, 4 p.m. They had had nothing since 4 a.m. Then we were out till dusk as Outposts, after which we lay on the rocks and slept heavily. No mess, no rations. Next day we were sent South of City to collect stragglers, arms, and men returning to give themselves up. We were out till 6 p.m. Dull and tiring work. This morning there is a Memorial Service to Gordon at Khartoum. Numbers were limited but I managed to squeeze myself in, and got up at 4 a.m. to go, but could not after all, as I was ill and in pain, but I got some opium and other medicine, and am now feeling all right again. I am very fit really. This is only an incident. I shall have nothing more of interest to write about. I wish I had seen the planting of the British Flag at Khartoum. It is going on now, but want to be fit for the march in state through Omdurman. As a matter of fact *we* did so yesterday.

Yours,

R. N. S.

I may as well give you the list of our horse casualties as that will show you, more than the men, what we went through: -

8 killed outright in action, 14 destroyed immediately afterwards. 44 gunshot wounds, and 53 spear and sword wounds now in sick Lines. Officers, 1 killed, 4 wounded. Men, 21 killed, 44 wounded. Total Men and officers killed and wounded 70. Horses 119; and all that out of 300.

It was an experience, and what struck me most was, you always hear that there are cases in every action where some men want dash and courage. In this instance I cannot quote *one*. I would if I could, because I value true statistics.

As far as Cavalry goes it is the biggest thing since Balaclava, and I am very proud of belonging to the 21st Lancers. Wise or unwise, it was a brave deed nobly done, and as Colonel Wauchope stated, he was so proud and pleased it had happened, as it proved that Cavalry still existed, and that we did not come here to play at Mounted Infantry. I must go now. I have to give in my return. In spite of losses in the Field, I can march out 28 horses and 27 Men fit, out of the 38 I started with from Cairo.

It is like the Infernal Regions. I never saw anything so disgusting. Crowds of horses and donkeys all died any time during the last 2 weeks, the Tomb has been badly knocked about by the Gunboat shells. I believe the Soudanese raided and slaughtered, the night after the battle to a great extent. I am very glad. If I had my way, every man we captured on the battlefield should have been shot at once then and there, cold blood or not. If you had seen the condition of our dead you would have said the same. We appear to be the only lot who had any really hard fighting and suffered to any extent.

Lieutenant Angus McNeill.

CHAPTER SEVEN:
The Battle of Omdurman

Lieutenant Angus McNeill
of the Seaforth Highlanders

Extracts from Diary, accompanied by drawings.

[Collection Mrs. Barbara McNeill]

Winston Churchill asks if the 21st Lancers have passed this way.
Drawn by Lt. Angus McNeill.

Lieutenant Angus McNeill was given this signed photo by his school-mate Winston Spencer Churchill as a memento of their experiences in the Omdurman campaign.

LIEUTENANT ANGUS MCNEILL

THE BATTLE OF OMDURMAN

INTRODUCTORY NOTES

Born in 1874, the son of Colonel Duncan McNeill of Colonsay, he was educated at Harrow School and enlisted in the Seaforth Highlanders in 1895. McNeill served in Crete in 1897, and went on with his regiment to participate in the Sudan campaign, where he saw action at the Atbara River and at Omdurman. He served in South Africa in 1899 and 1900 in command of Montmorency's Scouts.

In 1907 he married Lilian Findlay, a widow. They had one son, John Malcolm McNeill. In world War I he was attached to Lovat Scouts and mentioned in despatches five times. In 1918 McNeill was awarded the Distinguished Service Order. After the war, he commanded a Territorial Army Brigade in East Anglia. In 1922, he was sent to Palestine to form and command the British Gendarmerie in Palestine. He held this position for four years, and then retired in Palestine. He died in Cyprus in June, 1950 and is buried there.

During the Omdurman campaign, McNeill was attached as Orderly Officer to General Gatacre. In the confusion of the assault, he was instructed to assist a wounded officer, but finding there was little he could do, he joined men of his own regiment and men of the Cameron Highlanders in battle.

McNeill kept a diary throughout the campaign, and was a prolific illustrator of his own letters back to his family. Some of these sketches found their way into the contemporary illustrated press. However, it was his former schoolmate at Harrow, Winston Spencer Churchill, who found the best use for McNeill's artistic talents, commissioning McNeill to provide illustrations for Churchill's definitive history of the campaign, entitled *The River War*.

In his preface to the two volume history, dated September 25, 1899, Churchill comments: "I will not venture to pronounce upon the artistic value of the sketches with which Mr. McNeill has adorned the account: but I think they are in every detail scrupulously accurate." We are grateful to Mrs. Barbara McNeill for permitting us to quote from the diary of her husband's father; and to the Churchill Estate for permitting Mrs. McNeill to share with us the drawings still in her possession.

Saturday, 6 August
Started with all the Brigade Transport from Darmali. Owen also with all the Maxim Battery mules. He takes command as far as Wad Habshi. Marched at 1.45 and about 4.20 arrived at the cavalry camp about 1 mile north of Dakeila. Were prepared to cross next morning. Found the 32nd here in the middle of the River crossing.

Monday, 8 August
Stood by all day ready to cross. At last about 7 p.m. all the camels were over. I then took over a boat load, i.e. 22 mules and 3 horses. Very dark. Picketed animals first where we landed and waited for daylight to see where we were.

Tuesday, 9 August
By 5 a.m. Owen had started over another load and my first lot had got picketed into camp. By 11 o'clock we had the whole lot settled down and soon had nosebags on. We lunched with Young in the EA whose battery is alongside us. I also dined with him in the evening. Saw a boat going up with the 40 pounders. The animals of the 87th are now all on this side.

Wednesday, 10 August
Started all hands to work early saddling up which proved rather a job. Then about 6.45 took the whole show out watering order. The syces are an unruly lot and no mistake. Kourbash is the only thing.

Thursday, 11 August
Had the whole lot out again morning and evening—are getting some discipline amongst the devils. The native sergeants are rather good men and carry out any orders they happened to understand with alacrity.

Friday, 12 August
The 21st Lancers were crossing all day. By evening the whole of the 1st Squadron had crossed. Fowle, Kenna, Montmorency, Protherosmith, [sic] Jack Brinton-Price, Robert Grenfell and Col. Martin Commanding. We had the usual parades carrying the loads which we shall have on the march. In the evening Christie, orderly officer to Wauchope, arrived with the GOC's horses. I went down to help him and it was pitch dark before we got everything into camp. NB: We are doing ourselves thundering well here - a little mess of 4 - Owen, Christie, Russell & self.

THE BATTLE OF OMDURMAN

Saturday, 13 August
Much as usual. In evening saw the 1st Brigade pass in the barges—very slow progress they were making too!

Sunday, 14 August
Had the whole Div. Transport out at 6 a.m. and practiced formations for the line of march.

Monday, 15 August
2nd Squadron of 21st Lancers crossed the river. All made preparations to march early next morning. Christie and self crossed over to Atbara to get a few things and make some arrangements. Lunched with the Headquarters staff and crossed back again in the evening.

Tuesday, 16 August
Paraded at 6 a.m. and formed up on the desert clear of the bush. Waited three-quarters of an hour for the 21st Lancers who eventually turned up—having left 50 men behind to "clean up" camp! The remainder having had no breakfast before starting. Result—one man got a touch of the sun and is not expected to live. Got into camp about

Bivouac of the 21st Lancers: On the way to Wad Hamed.
Drawn by Lt. Angus McNeill.

12.45 but owing to disgraceful dithering on the part of the authorities our camping ground was not told off to us until two and a half hours later!—during which time the mules stood about with their heavy loads on. The place was full of scorpions and several people were bitten.

Wednesday, 17 August
Marched at 5 a.m. and after a very long and dusty march reached camp by a circuitous route at about 2.30. But no peace for the wicked—we had just watered and fed our animals, but luckily had not unsaddled when an order came to march at 4 p.m. and go round a lake to get to the river bank for our forage and rations—about 4 miles. The 21st have left 10 horses and shot 2.

Thursday, 18 August
Marched at 6 a.m. and after about 16 miles of it got into camp about 1 p.m.

Friday, 19 August
Marched at 5 a.m. and reached Megawiel—a charming camp which had been previously occupied—at 11.30 a.m. Here we spent the whole of the next day. The 21st sent 8 men and 7 horses down by a boat which called in the evening. The mules are very fit—so are we.

Saturday, 20 August
Spent a peaceful day, poking about the lines etc. After lunch a steamer came in and stopped for wood with a half battalion of the 5th Fusiliers on board and Gen. Gatacre.

Sunday, 21 August
Marched at 5 a.m. and reached Metemmah about 12 noon. Here we halted 'til 3.30 p.m. No shade for the animals whatever and only a few trees for the officers and men. Was too slack to go over beyond the town to see the site of the massacre. Marched at 3.30 p.m. and only went about two and three quarter miles. Most ridiculous rot! But such might be said of many other things on this march! Young's battery lost itself.

Monday, 22 August
Marched at 4.30 and reached a most shady and excellent camp about the middle of the Nasri Island bend about 12 o'clock. Here we made ourselves comfortable for the rest of the day. "Frankie" [a mule] got a go of Sandcholic and was very bad.

THE BATTLE OF OMDURMAN

Tuesday, 23 August

Marched at 5 a.m. for the last time and reached Wad Hamed camp at about 11.30 a.m. Some of the going on the way was fearful—great rocks and stones and narrow paths. Glad to say have lost no mules on the way. "Frankie" very bad—can give him no relief.

Wednesday, 24 August

The whole army was to be out early for a parade in marching formation with Transport, etc. Got up at 3.45—quarter of an hour before reveille—and found my way with some difficulty to the camel lines—blowing a fearful sandstorm which presently turned into rain—real good tropical rain. Managed to secure 32 camels and dragged them back to our lines losing our way many times en route. Had just got them loaded when the "No Parade" went. But not before I was wet to the skin. Spent the rest of the day getting the transport together and preparing for the march tomorrow afternoon. 2 Native Brigades marched out in evening.

Thursday, 25 August

Struck camp at Reveille—Heaven knows why! However there are the men sitting in the sun all day. Spent a long time in the transport lines. All the mules fit to carry loads I am glad to say. "Frankie" is out of danger and very much better this morning. The 2nd Brigade left at 5 a.m. Marched about 4.30 p.m. and went 6 miles, halted near the river bank for the night. The whole of the Rear Guard was lost in the desert and only rejoined in the morning.

Friday, 26 August

Started at 6 a.m. and marched another 6 miles or so to where the 2nd Brigade had got the day before. A very shady bivouac and close to the water. Here we remained all day and about 4.30 marched off for a place among the hills where we were to bivouac without water for the night. This was the most awful show I have ever seen. What the reason was I don't know but the fact remains that the men in both Brigades were falling out like flies. I was of course in rear with the camel transport. Smiler Kennedy was in command of the rear guard and made me stay behind and help with the cripples. We eventually got every one into camp by 9 p.m.! May I never see such a disgraceful and lamentable exhibition again. There were many cases of cramp, so severe that the victims could do nothing but writhe on the ground. What caused this I do not know. We bivouaced in square for the night very short of water.

LIEUTENANT ANGUS MCNEILL

My mules could only get half a bucket each—barely that. I was on patrol from 11–1 o'clock and have never felt so fearfully drowsy.

Saturday, 27 August
We loaded up and marched at daylight—another 6 miles or so and reached the river just opposite Jebel Royan where we found all the native army and the gunboats. The Native Regts. sent their bands to play us in—a great show.

Sunday, 28 August
All the native Troops marched out early in the morning—preceded by the cavalry and camel corps. The Eleventh Sudanese are a splendid Regt. Commanded by Jackson Bey, Gordon Highlanders. All the men have red hackles in the tarbushes and the Sergeants have sashes. We marched about 4.30 p.m. and got in fairly late after marching about 8 miles. Richie and Arbuthnot were sent onto a gunboat with the cripples.

Monday, 29 August
Got in late last night and no time to make Zareeba. Spent whole day in same place. Charming dust storm blew in a most persevering manner. Heavy rain in night. A dervish threw a spear at a Guardsman on piquet last night and an officer attempted to fire his revolver which did not go off!

Tuesday, 30 August
Started loading camels in the dark. Pouring with rain. All the blankets weighed twice their usual weight and had to separate many bundles and carry as best as I could. Marched about 12.5 miles.

Wednesday, 31 August
Marched about 6 a.m. and eventually Zerebared in one large square. Large force of dervishes reported to our front by the cavalry and every precaution taken against a night attack. Was on patrol and it fairly poured. No sleep and no dervishes.

Thursday, 1 September
Partridge shooting begins—probably dervish shooting also. Moved at 6 a.m. and marched over the Kerreri ridge into the village of that name where we halted and proceeded to Zereba. Enormous dervish force reported by cavalry to be moving towards us in a long line. Great preparations for receiving them. However they never came on and we stayed outside the village all night and we Zerebared where we lay. They sniped a bit from the hill during the night.

THE BATTLE OF OMDURMAN

Officers watching Dervish patrols from Kerreri Hill.
Drawn by Lt. Angus McNeill.

Friday, 2 September
About 5 a.m. everyone was ready to move off or to await the attack of the dervishes behind the apology for a Zereba which we had hastily made the evening before. At 6.10 the cavalry came trotting back and reported thousands of the enemy advancing about 2 miles off in a long line or rather a series of lines with many flags and yelling like blazes. The camels and camp followers were immediately parked some few hundred yards in rear behind a small knoll. Also the Field Hospitals. The Gunboats had also taken up a position on either flank of the river.

At 6.20 we saw the first white flag appear over the ridge. At 6.35 the whole ridge was covered with dervishes and flags also steadily advancing onto the plain. At 6.43 the first gun was fired by the 32nd field Battery on our left at another large force of dervishes who had just appeared over the other shoulder of the hill. After this the action became general—the shooting of the artillery was excellent and the execution fearful. The Dervish right attack apparently gave up the idea of attacking our left, where the 2nd British Brigade were and proceeded to leisurely cross our front at about 1,000 yards - much to their subsequent discomfort. At about 7.10 a.m. a large force of dervishes were seen making their way along the hillsides to our right. Here were some native artillery and the Camel Corps who had rather a hot time 'til supported by 3 gunboats. The steady volley firing of the British Division and the persistent rattle of the maxims continued all along the line—every shot seemed to take effect. Presently the centre attack of the enemy stopped and they drew off a bit but only to collect in a khor and reinforced by thousands of fresh men they advanced again straight at us. Brave men they are—most certainly! But very misguided. Just at this moment a Dervish Emir mounted on a weedy arab cantered slowly to the front and coming quite close up to the line, turned and cantered along it in the most leisurely manner. I never saw him killed and do not know what became of him. The second rush of the Dervishes was also repulsed and heavy firing went on for some time. The whole plain was a fearful sight - simply plastered with dead and dying men and horses—the wounded attempting to crawl away. Meanwhile the left attack of the dervishes bearing the enormous green flag of the Emir Wad Hela—a most notorious Baggara Chief—having been well hammered by the gunboats, withdrew slowly and in perfect oder over the shoulder of the ridge. But a gunboat was sent downstream a few hundred yards to drive them back into the fight again—which they succeeded in doing. They then thought it not good enough and slowly retired and disappeared behind the hill to all appearances gone for ever. But from where I was I could see them reforming in thousands with their banners and above them all the great green flag of Wad Hela. And now for the most interesting part of the day.

The fight in the plain being apparently at an end and the dervishes in full retreat, the Sirdar ordered the whole force to move to the left and advance on Omdurman supported by MacDonald's Brigade on our right. This was accordingly done—but hardly had the force moved 300 yards than very heavy firing was heard from the direction of MacDonald's Brigade. The British Division immediately charged front towards the firing and went to the assistance of the Soudanese, who had suddenly been attacked by an enormous force of dervishes who had never been under fire—assisted by the whole of Wad Hela's men who had popped over the hill from behind. The Soudanese own that they were devilish glad to see us as some of the men had only 3 rounds left and were very hard pressed. The second fight lasted for a good long time and the hill on our left was cleared of the enemy who were driven

THE BATTLE OF OMDURMAN

across the plain and suffered fearfully. They were now utterly broken and for the first time *ran*. Earlier in the fight they had merely turned and walked to the rear. About the time this second phase began the 21st Lancers were moving round to the South of the hill with orders to turn back any fugitives into the fight. They saw about a couple of hundred (apparently) dervishes standing a little way off who opened a heavy fire upon them. The Lancers immediately formed from column of troops into line and charged them. When they got about 50 yards from the dervishes, suddenly they saw a deep Khor with about an 8 foot drop in front of them filled with thousands of spearmen. There was nothing for it but to go on so in they jumped and cut their way through! They lost a lot of men killed or wounded - about 69 I am told. Young Grenfell in the 12th was literally cut to ribbons. His horse fell in the Khor and before anything could be done he was set upon and cut to pieces—poor chap. Brinton, Nesham and Molyneux were all severely wounded with sword cuts. It was a grand charge but did not do much good really. However the Regiment are delighted at having had their chance and taken advantage of it.

Tullibardine extracting a bullet from leg of a wounded Dervish.
Drawn by Lt. Angus McNeill.

This time the fight was really over and the army advanced on Omdurman. Halted for a short time in the afternoon outside the town to enable the men to get some food. We entered Omdurman without opposition just at sunset. The Sirdar and Slatin Pasha rode straight into the Mosque after the battle with a small escort of Cavalry but unluckily just missed the Khalifa and his chief Emir Anis—who had ridden in on donkeys to pray! The Camel Corps and native cavalry pursued the enemy all night. We bivouaced in an open space in the town, all dog tired!

The Soudanese troops and Jaalin friendlies committed the most fearsome atrocities all night and murdered, pillaged etc. over the whole of the town. Many hundreds of Baggara were killed and I fear a lot of peaceful Jaalins.

Thus ended the eventful 2 September - also a Friday. The Battle of the Atbara was on Good Friday.

Saturday, 3 September
The British Division moved into an open space on the outskirts of the town by the river early in the morning. The cavalry and camelry are still pursuing the scattered dervishes.

Sunday, 4 September
Most of the officers and detachments of men from all the British forces went in steamers to Khartoum to attend a Memorial Service held in Gordon's Palace gardens. The British and Khedival flags were hoisted side by side and the troops cheered. 21 guns were fired. In the evening the Sirdar spoke a few words to all the native troops on parade.

Monday, 5 September
The British Division route-marched round the Town of Omdurman— How it does stink! The market place is full of prisoners—many of them wounded. In the evening self, Gaisford and Ritchie rode in to see all the sights. Got pieces of the Mahdi's Tomb etc. Saw the Biet-al-Maua or Arsenal much to the rage of Maxwell Bey who said they had no business to admit us!

Tuesday, 6 September
In camp horse trading with the Egyptian cavalry.

THE BATTLE OF OMDURMAN

The Seaforth & Cameron Highlanders going down the
Nile in Gyassas after Omdurman, September 1898.

Drawn by Lt. Angus McNeill.

Wednesday, 7 September
Embarking horses and mules to go down river. A steamer arrived from
Fashoda full of Dervishes who gave themselves up. They say that
Fashoda is occupied by the French! The Sirdar himself with 4 gunboats
is immediately going up to verify the report.

Thursday, 8 September
We got orders to embark in 5 gyassas and got away. No wind, and we
drifted down the River and slept on the bank.

Friday, 9 September
Still no wind and we drifted down on the current.

LIEUTENANT ANGUS MCNEILL

Saturday, 10 September
Under way at 6 a.m. and floated down to Nasri Island, where we were to collect all our kit and possessions from Wad Hamed. However, we learned that it had all gone to the bottom of the river - including my new gun.

Sunday, 11 September
A splendid breeze, and we had a good run - nearly to Atbara.

Monday, 12 September
A fair breeze and we had a fast run to Abu Hamed by the evening.

Tuesday, 13 September
A good journey. Wadi Halfa at 9 p.m. and were embarked on the *Hannek*—towing 2 barges—nearly collided in the dark with another steamer coming up.

Wednesday, 14 September
Had a ripping sleep and got much refreshed. Stopped at Korosko and sent some telegrams and bought eggs and milk—great luxuries. Arrived late at night at Shellal and disembarked.

Thursday, 15 September
Entrained and traveled all day and night to Luxor.

Friday, 16 September
Had breakfast and wash in the Hotel. The men got 2 hot meals. Entrained and traveled to Cairo.

Saturday, 17 September
In Cairo we marched to the citadel where we made ourselves comfortable.

Sunday, 18 September
Was told that I was to be Adjutant and thus to go on first leave, so sailed for England - arriving on 29th September and went on leave to Scotland.

THE BATTLE OF OMDURMAN

Sir Archibald Hunter

CHAPTER EIGHT:
The Battle of Omdurman

General Sir Archibald Hunter

Letter written to his brother, containing detailed
descriptions of the military campaign.

[Anne S. K. Brown Military Collection,
John Hay Library at Brown University]

THE BATTLE OF OMDURMAN

INTRODUCTORY NOTES

Archibald Hunter was born in 1856. Educated at Sandhurst, he was gazetted to the 4th Foot in 1874. He was promoted captain in 1882. His first active service was on the Nile Expedition of 1884 gaining a brevet as major the following year. In the same year he was severely wounded at the battle of Giniss, and again at the battle of Toski in 1889. From 1884 until 1899 he served with the Egyptian Army. He obtained a brevet as colonel in 1894 and two years later served with Kitchener at the battle of Firket. At Omdurman, he commanded a division, and following the fall of Khartoum he was appointed K.C.B. Following a command in India, he saw action in the South African War. Prior to World War 1, he held various commands and from 1915-1917 helped to train the new armies for the Westerm Front. He retired from the army in 1920 and died in London on 28 June 1936.

The item published here is a five - page typed letter sent by Hunter to his brother Archie, who forwarded it to another relative. It was published previously in Duncan Doolittle, *A Soldier's Hero: General Sir Archibald Hunter* (1991). A further account of Hunter's role at Omdurman can be found in Archibald Hunter, *Kitchener's Sword-Arm: The Life and Campaigns of General Sir Archibald Hunter* (1996).

Khartoum, 14 October 1898.

My dear

Since 2nd September is a good long time, but till now I have made no effort to write an account of the fight from my point of view. For one thing I have been very busy, for another I have had a dose of fever, to which I am a stranger and it has pulled me down somewhat. In any case, no two people see the same phases in the same light at the same time.

I left the Atbara on August 2nd earlier than I expected, and formed a camp 56 miles north of Khartoum—Here all the army practically concentrated. I then marched 24 miles further and we again concentrated. After this we marched as one army, encamped in a closed up laager formation at night so that we could not be rushed. The army marched in echelon of brigades from the left, British next the water, as they drank the most, my division on the right towards the desert. My four brigades were disposed thus. Maxwell's on the right of British, then Lewis, then MacDonald's, Collinson's Brigade was in reserve, in rear of Maxwell with all baggage, British as well, and reserve ammunition and hospital stock. Each brigade had a battery of artillery of quick firing guns.

On September 1st we crossed Kerreri Ridge about 9 A.M. From the top I could see Omdurman. We chose sight [sic] for camp & formed it on the closed up principle. While I was seeing to this the Sirdar and his staff rode forward to a hill Sarghum, called by us Signal Hill, where the 21st Lancers had established their signallers and mounted it. I finished my work and galloped forward to get a good look, when I met Sirdar just come down from the Hill, looking as if he had seen a ghost and no wonder, for he said the enemy were only five miles beyond the hill, advancing 50,000 strong against us. I said "Come on back and we will get into fighting formation and fill all tanks and water bottles before dark and entreanch [sic] ourselves and it will be all right." So we got back and I got out the mounted officers and were speedily in a position to receive an attack.

So long as enemy came on in daylight I had no fear. But my conviction till I die will be that if he had attacked us in the dark before dawn, with the same bravery he attacked us next day by day-light, we should have been pierced, divided, broken and rolled into the river. Few people can realize and still less know from practical knowledge what happened when an enemy gets inside your formation. Friend kills friend, contrary orders are given, bugles are sounded to everyone's confusion, all is dark and dusk, and roar of animals and shrieks of dying & wounded, and clamour of natives, and shrill yells of enemy,

THE BATTLE OF OMDURMAN

and curses and prayers and a bable of confusion and horror.

However, we were spared all this by the enemy waiting for the light. When the sun rose on 2nd September '98, I was never so glad in all my born days.

My division and staff took it in turns to keep watch. There had been a few shots fired in the night not by my division. By six o'clock firing began. The British & Maxwell's brigade received the first attack and beat it off handsomely. Nothing could get near our breach loaders and Maxims. The lead belched forth was like a deluge of rain. They faced it like men and died shouting out their belief, not one whit intimidated by all our superior weapons, marksmenship [sic] and discipline. What with sick men behind on gun boats etc. the enemy were three to one. From earlier than 7 A.M. a green flag (Ali Wad Helu) had been passing across from our left front, passed our front and round and abreast of our right at about 2,000 yards distance. As they got round towards the river, the gun boats down stream of us, and the horse artillery guns started them well. From the moment they had been under fire of our artillery, they had been salvoed with buckets of iron and lead, so I am sure we took pretty heavy toll of them. Anyhow they turned back, some 8,000 men and took shelter behind a high hill right in our front.

1 & 2 B mean first & second British brigades, the other numbers refer to their numbers in my division. I show them as we were in Camp, and as we ought to have been in Echelon. 1 means MacDonald's Brigade, 2 Maxwell's, 3 Lewis's 4 Collinsons. You will notice 1 and 2 British Brigades had only to step forward to be in their position in Echelon. Maxwell had further to go. #3 (Lewis) had much further to go and MacDonald had to make way for Lewis to enable latter to get into place. Sirdar was with British. He was impatient and has bad sight anyhow. I asked him to give me time and reminded him of our friends behind hill A, who were still there. B is Signal Hill. Now, instead of being as in theory we ought to have been when we advanced owing to the hurry and skurry, to the delay caused by a lot of men who had shammed dead jumping up in front of Maxwell's brigade, we were not as shewn, but we were as I have traced.

Then out on top of MacDonald swarmed the mob behind A, and here ensued the best piece of drill and the finest piece of square stand up fighting of this campaign since the Atbara. MacDonald changed front and best [sic] them off alone, I sent the Lincolns to him but he did not require them. Then the Cavalry finished them off. By the time we got abreast of the steamers up stream it was one p.m. By the time I had collected the wounded, scoured the ground, mind you a fairly extensive one, for lost sheep and burried [sic] the dead, it was 2:30 p.m. So, I galloped on then quite happy that my Division is all correct. Maxwell's brigade was with the Sirdar, Lewis had gone for water, MacDonald was following him, and Collinson was safe with the transport too.

I picked up the Sirdar just as he was nearing the Khalifa's enclosure. I don't know what he felt, but I know how I felt and how he looked. I told him he was Lord Khartoum if he cared to be and said I hope Government would give him a big sum down. The campaign was over and we could now enjoy ourselves like boys ratting in a stock yard. And we did have an afternoon, poking into houses, in and out of narrow allies [sic], kicking down doors, forcing gateways, chasing devils all over the place, most surrendered, but we had to kill some three or four hundred.

However, to make a long story short, when the sun went down everybody wanted to know where to stay for the night, what were the orders for tomorrow, how about pursuit, &c. Leaving the Sirdar to liberate the rogues and blackguards (most of them) in prison I rode to the out skirts of the town and found a place to camp, and got most of them out of there by mid night. MacDonald's Brigade was tired and preferred to rest in the main street. (The cunning beggars, the blacks did nothing but loot the prettiest slave girls and best trophies to be had.) It was past 1 A.M. when we went to bed. Our transport had got stuck with MacDonald's brigade. Smith Dorrien of the Derbyshire Regt. gave me a mug of soup and a mug of the best champagne, and both were delicious. Whiggham [sic] of the Warwicks (attached 13th Btn.) lent me a blanket and a bed and I slept till dawn like a top, after one of the best days I ever passed.

Kitchener deserves all he gets. He has run the show himself. His has been the responsibility, some of us have helped too. And none has reasons other than to be proud. We have done what we said we would and thank Goodness the loss of life has been extraordinarily small.

The tactics of the enemy have helped us. Poor Devils, they tried to draw conclusions and they nearly hit the right one. The Khalifa summed up the fighting recently and said, "At Firket we were surprised, and afterwards fought behind rocks and in houses, at Hafir and Dongola the gun boats played Hell with us. Abu Hamed, we got into houses and were attacked and defeated. At Atbara Mahmoud reserved his fire and let the enemy close to him before he fired. [Note. Hence the shocking wounds and large number of amputations and deaths as compared with 2nd September.] "Now" said the Khalifa, "I will alter all this. I shall first fire (Hence all the shots were nearly spent before reaching to us, for he began at 2000 yards and over.) "Then I shall go back to the tactics of the Victorious Mahdi over Hicks and when they are confused with my firing and are all wounded and afraid I shall surround them and charge, and shall kill them all and shall return to pray in the Mosque at noon."

If he had surrounded us on three sides first and then charged altogether he might have given infinite more trouble. And if he had hurried up on night of Sept. 1st, surrounded us, closed in on us, and fired at us out of the broken ground, and then rushed in and penetrated then I say again and I know it is true we should have been licked. Some of course, would have escaped. Groups would form and fight their way to the boat etc. and so got away. There are scores and hundreds of incidents that remain to be told and that will keep till later.

The capture of Signal Hill by Capt. Capper detailed from 13th Btn. by Maxwell, was a dashing and very spirited piece of soldiering. It was baptism to a good many. We can never be sufficiently thankful that it was the grave of so few.

Well, then on 3rd Sept. the first thing was to find a camp for ourselves on clean ground & near water. This I did and we stuck to it. The town of Omdurman was too filthy for words. Many of the dead were carried in by night by their women folks and buried under the flooring of their huts & houses. Many wounded in the early part of the fight had got back to the town and died there. No! Omdurman was not a bouquet of violets, I can tell you.

Well on 10th Sept. Sirdar went off to the White Nile. On 19th I went up Blue. I did what I had to and got back here in 2nd Oct. Meanwhile owing to events toward Gedaref a force under Genl. Rundle had to be organized in Sept. [3 Oct] Sirdar left here by dint of express trains suspended traffic and everything laid on got to Cairo in 73 1/2 hours from here, including all stopages. The vast hords [sic] swept together into this shark's mouth are now tripping away hither and thither to their old home and the place will soon be reduced to practical limits for dealing with.

All vestige of responsibility amongst the people is dead. They were serfs, dirt under the floor of their masters. Hence there is nobody and nothing to appeal to as an assistant towards establishing a system of law and order. However, all will come with time, patience and given money and fair play. Some people imagine Khartoum will be rebuilt, trade will revive, peace and plenty be the order of the day, feuds forgotten, civilized rule be established and reverenced, all by a waive [sic] of a wand or by the raising of a flag here or there. They have had

GENERAL SIR ARCHIBALD HUNTER

14 years of Dervish rule, after 60 years of the Turk. And it will take 10 years to put things straight.

We have begun well, it could not have had a better prelude than by a big fight. They all thought they had us in their grip. As they came on in the early morning chanting their prayers begging for Victory in beautiful language, infinitely more eloquently than anything except the Psalms of David, our Cavalry & Camel Corps and Horse Artillery gradually retired. They construed this to be a victory already, and a few skunks made it the excuse to galop back to town and show off before the women (can't you imagine them, the peacocks that strut all the world over, we have plenty of them and I know a good few) shouting "El Din Nessret" (the faith has conquered). What a sell to them later on.

The 5–inch mortar battery with Lyddite shells is a perfect engine of destruction. In scientific and practical hands, as was #37 Battery under Major Elmslie, it shows us what can be done. If the Khalifa had chosen to hold the houses on the outskirts of the town and have made a house to house defence to coin away our easily fascinated men, then it would have been quite another affair. As regards Fashoda I am not in a position to discuss it, I wish I were Prime Minister for ten minutes.

Khartoum is a complete ruin. It will be rebuilt, Omdurman will be strongly garrisoned and otherwise it will be gradually obliterated. The Mahdis tomb was a splendid target and was hit plumb in the center of the dome at the 3rd round. It is beautifully built of red brick and lime and took some demolition. You are at liberty to assign any cause you please to its removal. We may say that so long as it stood it was a menace to our rule and an inducement to a removal of fanaticism. We may say that in its semi-demolished state it was a danger to life and living, anyhow so long as it stood it was a conspicuous memorial to celebrate the victory of the Savage over us, and now that it ceases to exist our disgrace may be forgotten and atoned for. The poor devils bones are gone too and quite right. Many folk wonder where they are, so just let them wonder. I wonder what happens when you can't find your complete set at the Last Parade.

(Capt. Smythe, Queens Bays, one of my galloper, deserves the V. C. The special act of bravery I allude to shews Burleigh of the *Telegraph* (read his letters and Jupiter and Mars are flea bites to him) and Rene Bull in such a poor light and there is no genuine terror in home circles of the Press that I firmly believe that nothing more will be heard of it.

Our reception up Blue Nile was enormously enthusiastic. The people were almost delirious with delight. Forest has usurped all the old cultivation and the people have been mostly killed, the manhood killed, the women swept into the Harems of Omdurman. They will shake themselves down again in time in their old places, and the race will revive. Quite a different people and country and scenery, ample game abounds, but country too thick yet to see.

Our concentration was made at an earlier date than I calculated but it was made at the expense of one of the conditions I stipulated for and that was three month's food and forage to be placed above Shabuka [sic] before we moved on. Mine was the safest way, the Sirdar's was the quickest.

It must have been a great relief to you all at home to get the news.

Yours very sincerely.

(signed) A. Hunter.

CHAPTER NINE:
The Capture of Gedaref

Major Henry Merrick Lawson

Letter to his Sister; 5 December 1898.

[Jean S. and Frederic A. Sharf Collection]

INTRODUCTORY NOTES

The garrison at Kassala learned on 5 September, 1898, that the British had won a great victory at Omdurman; and on September 7th the entire Kassala garrison was ordered to march for Gedaref. Approximately 1,350 soldiers accompanied by seven British officers (one of whom was a medical doctor) participated.

Churchill in *The River War* characterized this expedition as "reckless... and discreditable to those who ordered it"—while praising the participants for brave and resourceful behavior in the face of a much stronger enemy. After arduous and continuous marching, the expedition arrived before the town on 22 September, and found an army of 4,000 men advancing towards them.

The actual fighting was marked by exceptional bravery on the part of Dr. Fleming, whose primary responsibility was to guard the baggage and the medical supplies, and who found himself under direct attack. When the town surrendered at noon, nearly 10% of the British expedition were either killed or wounded!

On 28 September, Emir Ahmed Fedil; attacked the town supported by an army of almost 7,000 men; when his attack was repulsed, his army retired and refused to enter into further fighting. He continued to menace the garrison at Gedaref until a relief expedition arrived on 22 October; at which time he retired to join the Khalifa in Kordofan.

On Saturday 10 November, 1898, *The Daily Graphic* printed Kitchener's official account of the fighting at Gedaref, as follows:

> "Lieutenant-Col Parsons speaks highly of the way in which Maj. Lawson, Royal Engineers, commanded the irregulars, Capt. McKerrell, the 16th Battalion, and Capt. Wilkinson the Arab Battalion, and also of the services of Capt. Fleming, R.A.M.C. in charge of the medical arrangements and baggage guard."

Born into a distinguished Irish family in 1859, Henry Merrick Lawson attended Cheltenham College, and the Royal Military Academy at Woolwich. He joined the army in 1877 as a Lieutenant in the Royal Engineers.

Lawson had served with distinction in prior Egyptian campaigns. He went to the Sudan in February, 1884 with Sir Gerald Graham, and earned honors at the battle of El Teb, February 29, 1884. He participated in the Gordon Relief Expedition of 1884/1885, serving under Sir Herbert Steward at Abu Klea and Gubat in January/February, 1885.

MAJOR HENRY MERRICK LAWSON

Lawson returned to the Sudan in 1898, proceeding in April to Kassala, an important garrison commanded by Colonel Charles S.B. Parsons. He documented his experiences during the spring and summer of 1898 in an article published in 1899 in the *Royal Engineer's Journal*:

"The readers of the *Royal Engineer's Journal* may care to hear something of recent events in the Eastern Sudan, where we are having a little campaign all to ourselves, and with no newspaper correspondents to chronicle events. The writier arrived at Kassala at the end of April last, just as detachments from its garrison were returning after a successful visit to the Upper Atbara, where between Fasher and Ossobri they completed the dispersal of the fugitives from Mahmud's army, and brought many of them back as prisoners to Kassala. A period of inaction followed, broken so far as regards the writer, by a reconnaissance visit to the Atbara in May, which resulted in his being the only Egyptian casualty in a skirmish with Dervishes. Nature, however, aided by the best and kindest of medical treatment, worked wonders, and before the end of June I was as well and strong as ever.

"As the days went on our minds at Kassala were continually exercised as to the part, if any, we were to play in the coming campaign. With but a fortnightly post, and with a long, expensive, and circuitous telegraphic connection via Massowa with the outer world, we were very much cut off, and so far as the Nile was concerned we gleaned most of our news out of the English papers. It was very tantalizing to be at once so near and yet so far. When August came it was obvious that we were not to join in the advance on Khartum, and that our only hope of action lay in the Eastern Sudan. Our eyes turned naturally therefore on Gedaref, where, at a distance of some one hundred and thirty miles south-west of us, was assembled the army of Ahmed Fedil, reputed to number from five thousand to six thousand men. As the greatest amount of fighting men we could withdraw from Kassala for offensive purposes did not exceed one thousand four hundred, it was clear that so long as the bulk of Fedil's army was at Gedaref we would have to remain inactive; our hope, therefore, was that the Khalifa would withdraw some at least of the Gedaref garrison to assist him at Omdurman. Our intelligence patrols brought us word on many occasions that orders had gone to Fedil to come to the Khalifa, but for a long time he preferred the security of Gedaref, and it was not until a few days before the fall of Boga that Fedil marched west to the Blue Nile. On the 5th September we got confirmation of this intelligence, simultaneously with the news of the Sirdar's victory of three days before, and on the 7th we started for the Atbara."

Lawson's article, and his four - page letter to his sister Eva in Ireland which follows, are reminders that military actions in the Sudan in September, 1898 were not confined to Omdurman.

Kassala
Dec. 5 (1898)

My dear Eva

I have to acknowledge Alice's of 15th & 19th Nov. & yours of 17th & 24th, all of which came last Sunday—our Suakin post went on Tuesday, but I did not happen to be able to write, so this will go via Massowah, and I daresay will reach Ireland as soon as it would have done via Suakin.

We have been cut off a good deal from the outer world since I last wrote, as our telegraph line to Suakin broke down between here and Tokar & it was 8 days before it was repaired, while just at the same time the alternative line via Massowah broke between Massowah and Perine, so we felt really quite isolated. Communication was at last re-secured two nights ago and the first thing we heard of was the Gazette of Sat. last 17th [Nov.] with our various rewards, with which we were gratified.

We think our Commander Parsons might have been given a CB in addition to his Brevet Colonelcy, and we are sorry that Fleming our Doctor has got a D.S.O. and not a promotion. It would have meant a great deal to him to have been promoted as he entered the army rather late, after being a house surgeon in a big Edinboro' hospital, and promotion would have more than made up for this. They don't like promoting Doctors as a rule because they cannot give them brevet promotions, as with the rest of the army, and any promotion for them involves their stepping over the heads of doctors senior to them. This would however have been quite justified in Fleming's case as his professional qualifications are so good—doubtless far better than the great bulk of his seniors.

I am very glad to get my Lt. Colonelcy, although it is no pecuniary gain. Still it may be of advantage in the future, & where so many have been getting it, it is pleasant not to be left out. If they only date our promotions the same day as the Omdurman ones it will be all right—otherwise those in the Omdurman Gazette would go over our heads.

I am so sorry about Kincaid; I gather he is at Cairo still & fancy that he will have to go home from there.

MAJOR HENRY MERRICK LAWSON

The Sirdar arrived at Cairo a week ago & still I have had no news about my getting away. The only thing is to wait the course of events. I see that he & Lord Cromer go up to Khartoum just after Christmas. I wonder have they some surprise ready for the New Year in the way of a proclamation putting the Southern Sudan under England on that date—we shall see—I am sure the Sirdar must be glad to have got to the end of his feastings at home. He appears to have been the greatest "lion" for many years past.

I had a letter from Mrs. Collon last mail. The rooms are still let so that I am not losing money by keeping them on. Excuse this dull scrawl from

Your affectionate brother

Henry Lawson

CHAPTER TEN:
Return to Omdurman, 1899

Lieutenant Colonel Harry Finn

Journal of travel up the Nile exactly one year after the campaign.

[Jean S. and Frederic A. Sharf Collection]

INTRODUCTORY NOTES

Following the battle of Omdurman, the 21st Lancers returned directly to Cairo. Within a month of their arrival in Cairo (26 October, 1898), command of the Lancers was turned over to Walter George Crole Wyndham, who was promoted from Major to Lieutenant Colonel; on that same day Major Harry Finn was named second in command. While he was not given any promotion in rank on that day, on 16 November, 1898 he was breveted Lieutenant Colonel.

In the Sudan, British technicians and British officers assigned to the Egyptian Army were busy organizing a civilian government and planning the creation of a modern country; the officers were also training native troops and organizing expeditions to find the Khalifa. Meanwhile, the Lancers were only drilling and on manoevres in Cairo. Lieutenant Colonel Finn yearned for some real action.

In July 1899, Finn applied to Acting Sirdar John Grenfell Maxwell for permission to make a 6-week round trip from Cairo to the Sudan. His motives were varied, ranging from a simple desire to observe the progress of modernization taking place under British rule to a nostalgic wish to revisit sites of the 1898 expedition, and celebrate the first anniversary of the Omdurman battle at Omdurman. An unstated objective, perhaps the most powerful of all, was a hope to attach himself to a successful expedition to find the Khalifa.

Finn received this permission on 4 August, and hastily arranged an immediate departure from Cairo. He commenced a journal to record places, people, and events—a journal which can be read as a unique travelogue, as well as a celebration of British progress in civilizing the Sudan.

Finn carefully records the names of more than 65 men encountered during this trip. Since so many of the men mentioned by Finn in this account were British officers serving in the Egyptian army, it is useful to briefly describe such service.

The British were given the responsibility for organizing and training a new Egyptian Army by Khedival decree on 20 December, 1882, and the very next day the first Sirdar, Major General Sir Evelyn Wood, commenced work. Service in the new Egyptian Army was attractive to the British military: they were immediately given a higher rank in the Egyptian Army than the rank they held in the British Army; the pay was considerably higher; and there was a good chance to see action. Thus, from the start, a highly qualified applicant pool existed, and it was possible to maintain rigorous standards for selection. As an example,

LIEUTENANT COLONEL HARRY FINN

successful applicants were required to pass an examination in colloquial Arabic within six months.

The selected British officers were primarily responsible for training battalions of Sudanese soldiers who served in the Infantry, the Camel Corps and the Cavalry. Most of these officers were bachelors, with a love of sport and adventure; and a strong feeling of cameraderie developed among them, which is reflected in Finn's account.

Within one year of the establishment of Anglo-Egyptian control over the Sudan, war broke out in South Africa and many of the best British officers left the Sudan to serve in the Boer War. Many of those who remained were needed as administrators in quasi-civilian jobs.

This Journal communicates a very direct sense of what it was like to serve in the Sudan in 1899, and what it was like to visit this remote part of the British Empire. It must be pointed out that the Sudan is entirely seen in this Journal from a British 19th century colonial perspective; it is unfortunate that we cannot include a comparable account from the Sudanese point of view!

Friday, August 4:

At about 6:45 PM, Wyndham and I had just finished a round of golf at Ghezirih when Le Gallais drove up and told me Maxwell had wired his consent as Acting Sirdar for me to enter the Soudan. Wyndham agreed to my starting that night with Mahon, who was leaving at 9:30 PM. Le Gallais drove me to the Club where I left a couple of messages and then out to Abbasiyeh, thinking out plans along the way.

Luckily my servant Baddelen was in; he packed kit for 6 weeks while I wrote a couple of letters, signed mess bills, handed over the Printing Press & Vedetts to Brinton whom I found in the Mess; sorted Mess and Rifle Meeting papers & left them respectively for Clerk & Eadon. The Mess Sergeant put up whiskey, soda & sandwiches for the train.

Wyndham came up & talked over the journey with me & gave me a £5/ note to buy arms, etc. for the Sergts.' Mess. I also promised to get some for Eadon & Hutchison who were at dinner when I went out. Got to the station at 9:10, the first to arrive. Not a bad performance (Trumpeter!!) as Ghezireh is 6 miles from Abbasiyeh & the station a good 3 miles.

Our party consists of Mahon (8th Hrs.), Vandeleur (Scots Feds), Wemyss (Royal Scots), all Gippy Army—and myself. The train left at 9:30 PM for Luxor, Le Gallais saw us off bringing me his hurricane candlesticks & leather case with a supply of candles—good man! Each of us had a compartment in the very comfortable new sleeping car running between Cairo & Luxor. A Dover man named [—] was the attendant. We reached Luxor at 1:15 PM Saturday 5th after a very dusty ride, too hot to have anything closed.

Saturday, August 5:

Put up at the Hotel Luxor, not a very bad one, wrote letters after a tub & lunch & then rode donkeys to the ruined temples at Karnak. Wonderful ruins, bound to interest anyone. We had a capital Arab guide & made the most of the short two hours daylight left. One could not get away from the query how such enormous blocks of stone had been raised to such heights & laid so truly. The towering columns make one feel very small. Much of the carving looked as if it might have been done only yesterday, so clear and perfect was it. Some of it was coloured green, red & blue; in several instances the colours were nearly as good as ever. One of the obelisks we estimated to be 100 ft. high, about 8 ft. square at the base diminishing to about 5 ft. at the top where it suddenly tapered to a point. It was one solid mass of granite from the Assouan quarries 80 to 100 miles distant. What an immensity of labour. It is said to have been the work of Queen Hatasu. Sleeping in the garden was rather spoiled by the sand-flies.

Sunday, August 6:

Up at 4.45 AM to get baggage at the Station in time for the 6 o'clock train; thanks to an indifferent staff and many passengers the train was 1/2 hour late in starting. Seven of us (one a fat native) were crammed up in a pokey carriage on this narrow gauge line from Luxor to Shellal for 12 hours! Only 100 miles!! Arrived at Shellal at 6.30 instead of 3.30. No one appears to take interest in this bit of railway. Arriving so late prevented our visiting the immense dam under construction at the south end of the 1st Cataract at Shellal. Must do this on the return journey.

Elgood (Cmdr., Assouan) had made good arrangements on transferring us from train to boat. That rail journey was the very mischief, luckily we were in a good humour, it was a bit amusing. Luckily we got some ice on the point of starting. The boat, the sternwheeler *Toski*, left Shellal at 10 PM, without a moon & with a heavy load (two gyasses & a barge lashed alongside) against a stiff current. We slept well that night on the top, that is on the roof of the upper deck. The "Restaurateur" was a Greek & did us not too well. Still we survived, read, played "Bridge," and yarned. The complete freedom from all duties, correspondence etc. was very acceptable. I much appreciated the difference between this journey in this way & in that of last year when there were 150 men & as many horses to get up safely and fit for immediate work.

Monday, August 7:

An uneventful day, gloriously idle.

Tuesday, August 8:

Much the same [as previous day]; we availed ourselves of an Engineer leaving the *Toski* a little below Korosko to send down letters. I sent them to K.E. [his wife, Kate Scott Finn] & Clerk. The engineer was taking down a tourist steamer, the *Esneh* belonging to Cook & Son, which had just been floated after grounding some time back. The current is not so strong as it was when we went up last year.

Wednesday, August 9:

The women & children of a long straggling village on the left bank were much excited by discovering we had on board a youth from their parts who was returning from a lengthened visit to Cairo. They followed the boat shouting & gesticulating in a frantic manner mystifying us entirely till the blushing youth was found shrinking from all this commotion. It was not convenient to land him just there so he was put ashore at another village higher up; the womenfolk there gave him a great reception. He wore the ordinary native dress, but was equipped with a portmanteau & a silver-mounted black stick, both of which looked incongruous amid such surroundings. Few men were to be seen; the women were taller than those lower down the river, they wore long galabeiahs of the popular colour—blue; their hair was in smaller plaits & hung round their heads & over their foreheads like so may rats' tails; their teeth were very white & prominent. The fringe of cultivation along this reach (Shellal to Halfa) is never very wide. The land looked good. The date palms were everywhere & were pretty with their ripening fruit, varying from brown to yellow, clustering among the large green fronds.

Thursday, August 10:

1.30 PM found us at Wady Halfa. Anley, the Consul, was soon aboard, looking a bit more "{——-}" than when we said "Goodbye" there last Sept.

Baring, Stanton, Wolseley, Douglas & others left for Cairo on our boat, off on leave. Macauley, Stevenson, Scott & Coutts, all old acquaintances, were at Halfa, so there was great havering. Posted letters & postcards to K.E. & others. Strengthened my kit at Walker's store. Vandeleur, our "caterer," laid in stores for the remainder of our journey to Khartoum. It was not convenient to visit Mahmoud, the Atbara prisoner, so must do so on the return journey.

Our train steamed out of Halfa on its desert journey to the Atbara via Abu Hamed at 5.15 PM. A great contrast to the start I made with my squadron from the same place in August last, when it was made at 1.30 AM immediately after a warm task in entraining 150 horses & mules & a cold drink was never more appreciated that I got at the Halfa Mess just before moving off.

Friday & Saturday, August 11 & 12:

We felt a certain amount of doubt about our engine this time which was confirmed by its being unable to get beyond No. 7 Station; it left us on the siding there & returned to No. 6 to re-fit. We had reached No. 6 at 8 o'clock that morning (Friday 11th) & had to pull aside for water & to let a train for Halfa pass. (A bath under the pipe for the elevated tank was worth a Jew's eye.) Maxwell's train from the South arrived about 8.45. He and the Doctor (Wanhill) much enjoyed an iced soda we were able to give them. I was glad of the opportunity for thanking Maxwell (en route home on leave) for letting me up.

It was 10 AM when we left No. 6 and 11.40 when we arrived at No. 7. Engine could go no farther—something wrong! Most amazing to be left stranded in the desert. The telephone running alongside the line reported the case to Abu Hamed (No. 10) & asked for our deliverance. We yarned, played "Bridge" & watched for help, but alas! it was not till 1 PM on Saturday 12th that we moved on again by aid of the engine taken off a "material" train which arrived from the North: No. 9 was reached at 3.40 same afternoon, where we were again stopped by telephone and the engine sent back to bring up a breakdown gang to repair a large breach in the line between Nos. 9 & 10. We had experienced a big dust storm blowing from the North the evening before at No. 7. Another & much bigger storm with lightning & rain from the South had passed over Abu Hamed & the heavy rain had breached the line North of Abu Hamed, hence our engine could not get to us from there. Here we were again stranded in the desert.

Sunday, August 13:

At about 4 AM the breakdown gang passed us, their engine returned & took us on at 5.40 AM; we reached the break at 8.45, leaving again at 11.30 AM. Adams, the Civil Engineer from Abu Hamed who was at the breach, came to breakfast with us & brought the unwelcome news of there being something wrong on the line some 60 miles South of Abu Hamed! A Berber train being lost on that section!!—but whether from its engine having gone wrong or owing to a break in the line he was unable to say. Here we are, 2 1/2 days out from Halfa & only made a little over 200 miles! We shall take three weeks getting to Omdurman; the Sirdar is telling them at home that Cairo to Omdurman can be done in 5 days! Any number of pelicans had collected in the vicinity of this large breach, also some solitary stork.

While at No. 7 we saw a couple of fast trotting camels going South, a short mile away. Vandeleur & Wemyss went out to them, three people were riding the camels. The party would not stop for V. but one man slipped off to answer questions, the others trotted on. This man said he was from Korosko en route to Abu Hamed, that the other two were his brothers, that they could not be delayed. V. thought the third looked like a woman; if she were it was quite possible she had been stolen. V. & W. returned to the train; meanwhile, the dismounted man was taken by Soudanese soldiers of the train and brought in. Mahon interrogated him and as he told a different story detained him on the train to go before the native official at Abu Hamed. The other two & the camels were seen, hiding behind some hills, later on. The biggest part of the breach was 200 yards long and the whole bit flooded was a mile from side to side. We were agreeably surprised by the rapidity with which the repair was effected. We are keen to get to Abu Hamed where we ought to ascertain what is wrong 60 miles South from there. The betting is the line has been breached as the telephone communication with there is broken! Thank goodness we have a good stock of provisions with us, so we shan't starve, the ice is holding out too. The 200 yards of embankment had been washed away no doubt because there were no culverts, though had there been it is possible they could not have saved the embankment owing to the large amount of water which collected so quickly. Two other breaches of 20 yds. each had to be repaired. This over, there was an easy run in to Abu Hamed where we arrived at 12.25 PM. No news as to what is wrong Southwards.

To take on all available working men our train had to be lightened. Wemyss' two ponies were left, much to his disgust. Altering the train & collecting the men delayed us & it was 3.25 when we left Abu Hamed. At 4.25 we reached Dagash where a wagon with a hot axle-box had to be emptied & left; a further delay of 1/4 hour. Halts had to be made once or twice to put up fallen wire-poles; eventually Shereik was reached at 6.30 PM, too late for Adams to go on an engine searching for the damage, so it was decided to stay the night at Shereik near the river. Our numerous natives secured the only good bathing-place in the river so Mahon & I enjoyed a splendid bath under the big hose used for filling engines, the man at the crank turning on a "shower" which nearly knocked one over. Here, as all along the line, there had been an unusual rainfall. It was pleasant dining outside, & Adams' contribution of fresh meat very acceptable. Rather a stuffy night.

Monday, August 14:

Under weigh at 6 AM. Adams & I riding on the front of the engine between the buffers. Very jolly in the early morning & quite cool when traveling at 35 miles or more an hour, which was the pace on the down gradients. A dog lay calmly in the middle of the track & only cleared just as the train was upon him. Adams shewed me the spot where one of the American engines left the rails and toppled over 60 yds. on, a little sand drifted on the rails was the cause. Halts again had to be made to repair the telegraph line. Abba Saleem was reached at 7.45 & left at 8.15. Adams on his trolley having been given a 1/4 hour's start. The fallen poles, 20 & 30 in a stretch, were put up occasionally, three men to a pole soon did the trick; it is marvellous they stand up so well. They look to be 20 ft. poles with only a couple of feet or so in the ground. A few miles short of Abadia we came upon a working party and their train from that station, they had just repaired a big breach; both trains went on and reached Abadia at 11.35 AM; delighted to learn all clear to the Atbara. The river at Abu Hamed is very pretty with its green islands reminding one of the Killarney lakes. The "dom" palm & prickly acacia are plentiful along the line now. We had [a] good view of the scene of the Abu Hamed fight, where Macdonald's brigade with Hunter in supreme command lost pretty heavily. Fitz-clarence & Sidney's graves are marked by white wooden crosses & enclosed by a wall.

A little delay at Abadia, then on again; about Berber there had been much rain, considerable floods still remain along the East side of the line.

Atbara, the end of our rail journey, was reached at 2.30 PM & glad we were. Only a couple of hours short of 4 days traveling from Wady Halfa to Atbara! 381 miles; very nearly, if not quite, a record.

Just one year today I arrived here with my squadron, 150 men & as many horses; that journey from Cairo took less than a day longer than this, altho' then we travelled by boat from Khirzam [Khizam] (N. of Luxor) to Assouan & marched round the cataract to Shellal instead of railing the whole distance as we did this time.

El Bimbashi Swabey is still Comdr. here; we were soon at his house to get & give news. Found Micklem (RE) & Hoskins there. Later, Swabey & I walked across the iron bridge under construction over the Atbara, a jumpy walk only sleepers, widely & irregularly placed, for a path. One of the others who started turned back & another clung to the framework till retrieved by a trolley; the sight of the rising Atbara rushing along 20 to 30 ft. below was a bit too much for them. The last span of the seven is being thrown across, the spans are 150 ft. in length, hence the bridge will be 350 yds. when finished and quite one of the finest structures in these parts.

The American overseers are a cheery lot, and carry on as child's play what looks to a novice a big job. It was rather fascinating watching the work & seeing how every piece of the huge frame-work fitted perfectly together. We visited the cemetery on the way back; then took a turn round the old fortifications, post office etc. No letters or telegrams. Mahon, Wemyss, Adams & I dined at Swabey's, a cheery party & a late one. Our kit had been moved aboard the *Fateh*, a gunboat commanded by Lt. Escombe R.N. which arrived today (14th). On arriving at the boat we found Escombe's gramophone going strong to the amusement of quite a large audience. Among the number were Sanders & Jackson who with 500 men 17th Battalion were en route from Omdurman to the 4th Cataract near Merowi [Meraui] to haul two steamers up the cataract.

Tuesday, August 15:

Busy getting supplies for rest of our journey. Posted English letters & one to the Colonel. Wired to Pirie to meet the Fateh at Wad Hamad. At about 10 AM the *Tamai*, small gunboat, arrived from Omdurman. Broadwood (Gippy cavalry) on board en route to Kassala via Berber as Acting Mudir. Not too pleased by going right away from everywhere— no chance of cutting in at the Cape or an Expedition against the Khalifa. Wellby, 18th Hrs. of Thibet fame also arrived by the *Tamai* having just completed a most interesting journey from Berbera through Abyssinia by Menelik's capital Abbis Abbaba; thence South down the east side of Lake Rudolf round its Southern extremity part of the way up its west side whence he struck out westwards making Omdurman by the Sobat and White Nile. King Menelik did Wellby real well for which much credit was due to Harrington and the prestige we gained by Marchand traveling thru Abyssinia after leaving Fashoda. Who turned the French out of Fashoda? The English! Then up went the price of English with Menelik. Wellby seems to have shot most things, and secured a lot of ivory. He might have shot many more elephants had he wished. A simple cut from a tin, on his left forefinger, did badly and he has lost up to the 2nd joint of it. He brought all his Somali & Abyssinian men with him to send back by sea from Suez. He had the best of luck with his animals, brought them right through to Omdurman where they sold well, thanks to his unceasing care of them.

The *Fateh* got off about 11.30 AM. Soon after starting one of the crew was badly hurt by the anchor falling on him. Looked like an internal injury but he means getting over it. These "blacks" mend wonderfully. Very jolly being on the river again & clear of the dust. The *Fateh* measures about 120 ft. in length, 24 in width & draws 3 ft. water. She is bullet-proof plated, mounts one 12 1/2 pounder Q.F., two 6 pounder Q.F. & three Maxim Nordenfelds. She is taking up two "sandels" (two-storied barges) & a gyassa, all laden with stores, & a few soldiers.

The *Fateh* tied up at 6.30 PM at Aliab, our first bivouac last year. What a ghastly place it was, black cotton soil with wide fissures, among shallow sort of khors which the rising Nile partly filled during the night, driving out the scorpions.

Wednesday, August 16:

Much time was taken up in "wooding" this morning & we did not start till 9.30. Passed Kitiab about mid-day—last year's second bivouac now nearly all under cultivation, the increase of cultivated land above the Atbara is noticeable, although the river is from 6 to 8 feet lower than this time last year. A native fell overboard today & tho' he could swim so well that he scorned to use the life-buoy thrown to him, the current took him down a long distance before he could make the bank. We tied up to East bank at 3.30 PM for more wood. Sowerby & Wollen R.E., who are constructing the Atbara-Khartoum section of the Railway, came on board. The heavy rain has played the mischief with the line, the rush of water from the very adjacent hills rushes down the khors sweeping away the embankments (built for the railway till the bridges can be put up) leaving rails & sleepers in mid-air across the gaps. While ashore we saw one gap 80 to 100 ft. across with 10 ft. of water below. A very great amount of extra labour has been caused in this way. The hundreds of natives employed live in & near the train which was this far, the two sappers [Sowerby and Wollen] being fairly comfortable in a goods van with their ordinary camp kit.

Thursday, August 17:
Started at 5 AM. Cool cloudy morning. The boats thermometers (2) registered 102° today also on Tues. & Wed.; while they rose to 110° on Mon; it does not feel anything like that, the head breeze takes off the heat a bit of course. Magamieh (our 4th bivouac) was reached at 12 noon. It looks well with its thousands of date palms thick with fruit & so much land under cultivation. It looking (sic) a jolly place for an hour on shore.

It was here on the return march last year that two or three of us saw Neufeld on the Northumberlands' boat en route to Cairo. He shewed me his manacles & told a few of his adventures. A "Stowaway" was sent ashore here as he lives in these parts, he was only a youngster of 14 or 15 so was given a biggish piece of packing case to help him in swimming to the bank, his only garment twisted round his head to keep it dry. At 3.30 PM we were at Shendy with its three very fine peepul (?) trees, fine trees for any place, but looking specially grand here with only low scrub near them. The old mud fort looks small & insignificant for the experiences it has gone thru. Gordon often mentions this place in his Journals from Sept. 10th to Dec. 14th '84. Shortly after we passed Metemmeh (west bank). The low island between it & our course was not visible last year I think. The large town with the palm grove on the river bank look quite pretty—rather different to their real state. The increase in cultivation continues and it only requires sufficient population to widen, to almost any extent, the belt of cultivation alongside this most fertilizing of rivers. The people have returned in considerable numbers; assured safety to inhabitants & their crops will lead to the return of many more.

One of the American engines on a siding near the river past Shendy looked solitary & out of place, the recent breaches in the line had cut off it & its train for a while. One might reasonably have expected to see alligators in the numerous sand banks & islands, but not one has been observed. Tied up at 7 PM.

Friday, August 18:

Started at 5 AM. After 1 1/2 hours stopped to "wood." Hoskins (who had joined us at the Atbara) went ashore & brought back a few doves for breakfast—poor little doves & awful brutes—still a bit of fresh food is very nice. The gyassas going down stream today were making 8 miles an hour with the current & good south wind. Fortnight today we left Cairo, long enough to have done London to Bombay. This journey tho' slow is decidedly pleasant on the river, we are a cheery party & I find it a nice change. At noon we stopped opposite "rail-head" which is some distance from the river-bank just here. Hoskins left us here to inspect some recently purchased camels & their equipment. Nasri Island today looked different to last year when the river was so much higher. At 2.15 PM we stopped to give mails to the *Nasr* [Nasir] (Fell R.N.), a sister gunboat, going north. We exchanged visits & found the balance of the 17th Battalion going down to pull the steamers up the Merowi Cataracts. Fell had a good collection of "heads" he had shot up the White Nile. Fifteen in all with specimens of water buck, Maaref (rare), Gazelle, Cobus & tetel. Cowan R.N. was on board en route to the Cataract to bring on the gun boats—he is the Admiral of the Nile Fleet. Tied up about 5 PM for wood & the night. Vandeleur & I had a two mile stroll up the East bank, came across land which had been cultivated a few years ago—jolly walk, the river was very pretty in the evening light. Everything made very snug, considerable promise of a storm which came off to a little extent.

Saturday, August 19:

Started at 5 AM delightfully cool morning (down to 70°) after a smart fall of rain. Reached the sand bank opposite Wad Hamed at 6.30 AM. Much disappointed by not getting up the inside channel, wanted to stay with Pirie & the Gippy cavalry a day or two; had to be content with sending him a note by the soldier orderly there to receive stores. The river banks are green now with grass & foliage of small trees & bushes, numerous islands give the river the appearance of a large lake; very pretty indeed; & this continues right up to the Shabluka defile, the approach to the entrance to the latter is not easy to discern there are so many (apparently) to choose from.

The entrance looked very grand as the steamer approached it & the river narrowed down. The four forts, three on the West & one on the East bank guarding the defile, have crumbled into a semi-ruinous state, they look incapable of standing long against our guns if the latter could get at them. It is said that high Nile partly floods them & that this had much to say to their abandonment last August. The defile is 6 to 8 miles from end to end, bare rocky hills rise on either side with just a narrow fringe of grass between their base & the water's edge; here & there this was a strip of blackened ground where the dry grass had been burnt for the purpose of getting a crop of young grass. About 2.30 PM we were opposite the striking landmark of Gebel Royan, the river makes a big bend here and the channel is considered the most difficult part of the defile, ridges of rock run awkwardly in the river-bed, necessitating a serpentine course. Tied up at 7 PM.

Sunday, August 20:

Started at 5 AM. Occasional landmarks were passed such as Gebel el Teik where the "A" squadron was on outpost duty on the { } of last August and Smyth's & Conolly's picquets got in touch with dervish patrols for about the first time creating increased interest. I can recall the scene of Clerk carrying an injured prisoner behind him on his saddle when we joined the bivouac that evening. Kerreri, Gebel Surgham & the country on our right bring back last year's exciting experiences on those plains, they present a very different aspect now. A greater contrast could scarcely be possible; 70 to 90 thousand men were then engaged in a very bloody fight (at least it was that to the losers, poor devils!) with the guns of a dozen gunboats sending screaming shells from the river & now it is perfectly peaceful & scarcely a thing moving beyond the bullocks turning a "sakiya" here & there & a number of the Camel Corps grazing. It was not possible to distinguish the ground over which we charged but the line of advance towards it could be easily made out.

Omdurman was reached at 3 PM, only a temporary halt to drop one sandel, then by the South end of Tuti island & up the Blue Nile to Khartoum to leave the other. Not time to go on shore—must visit this later. The new palace the Sirdar is building on the site of Gordon's is very large, three-storied—red brick with stone corners & ends; it will be visible for many miles. Returning between Tuti Island & Halfayah with strong current in our favour we were quickly back to Omdurman dockyard! Where our little quartette broke up—Wemyss crossing to Halfayeh to join his Battalion, the 18th; Vandeleur going off to seek quarters, Mahon & I making our way to Maxwell's quarters in the Sirdariyeh (Yakoob's old house; he was the Khalifa's brother and was killed on 2nd Sept. '98). I was introduced to Lewis Bey at present commanding here—then on to see Asser (officer D.A.G.) who has a room in the Khalifa's house overlooking the big square. A large stone in the courtyard wall of the Khalifa's house marks the spot where Hubert Howard was killed by one of our own shells on the evening of the 2nd Sept., most cruel bad luck after the many dangers he had passed thro', ending with a place in our charge.

We next went to the Club, where one of the Bands was playing a rather good programme. Here were several I knew—de Montmorency, Guest, Bray (Doctor) etc. Dined that night with Asser & had a great haver about India in general & Bangalore in particular. Slept outside, delightfully cool night.

Monday, August 21:

At 6.30 AM, Mahon & I on a couple of Lewis's ponies rode out to breakfast with the Camel Corps who are North of Omdurman near Khor Shambat. Henry & Guest only two fellows there. M. left soon after breakfast, I stayed on to be shown all round. Most of the camels were out grazing. Rather good equipment; the leather bags for men's food & camels' food, with water skins, are arranged so that each camel can carry 6 days food for himself & rider. A good-looking old Arab brought a smart camel for sale—which was tried & found very fast. £24 was the price; the camel was left with its owner, but later in the day he parted with it to Guest for £19. Very high wind got up so H., G. & I rode in by the river bank—a busy curious scene, especially one of the markets, a one-time slave market. Wrote letters all the afternoon for dispatch tomorrow. Rode to polo with Lewis in the evening. Not at all bad considering it has to be played in the desert without a suspicion of grass, or anything green. Howard's grave is near this side, also Howe's, a young R.E. Lieut. who was buried a few days ago only. "Enteric." Ordered a week's stores at Angelo's for a trip up the Blue Nile, start in the morning. We dined at home (Lewis's) with Fitton, Asser, Doughty & Vandeleur as guests. A very cheery party, followed by another cool night.

Tuesday, August 22:

Up at 5.30 & down to the river to the boat for Wad Medani. Glad to find the *Fateh* ready - Angelo's stores not required, one can be fed on the *Fateh*. Left Omdurman at 7.30 AM, called at Khartoum for another "sandel." The object of the journey is to bring away stores etc. from Abu

Haraz, a one-time station near Wad Medani. Escombe has never been up the Blue Nile before.

The difference in colour of the two Niles at their confluence is very great, the Blue being dark & thick with the water it brings down from the Abyssinian hills & on which the rising of the Nile practically depends. The river widens to 2 to 3 miles just South of the confluence, in fact the White Nile there is just like a sea; the opposite bank cannot be seen. The current of the Blue Nile is very strong, even with only two empty sandels the *Fateh* makes but about 6 miles an hour against it; after passing Khartoum there was but little cultivation up to mid-day—from then on it increased, varied with tracts of grass on which quite a number of cattle were grazing. Villages are few and stand back from the river. They looked fairly well off. The land should be easy to irrigate & made to produce crops. The river varies from 600 to 700 yds. in width with some splendid reaches in its serpentine course S.E. Just now (5.15 PM) with the lowering sun astern the view ahead is very beautiful without perhaps any special points in it.

At 5.30 PM we tied up to the Right bank opposite the large village of Nuba for wood. No means of crossing to go through it; tried fishing with a net, not successful, caught only two small fish—so took an hour's sharp walking exercise. "Wooding" took a long time; we had to stay the night & finish in the morning. It promised a blow, so extra hawsers were put out to make the boat secure; the *Alaskeh* blowing over & sinking a few miles N. of Omdurman has made them specially careful.

Wednesday, August 23:
Finished wooding & away at 7 AM. Delightfully cool morning. Cultivation along the left bank increases, it is principally dhoura. Very few birds to be seen, beyond numerous pelicans & a few geese. Nothing very interesting up to 2 PM when Kamlin, a large but poor-looking village on the left bank, was reached. An hour was taken here for wood; what a lot of wood these boats want. I set the small fry running races, got 40 or 50 of them together, had them started 200 yds. away & raced to me—first in got a piastre. The first race was a poor one, the kids, as a whole, stopped when a few yards away—but when they saw the boy who did come on get something they finished better the next few times; the little beggars enjoyed the tumasha, and the Mothers looked on with interest, but would not cut in for a race among themselves. From Kamlin till 6.30 PM, when we tied up to a grassy bank, the river was prettier and the many sakiyehs & shadoofs with increased cultivation on the left bank give it a rather prosperous appearance;

while the right bank was quite park-like with its grass and trees. The latter (Acacias) were a bit small for an English park.

Escombe & I took advantage of the rippin' good green "towing" path & had a fine walk before dinner. Looks like another storm, much lightning but with 4 hawsers to trees & ground anchors the boat can't come to much harm. Insects were annoying at dinner—which had to be eaten in semi-darkness; caught a couple of fine moths which were spoiled by too much curing. The Sergt. R. M. Art. on board had gun-drill today; the detachment shaped fairly well considering it was their first acquaintance with a 12-pounder. The Egyptians having such indifferent sight one can't imagine their producing good "layers." The Corporal of the detachment is a humorous fellow. I recognized him as the native who was of great assistance at the foot races today. He got a score of small boys in line & taught them to salute and the "turnings"; I never saw a funnier awkward squad. We have some good piquet after dinner.

Thursday, August 24:

The *Fateh* got off at sharp 5 AM. We ought to make Abu Haraz near the junction of the Rahad River, by 2 PM. A really marvellous sunrise; quite (to me) indescribable. River winds and narrows, with an occasional opening out in a wide bit. Much prettier with small trees & bushes growing down to the water's edge; good crops on the left bank. Liddell & Roberts R.E. hailed us asking to be picked up on our return journey. We drew in & tied up for them to come aboard for a drink, they are working at the telegraph which runs down the left bank. Reached Abu Haraz at 3.35 PM; the two sandels were left here to be loaded with stores for conveyance to Omdurman. No time to go to the village which consists of some hundreds of "tukhls" (grass huts). It was the headquarters of one of the Egyptian Syces for a while. The Rahad River joins the Nile just above this; it runs dry during the dry season but is said to get as much as 40 ft. of water when it floods about this time or a little earlier, with a current of 5 miles an hour. After a few minutes at Abu Haraz we went on to Wad Medani making that 3/4 hour later & commenced "wooding" at once.

I went ashore to see as much as possible of the town (?) which is the next largest to Omdurman. It covers a great deal of ground, boasts of a post office (we brought 3 bags of mails) a large mamorieh (police post) and a telegraph office; the young Egyptian tel. master spoke excellent English, got permission to leave the office & escorted me "round the town." The place is much like other villages only much larger & more thriving; altho' this was a market day there were not so many people about. The majority are working on their land owing to the rising of the Nile. Very little appears to be manufactured here, I got a couple of curious & rather well made earthen pots, reddish clay semi-glazed, one for water; the other, jug-shaped, is used in making coffee. They turn out a good kind of native shoe also. Half a dozen perfectly bare ostriches stalked about the open space between the village & the river—a trifle formidable to look at, but quite harmless. In a palm grove nearby there were the remains of a rather nice garden. The villagers crowded the bank by hundreds to take stock of the *Fateh*. They might never have seen a gun-boat before. Escombe does not like remaining the night near a village so "wooding" over (much too quickly to please me), we dropped down stream a bit & tied up for the night at a place about halfway to Abu Haraz; he went ashore with his gun but found nothing to shoot for the pot. I'm very disappointed by not getting to Roseries [Roseires] or even to Senaar [Sennaar], the most interesting part of the Blue Nile & where there is shooting; however this trip is pleasant & better than nothing.

Friday, August 25:

Three weeks tonight we left Cairo. Did not untie till 7 AM, as the sandels would not be ready. Hit it off just right; the last things were being put on board as we swung round a little above Abu Haraz & dropped down alongside the first sandel. I went ashore while the final business was being settled, wandered thro' the "tukhls"—overestimated them yesterday, still it is a large village. Got a good dervish sword & a stone necklace pretty cheap: Pt 40 & 30 respectively. The inhabitants looked not too thriving, the children though were in excellent condition but much more shy than the Kamlin youngsters. One of the Abu Haraz party has a very good specimen of the golden-crested crane, about 30 inches high, he is taking to Omdurman. They are common in these parts.

Going with the current we made 10 to 12 miles an hour instead of about 5 only—so we should reach Omdurman by noon tomorrow unless delayed for wood at Nuba. Tied up at 10 AM for a few minutes to take Liddell on board. At 2 PM we passed Kamlin. Tied up under the Right bank at 3.30 PM to avoid a big storm gathering ahead, it passed across to our left and Escombe went on again an hour later. Did not stop at Nuba but kept going till 6.30 PM when a good sheltered place under the Left bank with a big tree to make fast to was found; fortunately, for it blew a gale till about midnight, the usual dust storm first, followed by rain, the wind continued all night.

Saturday, August 26:

Started at 5 AM, and with the strong wind aft we made Khartoum by 8.30 AM. Left Liddell there and were tied up at Omdurman 1/2 hour later. Found several letters awaiting me—answered them ready for tomorrow's down mail. Persse was up from Wad Hamed. We went in the Sirdar's felucca to Khartoum in the afternoon. Drage Bey was out. Gorringe R.E. piloted us over the new palace and new Govt. offices. The former will be a very fine place with a grand view. The front part of the ground floor was the front of Gordon's palace, the rear of it and the two upper stories are all new work. It appeared to me to be excellently planned, it will be completed this year. One was much struck by the splendid way in which the hundreds of workmen did their various tasks; no loitering or hanging about but very much the reverse; and the whole under one white man only—Gorringe. I was "introduced" to a workman named Rehan-el-Teyieh, who states (& is believed) he is one of the men who were always with the Khalifa, that he never was from his side on the 2nd Sept. '98, that the Khalifa was not with the body of dervishes we charged & drove off—nor never was, but that the Khalifa retreated by the West to Omdurman. Rehan says the Khalifa blamed him (Rehan) for the people deserting him and used him very badly. At length he succeeded in escaping. This man was very positive—the Khalifa was not near us on the 2nd.

Good red brick is being used for the palace with a considerable amount of stone-work, the principal parts of the latter being made from a hard white stone obtained from quarries South of Omdurman; very difficult to get this year owing to the Nile being so low. Other stone is being brought from near Kerreri. The Sirdar is bringing with him a fine marble staircase—a present. We did not get to the Gordon College. Owing to the strong current we were more than an hour towing & rowing to Khartoum; we returned in half the time, very jolly sailing back. Lewis had half a dozen guests that night & the Frontier band gave rather good music. They had a capital programme of jolly old British tunes & airs & played it remarkably well. One did not look for such in the Soudan.

Sunday, August 27:

Lewis & I had a rippin' ride early—the morning was just about perfect. Posted half a doz. letters this morning. Lunched at the 13th Soudanese with Phipps (Dorsets), one-time ADC to Gen. Gosset, Commanding Dublin Dt. A quaint old native calling himself Sheik Ibrahim, came to shew curious silver things. Most amusing old fellow—full of wonderful stories which he tells in a thoroughly Eastern style.

He swears he & Slatin were syces together to the Mahdi. This is quite probable. Spent the evening with Asser who is down with fever. Dined with Ingle, 9th Soudanese, & yarned over recollections of life on the Dilwara and other places where we have met. The expected arrival of the Sirdar tomorrow prevents our proposed visit to the battlefield in the morning.

Monday, August 28:

Up at 5. Rode Asser's pony to the Camel Corps lines near to Khor Shambat, and saw the Corps at drill. Really very good & decidedly interesting though they were weak, only about 350 on parade. Each Company is divided into 4 sections, and drills primarily to our Squadron columns. Lewis, who had dined & slept there the night before, rode back with me at 11.30. Called at the 13th Mess later & got a good necklace from the old Sheikh who was there again; took him back with me to the Staff mess where Lewis, Fitton & a few others were lunching. They drew [out] the old fellow who gave a very graphic description of the battle of Omdurman—of course in Arabic, still by a word here & there & his realistic postures, I could get much of the meaning of his story. Went to polo at 4.30. Too much wind & dust to be good, still a couple of quarters were quite fast. Dined at the Staff Mess. News received of a little affair yesterday near {   } about 20 miles or so from Wad Medani. Mahomed Cheriff [Sherif], the 3rd Khalifa, & two of the Mahdi's sons who had submitted some months ago & professed to be quite content, had been allowed to go here from Omdurman. These people turned round & were openly preaching sedition, hence it was necessary to arrest them. When Smyth V.C. with a few police & 2 (?) companies 15th Soudanese went to this village to take them, the villagers opened fire & there was trouble; result, 1 Native Officer & 2 men our side wounded, about a dozen villagers killed, more wounded, & 65 taken prisoners. Mahomed Cheriff [Sherif] & the Mahdi's two sons secured, tried, condemned & shot on the spot. The prisoners arrived at Omdurman this evening.

Tuesday, August 29:

Up at 6, rode to the Duke of Connaught's landing stage to meet the Sirdar who arrived about 8.00, Hamilton, Milford & Graham with him. The usual Guard of Honour & a salute of 19 guns. Nearly all the Gippy officers were present, also the big natives with banners & a large following. The Sirdar seemed very fit & in great spirits. Breakfasted at the Staff Mess, then went to Khartoum accompanied by Lewis only. I had a good "post" by the Sirdar's boat. Later secured a rather good bow & arrows for 60 PT at the photographer's!! Lunched with Phipps, bought two good swords (80 PT each) from the old sheikh. Writing hard all the afternoon.

Called on the Sirdar later. He shewed much interest as to the best place for an obelisk to be erected; he is inclined to think at Khartoum in the enclosure which is to surround the Church, when the latter has been built, would be safer & preferable to putting it up over the grave where our men lie behind the place where they fell. It would be quite safe at the former—& possibly doubtful at the latter. Played turns at "Bridge" at the Club before going to dine at the Staff Mess.

Wednesday, August 30:

Rode Mahon's pony to the Soudanese Brigade Field-day. The 9th, 11th & 13th Battalions, 2400 strong. Lewis gave them a couple of hours good useful manoeuvering, ending with marching past the Sirdar, who was present all the time. The men were very steady, distances & intervals well kept; this was the more creditable on account of a very high wind which made the communication of orders very difficult. The march past was uncommonly good. The 13th in my opinion were a trifle the best. It was a treat to see such strong battalions on parade. The jolly old black is really an excellent soldier, just wants steadying under fire; he does like to get at his man. I was at the "Sook" from 10 till 11:30, picked up a few odds & ends but the people have put up their prices. Again lunched at the 13th. Secured a good necklace from Sheikh Ibrahim for 100 PT, a bit dear—but it is a very good one. Wrote letters. Sent off my bedding to the Camel Corps lines preparatory to going out there to dine & sleep. Left myself at 7 on the grey in spite of the threatening storm. It suddenly became dark—impossible to see the track except when lightning flashed & then it blinded one so—it was impossible to see at all. Finding myself off the line I turned towards the river, knowing I could hit of the C.C. Lines from it. The ground soon began to slope down & became rougher; at length, feeling not satisfied, I got off; & most providentially too, for we were on the edge of quite a steep excavation, a couple steps more & we should have had a serious fall. The grey moved —- right or left without the slightest hesitation. Getting nearer the water, I turned North again & hit off a path which proved a right one & I soon got near the lines & picked up a Camel Corps man to conduct me to the Mess. The storm passed by. I had a rippin cheery evening with Henry, Norbury, Guest, Ruthven & Page. (Mahon could not get out & Sterling funked the weather.) Turned in at 10.30, more than recompensed for the jumpy ride.

Thursday, August 31:

Everybody about by 4 AM. The Sirdar was inspecting the Camel Corps & the 10th Soudanese at 6.30 near the polo ground 3 1/2 miles distant. A perfect morning when I started after a useful "chota hazri" [light breakfast]. The Camel Corps had gone on. Found the 10th formed up in a line immediately in front of the centre of the Camel Corps line. 500 camels on parade; a very striking parade to one unused to it. After inspecting the 10th the Sirdar rode quietly down the C.C. line & took just 8 minutes. Inspection over, the C.C. broke into column of sections (8 Companies of 4 Sections each), did a little manoeuvering, finally forming "Mass," lying down, the whole dismounted & moved out to attack as a battalion, leaving the No. 3s in charge of the Camels. Driving back the supposed enemy they brought up their left & advanced some distance firing, supported by the 10th Soudanese. Firing ceased & the companies marched back to within 50 yards of the camels when "Mount" was sounded. The men ran like hares, each one to his own camel, and, in spite of what appeared "pandemonium," mounted ready to move off quicker than I can write about it. This finished the Camel Corps, "home" was the order for them, "trot" sounded & away they moved so quickly I had to gallop the grey to get a word with Henry at the lead of the column. The 10th Soudanese marched past the Sirdar on the way back to their lines; in spite of their having been up the Blue Nile & split up for some time, they made a good show & have very few faults in the march-past.

After breakfast I paid another long visit to the "Sook," secured one or two things. Sorted my plunder in the afternoon. Rode with Hamilton to polo in the evening. Back with Lewis to see the 11th Soudanese grand guard-mounting ceremony in the big square. A really good show which attracts many of all sorts & conditions from Lord K. down. Spent an hour with Asser (living in the Khalifa's house), who is down with fever, before dining with the Sirdar. Hamilton, Graham, Majendie & Parker were also dining. K. was in great form & 10.30 came much too soon.

Mahan & Mitford left today for the White Nile. Their object is not given out, but doubtless it is to ascertain the state of the river banks to as far as Kaka with a view of selecting the best place from which to start an expedition against the Khalifa, who is supposed to be near Kaka. Owing to an extension of leave not been practicable I was not able to accompany them on their 4 to 6 weeks trip; this is most mortifying as the run would be very interesting.

Friday, September 1:

5.45 AM found me at Lewis's bedside stirring him to start for the Camel Corps lines for "chota hazri" prior to visiting the battlefield. We had a selected party & looked forward to an interesting morning comparing notes. Lewis on the 2nd Sep. '98 commanded a Brigade, Hunter (10th Soudanese now) was on that day with the Seaforths; Henry with the Camel Corps, & Smith the Brid. Car. Young Guest—just out to join the C.C.—made the 5th to take photographs for us. We wasted no time over the ride to the C.C. & our "chota hazri" & were soon riding northwards by the west of Surgham towards Kerreri. Alas! A mighty storm upset our plans. It threatened from the North for some time heading towards the west—some hoped it would miss us, but it got nearer & at length we had to give up the idea of doing Kerreri where the Egyptian Cdr. & Camel Corps were early on the 2nd, & make Eastwards to the river; but even there, there was no escape for us; the storm "re-inforced" on the East, broke, & we got the full fury of it. We turned our horses' heads South & galloped along the line taken by the 21st when the Regt. left the Zareba the second time on the 2nd Sept. '98, and arrived at the scene of the charge at 9 AM, drenched to the skin. I dismounted and poked about the nullah and on either side of it, no trace of anything, just the skeletons of a horse or two. The cairns over our grave has well wall built of large flattish stones in the form of a cross, up to this it has been held sacred not a stone mis-placed. We galloped on to the Camel Corps lines, Lewis & I took a sip of old brandy and rode hard to Omdurman accompanied by the storm. I was to have crossed to Halfayah today, dined & spent the night with Matchett's battalion, but there was no crossing in the face of this "weather," so wrote all the afternoon, then rode with Lewis through the bazaars & suburbs till dark. In spite of the many small floods it was easy to see how wonderfully clean the city is now; totally opposite to the filth & putridity which existed a year ago. Dined at the 10th Soudanese with Hunter & de Montmorency; the former is a very keen & successful Shikari and I listened with interest to his hunting experiences.

Saturday, September 2:

The first anniversary of the Battle of Omdurman. A fine morning so I started on the grey at 5.30 to again go over the scene of the fight. Took "chota hazri" at the Camel Corps en route, and Ruthven's camera with 11 blank films all ready for action. This time made certain of our Khor by going there first. Took two or three shots at different parts of it and of the cairn, also of a small cairn marking the grave of a few dervishes;

a keen search led to my finding an empty Lee-Metford cartridge case, only one out of the good few our men fired there. It was easy to recall & picture last September there and again I marvelled how the Regt. was able to ride thru' hundreds of determined armed men strongly posted in such a place and again one felt proud to have been with the Regt. that did it without a thought. From thence I went to Gebel Surgham, climbed to the top & spent half an hour taking in the great panorama around me and in going over again all I saw last year, filling in, as well as possible, the great remainder, by recalling all one had read & heard. Descending by the N.E. side I passed over the ground where large numbers of the dervishes fell; here I had the luck to find two Remington cartridges, one exploded, the other not. So thoroughly has the "field" been cleared, only an occasional shell & a few bleached bones here & there are to be seen; these, with the large cairns over the buried dervishes, alone mark this big battle-field. I rode on nearly to Kerreri, then towards the river, hitting off the small entrenchment of the Zareba & then following it right round. Not having Lewis or Henry with me was a great misfortune; they could have explained so much one wanted to know, but both were too busy to come out, altho' today is a holiday by direction of the Sirdar. The Zareba ends, no trace remains of the thorn bushes, so I made my way to young Grenfell's grave. Found it in good order with its wooden cross and the flat stone on the grave, giving his age & date of death. I took a couple of photographs of this, & then turned Southwards, rode back by our Khor paying it a last visit.

Leaving Sandy Ruthven's camera en route, I reached the Sirdariyeh at 12 noon. Finding a boat for the North could not leave before tomorrow midday, I decided to pay one more visit to Khartoum and commenced the journey at 3.30 with Gordon (a young civilian) in Gorringe's felucca; at first all went well thanks to a North breeze, but when we had made a good distance up stream the breeze dropped, the boatmen were idle & stupid & so we drifted back nearly to our starting place! At length by rowing & towing they got us up & across to the Mogrim, the point where the Blue & White Niles join, at 5.00!! Nearly 3 miles separated us from Gorringe's and Drage's quarters; by the aid of first a bad & then a good donkey & a 20-minute walk I arrived at Drage's house a little before 6. A drink and another drink were most acceptable. G. was out by [but?] D. gave me some information I wanted & lent me his horse to ride back to the Mogrim, left there at 7 in a small barge (very like the Masoolah boat of the East coast of India) with several inches of water in her. The two men worked well & got me across in time for 8.00 dinner at the Staff Mess.

Only half a dozen dining, we remembered the last 2nd Sept. and drank in silence to those who fell on that day. Immediately on returning at midday I sent a wire of good wishes to the Regt. and "Veritas" to K. My thoughts have been much with the Regt. today. I hope the Sports & dinner went off right well & that the Reserve won the shield.

Sunday, September 3:
Rode with Lewis for an hour & a half before breakfast—wrote letters afterward. Lunched with the 13th. Packed kit & got a camel ready to take it to the *Nasr* (gunboat) expected this afternoon & to leave at daybreak tomorrow; by 5 PM it was plain she could not arrive today, so sent the camel away & went for a ride with Lewis who at last was persuaded to give me an account of his fight at (Roseires) on Boxing Day last year. A clinking good fight—hope to write down his story. Quite one of the best fights in the Soudan & very plucky leading & following. Dined at the 13th and spent another pleasant evening. These Gippy Army fellows have laid themselves out to make my visit here a pleasant one in every way & succeeded.

Expected to have slept on the *Nasr* and left at dawn tomorrow, but there is not a sign of her.

Monday, September 4:
Up at 5.30 & off to the shore on the grey, still no news of the *Nasr* so I took a long ride thro' Omdurman Southwards to our bivouac on the west side on the night of the fight, & then rode back to the big square by the route I walked on that night or rather tried to. Everything if not "another colour" is very different now. Breakfasted with Lewis, paid a last visit to the "Sook", secured two more necklaces. The *Nasr* arrived about midday, but was sent on to Khartoum with a couple of barges, and was not back when I arrived at the shore at 4.30, with my kit now much increased by purchases, & by presents of arms to the Sergeants by the Sirdar. Left Achmed Suleiman in charge & rode back to see the polo.

I took the opportunity of thanking the Sirdar for his present to our Sergeants; he said he was very glad to send them something—also that I had been able to see Omdurman & the Soudan again, & hoped I had enjoyed my visit. This last was especially nice of him as there is still more to be done with regard to the Khalifa, and outsiders are not just now wanted. I have, in spite of using a room in the Sirdariyeh, kept out of the Sirdar's way and never even hinted I should like a post of any sort in the Soudan.

I was Lewis's guest at the Staff Mess tonight; the little warrior was in great spirits by the receipt today of his copy, on a double sheet of vellum, of the House of Lords' "Vote of Thanks" to him & a few other seniors on account of their good services at the Battle of Omdurman. The vellum had a very swagger crimson leather case, the Royal Arms, etc. in gold on it. The thanks of the House of Commons will be in a blue cover, they say. A good few were dining, we had an extra cheery night, several songs with two or three excellent piccolo solos by Vandeleur. I am putting up with Hoskins as my kit is on the *Nasr*.

Tuesday, September 5:

Up at 5.30. Left at 6.30 on the grey for the boat as soon as the important letter from the Sirdar for Le Gallais reached me. Found Fell all ready, but some of his crew who were ashore kept us waiting till 7.15. Prendergast, 9th Soudanese, was down to see me off. No fellows could have been kinder than these have been to me, I'm sorry to have to say good-bye. Jolly morning, — have I taken a last look at Khor Sambat, Gebel Surgham, Kerreri, etc. We run quickly thru the Shabluka, that is the 6 or 8 miles of narrow defile where the water is always deep, only at the two entrances is the river un-navigable at low Nile. At 11 AM we tied up for wood and did not reach Wad Hamed till 2.15. Pirie, Conolly & Bulkeley-Johnson were on the bank. We yarned all the afternoon and rode in the evening. They (the Squadrons) have opened out and taken up much more ground than last year, even here the river being so much lower makes a lot of difference in the appearance of the place. Persse is not too well, & was not at dinner tonight. A rather hot stuffy evening. I have the use of Baring's hut but of course the only chance of sleeping was out in the open.

Wednesday, September 6:

Up just after 5 and out with Pirie & his Soudanese Squadron. Rode No. 1, a good bay who carried me right well. The Squadron went out as an Advanced Guard. Details pretty correct—a good direction kept and concentration at the very good. Drill followed, this was very creditable considering the short time the men have been in the ranks; half column & wheeling were well done—the wheels about were not so good. Advance in line, attack & pursuit were steady; the dismounted work surprised me, they did it so much better than one expected. No fuss or bother in dismounting & mounting, all quietly & quickly done; just a little careless in handling reins to No.s 3. The men rode very well, sat up without being stiff, & appeared to have rather good hands (the horses' heads were steady). Pirie is on capital terms with his Squadron, they should turn out a good lot. At present they have swords only—lances will follow later. Horses are in poor condition, the result of hard work with indifferent or no grass. The Squadron had two hours at this, then breakfast, after which we were at Stable till 11. The men shaped rather well here also—one fellow I noticed would rival an English groom in using the body brush. Stables over, Persse, who was a bit better, took me round the other Squadrons, sick lines, etc. These horses look better—having had less work than Pirie's & Conolly's Soudanese have. The sick horses have the palm grove which was occupied last year by the Mess. One or two serious only. Watched the shoeing for a few minutes, better than a native usually does it. Back to the huts at 12.15 after a warm morning. Just then the *Dal* appeared with Asser on board; Persse got him off to lunch & we left at 2 PM for the Atbara. It was bad luck being unable to see more of Pirie & the others, but it was not safe to wait for the next boat. Lewis, their Vet, arrived from the North this morning from English leave, had to go to bed seedy; another first rate chap.

The *Dal* (the boat the Duke & Duchess of Connaught used for their Khartoum trip) pushed on well till 6.45 when the Reis said he could no longer "read the river" owing to the blinding lightning, so we tied up at 7; and luckily, for shortly after & before the boat was secured the storm which had been threatening for some time burst with fury. Waves blew up like those on a small sea, causing the steamer & her two sandels to roll quite a lot. Made all secure—got dinner over sharp & turned in. Not easy to find a dry spot as the roof leaked in many places, however; the rain ceased before morning—although the wind continued to rock us.

Thursday, September 7:

At 3.30 AM there was less wind & we started again. A little more sleep till day-break, when it was perfectly charming—cool & nice after the storm. The Merowi [Meroe]* pyramids were passed in the distance, next the splendid palm groves of Magawieh; half an hour later we met the Khaibar and Amara, Southward bound. The latter is one of the two steamers (Amara and Amheb) which the 17th Battalion sent to Merowi [or Meraui]* to travel up the 4th Cataract. (*Two distinctly different places [author's note]).

Stopped for an hour at 10.15 to wood & again for another hour at 2.15. This "wooding" causes great delay, not too many can be spared for the task & those work as if time were no object. We ought to make Atbara by 5 PM today. Wonder shall I have the luck to catch an American engine for the desert journey.

Atbara 4.30 PM. Here we are too late, thanks to last night's storm, for the American engine which left at 2 PM, having been detained some 4 hours for me; beastly bad luck. No letters or telegrams. Hobbs, the new Comdr., and Nickerson (Doctor) are the only officers here; Newcombe R.E. is on the South side of the Atbara. Another good youngster doing the work of one 10 years his senior. He was over to get us all to dine with him, it was not convenient to Hobbs—so we stayed here & were treated to good banjo music & songs after dinner by Hobbs.

Friday, September 8:

After a splendid sleep in the open I got up at 5.30, travelled across the Atbara bridge to meet the engine Newcombe was sending to take me to his place. Very different track now; sleepers closer together & firmly fixed. Each span is 150 ft., making total length of the bridge 350 yards. The engine met me at the far side, we were soon at the "shops," considerable work going on; sleepers & rails for 35 miles lying stacked ready to go on—more to follow. Newcombe's description of the Atbara battlefield made me wish to visit it, but it could not be, 'tis {30} miles from here & requires at least two days on ponies—can't risk it. N.'s horse is quite the best in the Soudan, putting even Drage's in the shade. After breakfast we "engined" back to the North side. My train was to leave at 10 AM, then 1 PM; eventually it was 5.15 PM when it steamed out. It is a "material" train, and with so much stores, etc. to move, it is impossible to ensure anything like punctuality with this sort of train. The *Fateh* arrived from the South & left on her return journey today. Pretty warm here today—but not such a "scorcher" as the Sunday my Squadron arrived last August, when we were the whole day up to 9 PM crossing to the West bank, a steamer & some small gyassa to take everything dead & alive over; two or three men were bowled over by the heat & one horse went overboard, saddle & all, from "sunstroke."

Our engine, the "Debbeh," has a long train of 40 vehicles beside her 3 water tanks to drag to Halfa. She has a good reputation; let us trust to her playing up to it. Atbara was left at 5.15, Berber reached 6.30, left 6.45. Arr. Abadia 7.45, left 9.15. An hour & a half seems a long time for wood & water. I'm the only English-speaking animal in the train & not "having" any Arabic there is no means of finding out the reason for the long halt. At 10 PM we reached the Khor, the bridge over which had been destroyed by fire a fortnight or so back. It was a pile bridge & entirely of wood; how it was fired no one knows, possibly by some wandering Arabs cooking underneath it & not putting out their fire. It burnt & smouldered right away, consequently when a heavy train with no engines Northward bound came along in the middle of a dark night, there was a bad smash. The leading engine with its three water tanks took a big leap straight ahead into the gap, the rear engine & its tanks went to one side, the tanks coming next were piled on the top of the first cab. Several natives were killed & more injured, but altho' the engine driver & firemen went with their engines not one of the four was badly hurt! The Sirdar returning from leave was on the train going South next to cross the place, a narrow escape for K. A diversion was rigged up without delay & traffic resumed. It was not possible to get out all the bodies for 2 or 3 days. The stench was sickening, naturally. The engine of my train was detained till 10.50 PM in hauling up by a prepared ramp the foremost engine. This done, we went on again. Arr. Abba Saleem [Abu Selim] 11.45, left 12.15 on Saturday 9th September; arr. Shereck [Sherek] 1.55, left 2.55. Two more small stations and then Abu Hamed at 7.30 AM.

Saturday, September 9:

Adams was awaiting me here with an excellent breakfast under the front verandah of his house. Delightfully cool with a splendid view down the river studded here with islands. On again at 9.15; now followed the real desert journey. No. 9 was reached at 11.25 & left at 11.50, & so on thro' 8 and 7, arriving No. 6 at 5.10. Stopped till 6.45 overhauling the engine, took in water & coal. I had all spare soda-water bottles filled with the excellent well water here. Nothing startling occurred except that the cooking arrangements, being carried out in the interior part of an old engine on an open truck next to my carriage, were much interfered with by the dust storm which blew up just before we left No. 6. However, I managed to get a rough meal. The "Debbeh" fizzed along well & landed her load at Wady Halfa safe & sound at 5 AM Sunday, 10th September.

Sunday, September 10:

After moving into the Sirdariyeh and enjoying a tub, I went in search of Anley, the Commander. Found him at the North End looking round. Strolled with him till time to return for breakfast at 8.30; lot of convicts at work moving coal, all very bad characters, consequently heavily ironed. Moved into Anley's house after breakfast—to stay with him till the boat leaves for Shellal—he says on Wed. In view of this delay I replied to Clerk's wire this morning, asking if I wanted an extension, "Yes, till Tuesday 19th." Glorious morning here, cool breeze, Anley's large verandah overlooking the river is about perfection after 30 hrs. in the train. Breakfast over, we yarned for a while; then I was taken to see Mahmoud, who fought us at Atbara on Good Friday last year. A clean, well-bred, good-looking man, cheery & very well in spite of but little exercise. Thro' Anley I told him the story of Mahomed Cheriff's [Sherif] abortive rising & of his death & that of two of the Mahdi's sons. Mahmoud did not appreciate the news—declared that they were great fools. He probably thought that his period of detention would be lengthened by this abuse of liberty by Mahomed Cheriff [Sherif]. I took Mahmoud a packet of tea which much pleased him; he gave me his autograph & kissed his fingers after our goodbye shake of the hand.

Found a letter from K. at the Post Office, though they declared there was nothing for me—the idiots! Lunch, reading, tea, & then a long walk thro' North End to Tewfikieh, the native town; en route we passed the place where our Squadrons dis-embarked & embarked last year; the river is washing away the bank & a line of rails has had to be removed; then on thro' the Haraamat (married lines) & out to Tewfikieh. Very clean & an entire absence of bad smells, shews excellent supervision. Many Greek shops & cafes. In rear of one large cafe was a very fine young lion, confined in a small hut, having a couple of strong iron-barred windows. The lion was only a year old & came from Kassala District when quite a little cub; such a jokey chap, as full of fun as a kitten, played with my stick as a kitten would with a ball. The Greek owner said it had fever, but its coat looked the perfection of good health. I managed to rub its back & stroke its paw once, but had to be nippy about it. Sanderson, a civil engineer, and Tewfik Bey, an officer in the Egyptian Ordnance Dept., arrived with us, a very nice little party. Tewfik Bey is a most interesting old fellow & very good looking. Ismail Pasha sent him to England in '75 to learn all about arms, etc. at the Birmingham Small Arms Factory & at other similar establishments; he was nearly two years in England— visited London & all of our large towns & had many experiences which he related so well I wished I could write short-hand.

Monday, September 11:

Delightfully cool night on the verandah close to the river. Another glorious morning with a sunrise that held one for minutes. Wrote till breakfast at 8, then read till 10 when Anley was free for a while. Macauley & Stevenson (both R.E., the former Director of Soudan Mil. Railways) shewed me all over the railway workshops—very extensive and interesting. A large proportion of the "plant" was brought here by Ismail Pasha, and formed a nucleus for the present works. The principal workmen are French, Greeks, Italians & a few English; the larger number are Egyptians & Arabs, with a sprinkling of convicts. The wooden models for the "castings" are made by a clever old Arab; the "castings" themselves being turned out by a Greek whose best helper is a convict (a lifer for murder). New machinery is being steadily added. The "talent" is just now busy on an improved traveling carriage for the Director. One important feature is a new arrangement for admitting air while still excluding dust—a tremendous boon. Stores and all traffic for & from the Soudan pass thro Halfa, changing from river to rail or vice versa. So excellent is the system there appears no fuss or bother—all works out smoothly. About 250 convicts—heavily ironed, being lifers & in many cases murderers—do the greater part of the "coolie" work & get what they deserve, a hard time. Halfa is lucky in possessing many trees—principally a kind of acacia, also a good few gardens, all very restful for the eye & lessening the dust.

Anley & I did a long walk Southward in the evening, the belt of cultivation was very flourishing, the villagers should be well off. We looked in at the Serai, set apart for the Dongola refugees; only a few women there just now. We dined at the Mess with Macauley, Stevenson, Wanhill, & Sanderson. Very jolly dinner & a perfect evening on the verandah over the river. This verdict & sentence on Dreyfus makes me as much inclined to fight the French as the Boers.

Tuesday, September 12:
Up at 5.30. Anley had to take the *Semmeh*, which arrived last night, down the river to the village of Arjin to hold a sort of pow-wow & read a few new rules & laws to the villagers, who have recently been giving trouble in the way of disposing of their land. I accompanied him. The villagers, with the "Omdeh" (head-man), were assembled on the river bank to receive the "Mudir" (Anley); we were conducted to the village were [where] a sort of pandal had been erected and furnished with a divan & chairs & rather well carpeted. Anley got to work at once, the new rules were read one by one to the villagers seated around who were asked if they understood & did they wish to make suggestions. There was scarcely a dissentient. After this those who had complaints or petitions came up one by one & had them heard & adjusted. Two of the petitioners were very plain women. The Omdeh was a very tall Bosnian—considerable presence & evidently has much power over his village; his house was very well built & had one large room evidently used for a meeting-place to discuss village affairs. A great fight came off here in 1889. The dervishes were determined to get to the river. Col. Wodehouse had to prevent this; the fight lasted the whole day in and

about this village—a long straggling one by the river—at length the dervishes were driven back into the desert with considerable losses; the 10th Battalion, which bore the brunt of the first attack, suffered heavily, being quite out-numbered. They fought well & contested every yard of ground right back, even into the river itself. Nine o'clock saw us back to breakfast. Packed & sent things to the boat which left at 11 o'clock. Anley came to see the start. We had cast off when two letters for me were brought down by the Postmaster; a native waded & swam out with them. Stopped at the Post Office, Tewfikieh, & finally started for Shellal at 11.40 A.M. A perfect temperature going down the river with the North wind in our faces. It has been an interesting day—bits of the river very pretty—others wild—gyasses heavily laden making good progress upstream with the favourable wind. Then the occasional halts on account of the post to leave or take on. Our reis is a fine fellow at bringing his boat up to bank with a bang; seemed rather proud of it. Made Korosko at 11 P.M. Sorry not to have had daylight to look over the place. Toski a few hours later.

Wednesday, September 13:

A perfect morning, just wanted another here to share it. More scenery to please the eye. The crops are looking well. Passed one or two notable places for tourists judging by the white numbers such as "11 8" on the rocks here & there. Reached Shellal at 11.15 AM. A very civil note from Elgood, Cmdr. Assouan, was awaiting me, saying come on by the train at 12 noon in the special carriage sent for me, he had arranged to shew me the dam in the afternoon. Room ready for me, etc. Very nice indeed. I telephoned my thanks & acceptance—enjoyed a whiskey & soda at the Hotel (?) while the fatigue party moved my "afsch" (baggage) from boat to train. E. was at the Assouan Station to take me off to lunch. Found him capital company—keen soldier, good at languages & a great amateur actor. There were so many people & places we both knew that yarning after lunch lasted to tea time & we made a rather late start for the big dam, a 3 1/2 mile ride thro' the desert along the right bank of the river at some distance from it. Much blasting was going on. I was greatly impressed by the immense mass of masonry—every block of granite in it being laid in Portland cement. Just now the construction is stopped owing to the high water; at low Nile it will re-commence. The broken rocky river bed & the swiftly running water dashing over & around the rocks made a most impressive sight. Pirie's old syce appeared & came up to enquire about the Regt.—& his medal! I rather wished the ride home had been longer, it was a perfect time for being out in the desert, very cool, and enough moon to see things. Dinner at 8.45 in the Mess garden. Till now I had no idea Assouan was so pretty. The Esplanade is coming on well with its trees growing & thriving. The Sirdar's and other green islands over towards the opposite bank shew up well with the high sand hills for a background.

The old Mess-house & Officers' Quarters stand in really nice gardens. Good shrubs—fine trees—excellent gravel walls—all well kept. The stone floor, old dresser, & deep windows of the "dining" room reminded one of an old English kitchen. Elgood turned in at 10.30. I enjoyed a half-hour's stroll up & down in the moon-light—it was rippin'—before going aloft to my bed at the top of a high house. Delightfully cool out there—not a mosquito or sandfly.

Thursday, September 14:

Up at 5.30 to find quite a nip in the cold tub. It was nearly seven o'clock when we started our ride Northwards. Visited the Camet prison—Hospital and the Old Soldiers' barracks, all very good & in the best of order. The Egyptian officer in charge of the prison shewed much keenness for every detail to be seen, & would have my signature in the visitor's book!

One of the convicts in Hospital was a sickly-looking youngster of 19, doing 57 years for slave-trading (bagged a boy & sold him). They have good iron bed-cots & the usual furniture of an ordinary hospital and are quite as well done as they deserve. The old soldiers—who by the way do not get pensions—are employed here on guard duty; good old Soudanese who have seen a deal of fighting & many of them wounded. Their Barracks appeared comfortable & were very clean & tidy. The old black loves to be noticed, over & over again. I regret being unable to talk with them & so gain an insight into their many & varied experiences. The outside was all I saw of the monastery or convent, whichever it may be.

After breakfast my kit was sent on board the Niagara ready to start for Luxor at 12 noon. On the "grey," escorted by a couple of police, I poked about the bazaars—succeeded in picking a few things such as camel sticks & a good kourbash. A dervish sword without a scabbard was offered to me at £21/-!! The seller is keeping it for the tourists next season. Such things will command high prices until there has been another brush with the dervishes. I felt complimented by not being offered any of their home-manufactured arms. A tremendous trade appears to be done in gaudy English handkerchiefs. Elgood saw me off on the *Niagara* at 12.15. Much regret not having one more day at

LIEUTENANT COLONEL HARRY FINN

Assouan to visit the Sirdar's island, & the old ruins & tomb on the opposite bank—belonging to Gen. Grenfell. Hope to fit in a visit to Thebes from Luxor tomorrow before leaving for Cairo. It is splendid going down stream with this head breeze; company would add greatly to the enjoyment of this trip. The wide strip of cultivation on the right bank with its fringe of date palms and the irregular line of hills beyond with the light of the setting sun combine to make a wonderfully pretty picture. An occasional halt to put off or take on passengers. Just as the light was failing a priest had to get ashore at Edfou—an awkward part of the bank was chosen for the holy man to land, he & his belongings narrowly escaped a ducking. Esneh was reached at 10 PM, tied up for the night. The native passengers went ashore to sleep. My fine large cabin was quite cool.

Friday, September 15:
I awoke to see the boat start at 3 AM; pity these people cannot work without shouting or singing (?). At 6 I was up to enjoy another lovely morning & to wish that this boat were going right thro' to Cairo; far & away pleasanter than the dusty, stuff[y] train. A large place with 3 or 4 tall shafts was reached at 6.15, the natives called it Amarinth, and Luxor an hour later. The Anglo-American Company's Agent, a Copt, was soon on board & put me in the way of crossing to Thebes; while the dragoman was away to arrange boat, etc., I breakfasted off several hard-boiled eggs, cold potatoes, jam & bread and soda water. Millet gone bad, the balance of my fresh stores from Assouan. Pity this boat is so old & was so lightly made, the engines are powerful hence there is a continual shake & rattle; one gets used to it, but appreciates the quiet which reigns when the boat is not on the move. This visit to the old Temples will be warm work, there is every promise of a hot day; as much as possible must be seen in the 5 hours or so available. The Cairo train leaves Luxor at 4 PM.

Khirzam [Khizam] 6 PM. Rather a change of programme—I did not contemplate re-visiting here. It was 9 AM when we left Luxor for the other side of the river. A small sailing boat with a man & a boy carried the party over: the dragoman, two donkeys & their boys, a boy from the boat with a basket of hard-boiled eggs, limes, bread & soda-water (no whiskey). A cool breeze against the current took us across in about 20 minutes. A longish ride brought us to the first lot of temples—I omitted to take notes of the guide's explanations of these & do not recollect who built [them]; we spent a little time among them & they interested me in one point I recollect; they were said to be connected by an avenue of sphinxes with a similar avenue from the Karnak temples on the other side of the river. From this spot we went to a village where Hassan Hasni, the Inspector of Antiquities Konah, lives; the dragoman, Mahomed Kalil, gave him a message from the Coptic agent which resulted in his giving me his card. This proved an open sesame to all the places I wished to see; the keepers unlocked the iron gates & all was made easy by it.

A hot ride of half an hour or more up through the hills brought me to the Tombs of the Kings or rather among them. I know practically nothing of these Kings, their works or their carving, therefore I will not attempt a detailed description of what I saw. A good Baedecker would be useful from which to crib a few extracts, unfortunately there is not one handy.

Time being limited, the dragoman was instructed to take me to two or three of the most important Tombs. He started with "Tomb No. 6. Rameses, Ra-nefer-Ka XX Dynasty"—this is a facsimile of its description as given in white letters on a black board hung over the entrance, which called to mind the { } board in an Indian barrack. We turned off the track, went a few paces along a cutting, then down a flight of steps which, like the whole of each tomb, were cut in the solid rock of the hills. Then followed a hall 12 to 14 ft. high & 8 or 9 wide, the walls & ceilings covered with beautifully-executed carvings, many of them coloured. My guide (the dragoman) had his history of all these and commenced with it without delay; some of it was not interesting to my unprepared mind; this he discovered without shewing much disgust; he contenting himself with answering questions and volunteering information only on some really "big thing." At the end of the hall was a downward slope, then more steps & another slope, all into the heart of the hill, till the sarcophagus, or the excavation where it had been, was reached.

King Rameses (this one's particular number was not given) frequently appeared among the carvings, offering sacrifices to or receiving presents from the gods. Lotus, papyrus and the symbol of the key of life were principally used in the above ceremonies. The sacred boat is often portrayed, also the serpent who is used in various ways in passing on the great king to his last resting-place. Bad people & enemies were shewn head-less, or on their heads with heels in the air, in either case their hands were tied behind their backs. Others who were not very bad (*vide* the guide) were horizontal. One scene shewed the King administering justice by the aid of a pair of scales on a man's shoulder. Those for the test are advancing in single file up to the King. The guilty were being removed by means of a boat containing a pig. (The guide explained that the pig was of much importance in the case) while the "all rights" were formed, in rear of the king, in column of sections similar to the diagram in the Cavalry drill book—ready to march aloft.

A few of the carvings as explained by the guide were very quaint. I was sorry time did not admit of taking notes. We were well equipped with candles but a large stock of magnesium wire would have been useful; it is essential to seeing the beautiful ceilings of the innermost "rooms." The "batty" smell was less than I expected. I was much impressed by the brilliancy the colours still retain. Also, by the way, an odious comparison, certain persons had traced their names by the aid of candle or torch on the ceilings of one or two low pitched rooms. Much damage has been done to the carvings, etc. by hacking and cutting. This is said by the guide to have been done before the tombs were opened up to tourists.

Tomb No. 9, Rameses VI of the same dynasty, was similar to No. 6 and yet probably very different if detail were compared. No. 17, the tomb of Settu I, 19th Dynasty, is quite the largest I saw and descends deeper; unfortunately only one bit of magnesium wire was left for the place where it was most wanted; still, I got a glimpse of the magnificent ceiling. Apparently the whole of this tomb has not be[en] cleared out. I went as far as possible, further than the guide approved or would venture, he beseeched me to return as the roof was unsafe. It looked so & I did not tarry. These sort of fellows generally know best only one hates advice from them. On getting out of this tomb into the fresh air (a bit like that in a medium sort of furnace) a halt was called for eggs, bread & soda-water before making a fairly stiff climb over the hill & down the other side to the Dir-el-Bahar-ri (?) built by Queen Hatasu, 18th Dynasty, {1600} B.C. The guide thought it a cracked thing to foot it all the way but it was a good change and the wild scenery could be better seen in that way.

From the height overlooking Queen Hatasu's temple the drop is very deep and perfectly straight & a grand panorama is to be enjoyed. How much grander it would have been if hundreds of acres now dry & brown were under water, as was the case last year. Queen Hatasu's temple is not under-ground but built against the straight side of a very high hill. It seems she incurred the serious displeasure of a nephew (?) who succeeded her and he caused every figure of her, her name & symbol wherever they appeared in this temple, to be erased. The erasures are evident, whether deserved or not is another matter. She built much & well. The guide said an avenue of trees & sphinxes alternately went from this Temple to the Nile and followed from the opposite bank up to [the] Temples of Karnak. This seems probable. The watchman here treated us to a drink of cold & pretty clear water, said to be from a well; I asked no questions. It is reported that Queen Hatasu's tomb has never been found. (Wonder how many "inventions" the guide has told me today.) From here we rode on to the Temple of Rameses II the Great. This temple is also called the Ramaseum, & is above ground. On one large wall is an immense battle scene shewing Rameses fighting his enemies with considerable success; the carving is splendidly done, many of the belligerents are in weird positions & a good few in sore straits. Rameses in his chariot & drawing a tremendous bow is a big giant compared with all others in the picture & much larger than the lion shewn in a bounding position by his side. (A smart polo pony & a kourbash would have been useful at this temple; a half score of young Ishmaelites wanted licking.)

On again to the Palace & Temple of Rameses III called Madinat Habu. Very fine pillars, archways & carvings. Enormous blocks similar to those at Karnak; here again some good fighting was permanently recorded by the same beautifully executed carving. A stone staircase enables one to get more than half way to the top of a gateway. On one side of an open courtyard are the remains of gigantic figures, one alone has been left nearly complete, the others have lost an arm, a leg, a head or one side of the body, still they are imposing.

There now remained the two colossal figures of Amenhotep III to see, these are in the middle of cultivated land (now bare & brown) & said to be over 60 ft. high. They look it; even at a considerable distance they look enormous, 'tis a pity they have been damaged so much. Two large carved figures on one side are shewn having what looks to be a "tug-of-war," near the figures are lotus representing the Lower Nile and papyrus the Upper; the guide explained the tug of war is to haul away the barrier separating Lower and Upper Nile. These last three places had to be scamped & even then it ran the train too close; the boy from the boat, less used to walking bare footed on hot sand & rocks, was going a bit short, so we could ride only foot-pace to the river. The breeze too was less favourable going back, we were more than half an hour crossing. By this time I had determined to break journey at Keneh to see the Dendera Temples across the river from there, and to do this, to stay the night at Luxor, leave by 10 AM train tomorrow Saturday, get out at Keneh, do the Temples, and on by the evening train to Cairo, due there early Sunday morning.

On leaving the *Niagara* this morning she was to remain at Luxor till starting back to Assouan Saturday. On returning to her this afternoon she had steam up ready to start for Khirzam [Khizam] (down stream) returning early morning. I was welcome to remain on board, this was better taking it all round than putting in the night at Luxor, so here I am enjoying one more cool night on the river. The Company's Agent, Mr. Besada Hanna, is on board. He is the son of a Coptic priest who was born at Luxor. This son seems to have acquired considerable knowledge of our Established Church & tells me it & the Coptic are similar. He explains their priests may marry but once, a priestly widower may not enter the matrimonial state a second time. He further explained that their Lent was 40 days duration only, but has been increased to 55 days as a sort of penance to admit of the marriage of cousins being legal! A bit curious, this.

Khirzam [Khizam] brings to mind the grit our men shewed here on the way South last August. 150 horses & tons of baggage & stores had to be detrained & embarked; a miniature dust-storm was blowing the whole time my squadron was carrying out the change, dusk fell before it was finished—but it was done & well done, without my hearing anything but cheeriness; probably the good prospect ahead had a little to say to this.

Saturday, September 16:

A good cool night was followed by a delightful morning. Left Khirzam [Khizam] a little before 6 AM & thoroughly enjoyed the run up to Luxor where we arrived about 7. Got away on the 10 AM train for Keneh; little Besada Hanna was very attentive & promised to see that the rail-way people did not leave any of my heavy baggage behind—it was coming on the 4 o'clock express.

Arrived Keneh at 11.20; away at once on donkeys to the river; the route lay thro' this rather important town. Crossed a wide canal on the opposite side; then a raised road led through good cultivation. This road with its avenue of trees appeared to be a sort of "Mall." We luckily found a boat just starting for the opposite bank & they could just make room for the two donkeys, their boys, Mahomed Kalil & myself. Fifteen minutes took us across—then, armed with a couple of sodas & Hassan Hasni's magic card, we started on our ride to the Dendera Temple. Soon passed thro' two villages; any number of women about who "skooted" like rabbits as we approached, only the very young & the very old sat tight with their faces covered. It is the sort of thing one is used to, but I never saw such very "particular" people before. One of the irrigation canals ran alongside the track. Many "shadoofs," the primitive way of raising water by hand, have just been built along its banks; these were in full swing getting water on to the land; the only possible way with this low Nile. A pound & a half bunch of really good grapes were useful during this ride. Half a dozen ferocious-looking dogs baited us at the last village we passed—reminded one of an Indian "busti" in that respect. No village there would be worthy its name without a {doz.} of pariah dogs to yelp at a stranger. Goulahs (Earthen jars) large & small are so plentifully made in & about Kenek that the village compound walls are made of them. They are used like bricks; look a bit odd.

Today's ride was much more interesting than yesterday's, still one was not sorry to get into the shade of the first large Court of the famous temple. In this court were eighteen grand stone columns in 6 rows, these supported a very lovely roof. Each 6 ft. in diameter & standing on a base 9 ft. in diameter—I estimated their height to be not less than 40 ft. Four faces round the top of each pillar, representing a god or deity of sorts, had their noses & lips chipped off, a beastly shame whoever did it. Mahomed Kalil had two or three theories regarding this damage. This temple, built by Ptolemy 13th, seems to be the finest I have seen. In spite of much damage the carvings are still very wonderful and I spent an hour & a half wandering about the rooms, halls & passages; one of the latter was quite underground; we went down a short flight of steps and then thro' a very small aperture, about 2 ft. square, possibly 30 inches, in the thick wall, down more steps into a passage running right & left, each end closed. The carving here was very good and but little damaged; 'twas too stuffy to stay long, still there was no "batty" smell, this was pretty bad in some part of the temple, especially when ascending by a stone walk which reminded me of going up the Campanile at Venice, only this latter is not infested by bats. A steep iron ladder of 20 steps (so hot from the sun's rays I had to use my handkerchief in gripping the handrail; Mahomed Kalil took the tail of his "galabeiah") took one to the highest part of the roof, whence a fine view was obtained, spoiled again by the scarcity of water—too much brown land was visible, all should be flooded.

I felt tempted to ride on to three or four large white tombs of Sheikhs (quite modern) but I wished to ride thro' the Keneh Bazaars so had to resist. My donkey was great at "lepping" the numerous channels for conveying the water to the various patches of cultivation; the native is very clever in this manner of irrigation, gets a "fall" for the water where everything appears quite flat & level.

In spite of an almost empty boat we were 40 minutes in getting back—the wind was light and the boatman an idiot. We made at once for the bazaars, nothing very wonderful. The amount of cheap English

& European goods struck me. Handkerchiefs, beads, looking-glasses and such like fairly stocked the shops. Only one specimen of the donkey-saddle cloth made at Keneh was to be seen—human nature of course wanted much above its value, so it was left with H.N. Several quite large brick & stone houses were in course of erection. One of the Goulah yards was visited; great competition as to which potter was to show me how it was done. Not bad work, but after the old potter in the Sappers at Bangalore it was a bit tame. Ugh, such a dirty place, & the smoke from the small furnace was the filthiest possible.

Back to the Station by 4.30; sent telegrams to Clerk & Le Gallais about arriving in the morning. Had a tin of "Mutton Chops" heated in boiling water for dinner in the train; while this was going on there was a certain amount of humour obtained out of settling up with Mahomed Kalil; his account for the two days equalled an Indian butler's for detail, but to give him his due the prices were moderate; after being allowed just half of what he suggested should be his daily stipend & having a few lines written in his character book, he was so pleased (or pretended to be) that he declared he would go anywhere with me, & if I would take him to Khartoum he would give his services free. He was a capitally good young fellow. Spoke good English & understood it equally well and had a deal of what sounded like reasonable information about the Temples.

The Express came in and we left fairly punctually at 5.20 on the filthy, dusty journey to Cairo. The "mutton chop" tin contained 3 chops & rather tasty gravy. These, with a good quantity of dust, washed down with a couple of bottles of soda and whiskey, made a good square meal, the first solids since 8.30 AM when I breakfasted on two mugs of tea each with 6 raw eggs beaten into it. A fine sustaining meal; I strongly recommend it. But for the dust it would have been a nice evening, not too warm & plenty of moon. But oh! the dust, ugh! Vandeleur's Campaigning on the Upper Nile & Niger & practising hands at "Bridge" put in the time till 11.30 PM when I turned in & slept soundly till —?— when the compartment was invaded by a quiet man who soon slept after apologising for disturbing the peace. Six o'clock I dug myself out of the dustheap—obliged to have a couple of windows open for air—& got ready for de-training.

Sunday, 17 September:

Reached Cairo 7.30 AM after a very interesting & enjoyable 6 weeks. I'd like to do it again, if only to once more meet the many good fellows in the Soudan. Each one laid himself out to do me well and put me in the way of seeing all that was going on.

CHRONOLOGY OF FINN JOURNAL

August 4:   Departed Cairo at 9:30 PM by train with Mahon, Vandeleur, Wemyss.

August 5:   Arrived Luxor at 1:15 PM. Overnight at Hotel Luxor.

August 6:   Departed Luxor at 6:00 AM by train.
              Arrived Shellal 6:30 PM; Transfer to Nile Steamer *Toski*; left 10 PM.

August 7:   Cruising up Nile.

August 8:   Cruising up Nile. Stop at Korosko to transfer Mail.

August 9:   Cruising up Nile. Describes villages on Nile.

August 10:   Arrived at Wady Halfa at 1:30 PM.
              Departed by train at 5:15 PM for Atbara.

August 11:   Reached No. 6 Station at 8:00 AM; departed 10 AM.
              Arrived Station No. 7 at 11:40 AM.
              (Stranded in mid-desert by train breakdown).

August 12:   Departed 1 PM. Reached Station No.9 at 3:40 PM.
              (Stranded again by storms and breakdowns).

August 13:   Departed 5:40 AM; reached breakdown place at 8:45 AM. Departed at 11:30 AM, arrived Abu Hamed at 12:25 PM. Departed Abu Hamed at 3:35 PM, reached Shereik at 6:30 PM. Overnight at Shereik. Bathed under RR Watering Hose.

August 14:   Departed at 6:00 AM; Arrived Atbara at 2:30 PM.
              (Finn Recalls Arriving at Atbara on Same Day in 1898).

August 15:   Departed on Gunboat *Fateh* at 11:30 AM.
              (Wellby arrived on Tamai at 10:00 AM - Brief chance meeting for Finn).
              Arrived at Aliab at 6:30 PM - overnight stop.

August 16:   Departed 9:30 AM. Passed Kitiab at Noon.
              Tied Up at 3:30 PM for Wood and Overnight.

August 17:   Departed 5:00 AM. Passed Magamieh at Noon; passed Shendy at 3:30 PM; Passed Metemmeh. Stopped at 7 PM to tie up for the night.

LIEUTENANT COLONEL HARRY FINN

August 18:   Departed 5 AM; reached Nasri Island in early afternoon, and at 2:15 PM transferred mail to Gunboat *Nasr*. Tied up at 5 PM for the night.

August 19:   Departed 5 AM; reach sandbank at Wad Hamed at 6:30 AM, but did not stop there. Finn wanted to meet Pirie at Wad Hamed. Entered Shabluka Defile. Reached Gebel Royan at 2:30 PM, where Nile makes big bend. Tied up at 7 PM.

August 20:   Departed at 5 AM. Passed Gebel el Teik, Kerreri, and Gebel Surgham before arriving at 3 PM at Omdurman for a temporary stop, then on to Khartoum, and then returning to Omdurman.

August 21:   Rode at 6:30 AM to visit Camel Corps near Khor Shambat (north of Omdurman).

August 22:   Departed at 7:30 AM on Gunboat *Fateh* for Abu Haraz. Tied up at 5:30 PM opposite Nuba.

August 23:   Departed at 7 AM and reached Kamlin at 2 PM.

August 24:   Departed at 5 AM and reached Abu Haraz at 3:15 PM.

August 25:   Departed Abu Haraz for return to Omdurman. Tied up at 6:30 PM beyond Nuba.

August 26:   Departed at 5 AM for Khartoum and arrived at 8:30 AM for brief stop, reaching Omdurman at 9 AM.

August 27:   At Omdurman.

August 28:   At Omdurman. Camel Corps Drill.

August 29:   Arrival of the Sirdar at 8 AM.

August 30:   Soudanese Brigade Field Day; Parades in AM.

August 31:   Arose at 4 AM. Sirdar troop review at 6:30 AM. Shopping expedition to "Sook." Dinner with Sirdar.

September 1:   Visit to Omdurman Battlefield in storm.

September 2:   Departed at 5:30 AM for Battlefield. Found Khor of 21st Lancer Charge. Climbed to top of Gebel Surgham for Panoramic view. Took photos. (First anniversary of Battle of Omdurman; observed in Staff Mess.)

September 3:   Packed for return trip on Gunboat *Nasr*, due to arrive at Omdurman...did not arrive until next day.

September 4:   *Nasr* finally arrived at noon but went immediately to Khartoum; returned in late afternoon, at which time Finn's baggage and souvenirs were loaded.

September 5.   Finally departed at 7:15 AM, and reached Wad Hamed at 2:15 PM. Spent afternoon with Pirie, and remained overnight.

September 6:   Early morning ride with Pirie and Soudanese Squadron, and departed for Atbara on *Dal*. Tied up at 7 PM.

September 7:   Departed at 3:30 AM and reached Atbara at 4:30 PM.

September 8:   Departed Atbara by train at 5:15 PM, after all day wait for the train. Brief stop at 6:30 PM at Berber, then Abadia at 7:45 PM. Overnight on train.

September 9:   Reached Abu Hamed at 7:30 AM. Departed at 9:15 AM. Overnight on train.

September 10:   Reached Wady Halfa at 5 AM. Stayed with Anley until departure of boat.

September 11:   Tour of Railway workshops at Wady Halfa. Comments on Dreyfus sentence: makes him want to fight French, not Boers.

September 12:   Accompanied Anley on trip to native villages, where British authority needed to be exerted. Description of "pow-wow" with villagers. Returned to Atbara in time to depart for Shellal by steamer at 11 AM.

September 13:   Reached Shellal at 11:15 AM. Went by special RR carriage to Assouan. Overnight at Assouan.

September 14:   Toured Assouan. Departed by steamer *Niagara* at 12:15 PM.

September 15:   Arrived at Luxor at 7:15 AM, and transferred to boat for Thebes. Lengthy description of sightseeing.

September 16:   More sightseeing and traveling. Train to Cairo left 5:20 PM.

September 17:   Arrived Cairo at 7:30 AM on a Sunday morning.

CHAPTER ELEVEN:
The Kaka Expedition, October 1899
Captain Arthur Pirie

A detailed account written to Lieutenant Colonel Finn,
his former commander.

[Jean S. and Frederic A. Sharf Collection]

THE KAKA EXPEDITION, OCTOBER 1899

INTRODUCTORY NOTES

Arthur Murry Pirie was born 3 May 1869. He joined the 21st Lancers in 1889. He served during the Omdurman Campaign as Adjutant to Colonel R. H. Martin, with the rank of Lieutenant. His service during this campaign brought him medals and mention in despatches. In 1899, he was promoted to Captain.

Pirie remained in Egypt from the fall of 1898 until 18 June, 1904, serving with the Egyptian Army. He rose to the rank of Kaimakam in the Egyptian Army Cavalry.

He retired from military service in 1906 with the rank of Major. However, he returned to active service during World War I and was killed in action on 21 November, 1917 at Beylumia, Palestine.

The Kaka expedition was mounted to capture the Khalifa, who had escaped from Omdurman and fled south to the province of Kordofan. He consolidated his power in that region during 1899, and thus continued to pose a threat to British development of the Sudan.

In August 1899, the British Intelligence Department finally had reliable information as to the Khalifa's whereabouts, and the Army decided to mount an expedition to track him down. Troops were moved down the White Nile to a place called Kaka, where by October 20th there was a sufficient force to commence operations. They believed that the Khalifa was at Jebel Gedir, approximately 80 miles distant from Kaka.

The force under Sir Reginald Wingate set out for Kaka, but when they reached Fungor on October 23rd they received information that the Khalifa had fled into the desert. When Lord Kitchener, who was waiting in Kaka, heard this news he decided to cease operations, and return with his force to Khartoum.

The British soldiers in the Sudan were extremely frustrated by their inability to participate in a decisive battle which would once and for ever end the Khalifa's career; they were especially upset when they started to get news from South Africa, which indicated that many of their comrades were in a real fight.

On November 12, 1899, reliable sources in Khartoum received word that the Khalifa was marching north towards Omdurman in one final attempt to capture his former capital. Kitchener immediately returned from Cairo; an expedition was assembled at Abba Island on the White Nile. On November 21, 1899 the expedition departed; on November 24, 1899 the Khalifa's army was defeated at Um Dibaykarat, his camp seven miles southeast of Gedid, and the Khalifa himself was killed.

KAKA EXPEDITION, OCTOBER, 1899:
ACCOUNT OF CAPTAIN ARTHUR PIRIE

Sheik el Teib
Nov. 18th (1899)

My dear Colonel:

You are indeed a brick to write & wire before leaving. I got your wire at Kaka when on the way down, and your letter of the 24th when I arrived at Omdurman on the 10th of the month. As you know by this time, the expedition was a dismal failure, tho it was about as hard on the horses as it could possibly be.

As I told you, we left Wad Hamed on Sept. 27th and got to Omdurman on the 29th, [and] crossed over to the other side the next day, and then marched on October lst. [There were] Five Squadrons: lst, 2nd, 7th Egyptian, 100 strong each; 8th & 9th Black, 75 strong. The Hamlah Camel Corps & Artillery horses left two or three days before by march.

We had rather a jolly march up, except we were most awfully hurried, never having a day's halt from the 1st to the 18th, when we arrived at Mushra Zeraf 420 miles from Khartum. So the horses were not in the very best of condition at the end of it. It was fairly hot all the way. We used to start, as a rule, about 3 AM, sometimes 4 AM and march till 11. Sometimes again in the afternoon. They certainly are wonderful beggars the way they saddle in the dark.

We had one very bad march. We started at 3 AM to march 18 miles to a place called Renk, where we were to get 3 days forage and rations. When we arrived there about 8, all we found was a note to say that there was no mizel there, but it was 20 miles further on. The horses had eaten their last feed before starting that morning so we had to go on. We watered and grazed them till 9 and then went on till 10:30 when we were met by a couple of camel corps who had been sent back with biscuit for the men. It was beastly hot, so we off-saddled and the horses grazed. We ourselves were all right as the baggage came up and we had the mess. We marched again at 4:30 PM & went on till 10:30 PM. Awfully stuffy night, clouds of dust, & millions of 'squitos so it wasn't gay. We halted at 10:30 till 12, watered and grazed, & then marched again at 1:30 AM, and came upon some camels who had been sent out with forage. So we camped for the rest of the night & got in the next morning. It was 29 miles instead of 20 & we halted 5 miles short of the place. So the horses did over 40 miles without corn that day. They were rather done up at the end, but were all right next day.

From Mushra Zeraf we were taken up 30 miles by steamer and landed on the west bank at Kaka. We all got there on the 20th. All the infantry had been taken up by boat; one or two battalions marched part of the way. The whole army was concentrated at Kaka on the 20th: consisted of 2 guns, 10 maxims, 6 Black & 1 Egyptian battalion, 5 squadrons, 500 camel corps. The Khalifa was at Gedir, 90 miles away out west.

They said there was no water for the first 50 miles to a place called Fungor, so the army was to march across in detachments, [with] the Hamlah & Camel Corps working backwards and forwards with water. We left on the morning of the 22nd & marched 7 miles up the river to a place called Kurwa, where we start inland. 4 Black battalions had preceded us. We left Kurwa at 3 PM, rumors being about that the Khalifa had already bolted. We marched till 8 PM when we halted. We carried a few water skins for the men with the camels.

We were off again at 2 AM and marched till 7:30 AM when we caught up [with] 2 infantry battalions who were halted at a pool, where we didn't expect to find any water. Luckily, there was enough for the horses. It was 38 miles out from the river. We did another 12 and got to Fungor at noon on the 23rd. There we found Wingate & Taffy with the 9th & 10th Battalions, also news that the Khalifa had really gone. This was sent back to the Sirdar that afternoon and next morning (October 24th) orders came that everyone except us were to return: there were the 9th and 10th at Fungor, 2 Battalions at the pool 12 miles out, and the others had been stopped & never left the river.

We had the devil of a rainstorm that night of the 23rd, & got everything soaked, as we had 20 tents. However, these wonderful servants manged to give us a hot meal after and I drank real brandy & whisky alternately, so didn't suffer. On the 24th we were ordered to march to Gedir & confirm the news of the Khalifa bolting. We were to take two days forage, which really only meant one as the horses were on 1/2 rations from the day we left the river. We marched at 4 PM and went on till 8 PM, all thru bush, and a single file track. We had a guide with us, but the track was so bad he too lost his way, as it was pitch dark when night came on. We couldn't find water, tho we knew there was a watering place near, so we finally bivouacked in the bush in a small clearing. Of course we had no baggage with us so we didn't want very much room.

Next morning, we marched at 4 AM and got to the watering place in 1/2 a mile. This was a low rock about 40 yards long with a deep cleft about 20 long and thanks to excellent rain water we watered and fed there & left at 6 AM and did 21 miles into Gedir, thru a damnable country, a narrow track, thick bush or else high tall grass & mostly very rough ground. It was a hot day, & not much wind, & so the horses hardly got any air, as the grass was well over their heads.

We got to Gedir at 12:30 [PM] having had to walk the whole way. We expected to find water there, but devil a drop was there, nothing but a very deep well with very little water...a small outlay...you couldn't possibly water horses at it. We found that the Khalifa's camp was another 6 miles on and that he had gone a week before, and they weren't sure if there was water there, so it was no good going on.

We took the headman of Gedir & his secretary back with us, as they were wanted. They didn't seem to mind much. We left again at 4:30 [PM] & had to march all the way back as there was no water on the road, only a very small pool about 2 miles from Gedir, where we managed to water 12 horses [to] a squadron & that used it up. The horses that day did nearly 40 miles with no water from 6 AM till 7:30 PM, carrying about 17 stone, & one half rations & no time to graze. We lost 3 [horses] altogether: one of the 7th dropped at Gedir & was left in charge of the village; one of the 1st when we moved next morning to march back to Fungor; and one of mine dropped on the way back to Gedir that afternoon.

We got into Fungor the next day at about 2 PM as we could only march very slowly. I led a good bit of the way. Next morning we left Fungor & marched to the pool on the way to the river. This was almost dry & had just enough to water the horses some. We went on again in the afternoon & marched till 7 PM. We expected to meet camels with water for the horses, but as they didn't turn up we halted. Left again at 12 midnight & came on the camels at 2 AM. Watered all the horses & went on & got to the river at 9 AM next morning. Stopped there that day & marched into Kaka the next morning.

Found everyone gone except the 10th Battalion & the mizel. Next morning the 3 Egyptian squadrons marched as they were to go about 80 miles by road, and the rest by steamer to Omdurman. The 2 others were to wait at Kaka for steamers & go straight down. We remained till Nov. 5th & then two [steamers] came up & we got to Omdurman on the 10th. It was a damn poor show as you see. A lot of marching & hard work, all very well if you get a show for it, but sickening if you don't. But I'm very glad I was on it as I saw the country, tho it's all rather uninteresting after you got about 200 miles south of Khartum.

You find it very hard to get water as the sudd begins & you very often can't see the river at all, only an enormous long stretch of tall green grass from Kaka to Gedir. It was nearly all bush except a great grass plain about 20 miles across between Fungor and the river. We had two orderlies lost in it, poor devils. They were sent at night & never turned up. I expect they lost their way & got done up & must have died from thirst. They were Gypie.

We didn't disembark at Omdurman on the way down, but came straight down here-it's 20 miles north. They've got the railway opposite here & all stores are put on the steamer here to go up. So now no steamers run north of this & the telegraph on this bank is closed so Wad Hamed is entirely cut off. I'm sorry as this is a beastly hole, all stones and thorn bush. Not a square yard you can ride over & no grass & we've got no polo. There's nothing to shoot so altogether it's not gay.

We thought we were off again last week as the Khalifa is so pleased with himself at getting the best of Kitchener that he's marching north & is only a couple of hundred miles south of Omdurman & quite close to the river. Taffy is up there with two Battalions & we thought we were going but they stopped us. However, we may go yet. The Sirdar has been down in Cairo & passed today so Le Gallais who is in command has gone up to see him. I suppose he will do something.

I'm very sick about the Transvaal. Rome wrote & told me he was going & Kenna, P. Smith, De Moss. It's fairly damnable being stuck out in this vile country & having no chance of getting out to a real fine show like that. I hear our late old man has gone out. Is it him? What is he doing? I hear I have at last got my promotion. About time don't you think so. What are our last [ ] ones like. Thanks very much for getting me all the things in Cairo. Nason gave me the ammunition, & I got the Euchisma but no mess tins but I expect they'll turn up.

Best love to you & all the lads. Do write again soon & give me all the news of the Regiment.

For ever

A. M. P.

Please remember me most kindly to Mrs. Finn and all the Finnlets.

CHRONOLOGY
CAPTAIN PIRIE'S EXPEDITION

September 27: Depart Wad Hamed.

September 29: Arrive Omdurman.

October 1: Depart Omdurman. Cross River to East Bank. Eighteen-day march up the Nile River.

October 18: Arrive at Mushra Zeraf on Nile River.

October 20: Cross Nile River by boat to Kaka on West Bank.

October 22: March to Kuroe .... heading West towards Gedir.

October 23: Rendezvous at Fungor with Army of Sir Reginald Wingate. Approximately 30 miles from Khalifa's camp at Gedir. Received news that Khalifa departed.

October 24: Sirdar orders Army to Kaka, but Pirie is told to proceed to Gedir to make certain the Khalifa is no longer there.

October 25: Pirie Arrives Gedir at 12:30 PM. Khalifa's camp 6 miles further. Definitely abandoned October 18th.

October 26: Return to Fungor.

October 27: Marched towards Nile River.

October 28: Reached Nile River and camped overnight.

October 29: Marched into Kaka in the morning.

October 30: Army begins march Northwards. Egyptian Army leaves.

November 5: Steamers finally reach Kaka to take Pirie and Cavalry North.

November 10: Arrived at Omdurman. Did not remain, but picked up mail (Letter from Finn) and proceeded North to Sheik el Teib.

LIST OF WAR CORRESPONDENTS PRESENT AT OMDURMAN

BENNETT, Ernest N.	*Westminster Gazette*
BURLEIGH, Bennet	*Daily Telegraph*
BULL, Rene	*Black and White*
CHURCHILL, Winston S.	*Morning Post*
CROSS, Henry,	*Manchester Guardian*
GREGSON, Francis M.	*St. James Gazette*
HOWARD, Hubert	*The Times*
JAMES, Lionel	*Reuters*
MAXWELL, William	*Standard*
MAUD, William T.	*Daily Graphic*
OPPENHEIM, Lawrie C. F.	*(?)*
RHODES, Frank	*The Times*
SCUDAMORE, Frank	*Daily News*
STEEVENS, George	*Daily Mail*
VILLIERS, Frederic	*Illustrated London News*
WELDON, Hamilton	*Morning Post*
WILLIAMS, Charles	*Daily Chronicle*

BIBLIOGRAPHY:
PRIMARY SOURCES

Finn, Lieutenant Colonel Harry. *Journal: Return to Omdurman*, 1899.
[Jean S. & Frederic A. Sharf Collection
Chestnut Hill, MA 02167, USA]

Finn, Major Harry. Letters to his Wife.
[Jean S. & Frederic A. Sharf Collection]

Hodgson, Lieutenant Hamilton. Letter to his Father.
[Jean S. & Frederic A. Sharf Collection]

Hubbard, Major Alfred Edward. Diary Inscribed to his Wife.
[Jean S. & Frederic A. Sharf Collection]

Hunter, General Sir Archibald. Letter to his Brother.
[Anne S. K. Brown Military Collection
John Hay Library at Brown University
Providence, RI 02912, USA]

James, Lionel. Handwritten Telegrams on Reuters Letterheads.
[Jean S. & Frederic A. Sharf Collection]

Lawson, Major Henry Merrick. Letter to his Sister.
[Jean S. & Frederic A. Sharf Collection]

McNeill, Lieutenant Angus. *Diary*.
[Collection Mrs. Barbara McNeill, England]

Pirie, Captain Arthur. Letter to Lieutenant Colonel Finn.
[Jean S. & Frederic A. Sharf Collection]

Smyth, Lieutenant Robert Napier. Letter to his Sister.
[Jean S. & Frederic A. Sharf Collection]

SECONDARY SOURCES

Alford, Henry S. L. and Sword, W. Dennistoun. *The Egyptian Soudan*. London: Macmillan and Co., Limited, 1898.

Baedeker, Karl. Egypt: *Handbook for Travellers* (5th Edition). London: Dulau & Company, 1902.

Barthorp, Michael. *War on the Nile*. London: Blandford Press, 1984.

Bennett, Ernest N. *The Downfall of the Dervishes*. London: Methuen and Company, 1898.

Budge, E. A. Wallis. Cook's Handbook for Egypt and the Egyptian Sudan. 3rd Edition. London: Thomas Cook and Son, 1911.

—. *The Nile: Notes for Travellers in Egypt*. 8th Edition. London: Thomas Cook and Son, 1902.

Burleigh, Bennet. *Khartoum Campaign 1898*. London: Chapman and Hall Limited, 1899.

—. *Sirdar and Khalifa*. London: Chapman and Hall Ltd, 1898.

Churchill, Winston Spencer. *The River War* (Two Volumes). London: Longmans, Green and Company; Second Impression, 1900.

Doolittle, Duncan H. *A Soldier's Hero: General Sir Archibald Hunter*. Narragansett, R. I.: Anawan Publishing Company, 1991.

Hunter, Archie. *Kitchener's Sword-Arm: The Life and Campaigns of General Sir Archibald Hunter*. Staplehurst: Spellmount Books, 1996.

James, Lionel. *High Pressure*. London: John Murray, 1929.

Keown-Boyd, Henry. *Soldiers of the Nile*. Thornbury: Thornbury Publications, 1996.

MacLaren, Roy. *Canadians on the Nile 1882-1898*. Vancouver: University of British Columbia Press, 1978.

Maud, William Theobald. `Egypt and the Soudan in 1897-1898.' *Journal of the Society of Arts*, XLVII (December 9, 1898).

—. Reports Published in *The Daily Graphic*, 1898. London, 1898.

Meredith, John. *Omdurman Diaries 1898*. Barnsley, England: Pen & Sword Books Ltd., 1998.

Officer, An: `The Fall of Khartoum: Notes from an Officer's Diary during the War, 1898.' *Pall Mall Magazine*, XVII (Jan-April 1899).

—. *Sudan Campaign 1896-1899*. London, Chapman & Hall Ltd. 1899.

Scudamore, Frank. *A Sheaf of Memories*. London: T. Fisher Unwin Ltd., 1925.

Steevens, George W. *With Kitchener to Khartum*. London: William Blackwood and Sons, 1898.

Villiers, Frederic. *Villiers: His Five Decades of Adventure* (Two Volumes). New York and London: Harper and Brothers, 1920.

Watkins, Owen Spencer. *With Kitchener's Army*. London: S. W. Partridge & Co., 1900.

Wellby, Montagu Sinclair. *'Twixt Sirdar and Menelik*. New York and London: Harper and Brothers, 1901.

Ziegler, Philip. *Omdurman*. London: Granada Publishing, 1973.

DIRECTORY OF PARTICIPANTS

(Chapter Number in Parenthesis)

ADAMS, ———
(Civil Engineer)(10)

ANLEY, Frederick Gore
(1 June 1864 - 17 March 1936)
Served in Egyptian Army: 16 March
1896 to 2 December 1899. Governor
of Wady Halfa in 1899. Served in Boer
War and World War I. Final British
Rank: Brigadier-General. (10)

ARBUTHNOT, Kenneth Wyndham
2nd Lieutenant, Seaforth Highlanders,
19 July 1893; Lieutenant, 3 July 1895;
Captain, 29 April 1900; Brevet Major,
22 August 1902. Served with the
Chitral Relief Force under Sir Robert
Low in 1895 with the 2nd Battalion.
(07)

ASSER, Joseph John
(31 August 1867 - 4 February 1949)
Served in Egyptian Army: 23 January
1897 to 1914; Adjutant-General, 1907
to 1914. Served in World War I.
Final British Rank: General. (10)

BARING, Everard
(7 December 1865 - 7 May 1932)
Served in Egyptian Army: 25 June
1897 to 6 October 1899. Final British
Rank: Brigadier-General. (10)

BARING, Sir Evelyn, 1st Earl of Cromer
(1841-1917)
Served as British Consul-General in
Egypt from 1883 through 1907. (09)

BENNETT, Ernest N.
Correspondent of Westminster Gazette.

BEY, Jackson
(Gordon Highlanders) (07)

BRAY, Hubert Alaric
(18 July 1867 - 23 January 1935)
Member of Royal Army Medical
Corps. Final British Rank: Colonel. (10)

BRINTON, John Chaytor
2nd Lieutenant, 28 January 1891 with
2nd Life Guards; Lieutenant, 13 April
1892; Captain, 12 January 1899.
Charged with the 21st Lancers at
Omdurman and was severely
wounded. Aide-de-camp to General
French in the South African War,
won the D.S.O. [?Also acted as a
correspondent for Black and White
magazine?] (06, 10)

BRINTON-PRICE, Jack (07)

BROADWOOD, Robert George
(14 March 1862 - 21 June 1917)
Served in Egyptian Army: 23
September 1892 to 25 November
1899. Served in Boer War; died in
action, World War I. Final British
Rank: Lieutenant-General.

BULKELEY-JOHNSON, Charles Bulkeley
(19 November 1867 - 11 April 1917)
Served in Egyptian Army: 8 January
1899 to [?]. Killed in action in France
during World War I. Final British
Rank: Colonel (10)

BULL, Rene
(? - 14 March 1942)
War artist for Black and White,
commencing in 1896 with the
Turco-Greek War. Following arrest and
escape from the Turks, went to India
to cover the Tirah camptign in 1897
before journeying to Sudan to cover
the Atbara and Omdurman campaigns. During World War I he served
with the Royal Naval Volunteer
Reserve and was drafted for active
service in France in July 1916.
Transferred to the Royal Air Force in
1918. Worked with the Air Ministry in
1940. (08)

BURLEIGH, Bennett
(? - 17 June 1914). War
Correspondent for Daily Telegraph
from 1882. First covered the Egyptian
War of that year and was present at
Tel-el-Kebir. Covered the Nile
Expedition two years later and wit-
nessed the battles of El Teb, Tamai,
Abu Klea and Abu Kru. Other cam-
paigns included the Ashanti
Expedition, the Greek War, the
Spanish Riff campaign, the 1898
Sudan campaign, the war in South
Africa, the Somaliland Expedition, the
Russo-Japanese War, and the Italian
campaign in Tripoli. (08)

BURROWES, Louis Arunell
Lieutenant, 13 December 1897.
Served with Lincolnshire Regiment
from 1894 until 1901 when he
became a captain with the Middlesex
Regiment. Received clasps for the
Atbara and Khartoum. (02, 03)

INDEX OF NAMES

CALDECOTT, Guy
(? - 2 September 1898)
Lieutenant, Warwickshire Regiment,
30 January 1886; Captain, 6 August,
1892. Killed at Omdurman. (02)

CAPPER, Thompson
(20 October 1863 - 27 September
1915)
Commissioned into East Lancashire
Regiment in 1882, achieved the rank
of Major-General. Served with the
Egyptian Army from December 1897
until July 1899. Saw action at Chitral
in 1895, and at the Atbara and
Omdurman in 1898; won the D.S.O.
in South Africa. Mortally wounded
at the Battle of Loos in 1915 while
serving as GOC 7th Division.

CHRISTIE, William Charles
2nd Lieutenant with Royal
Warwickshire Regiment, 21 October
1893; Lieutenant, 12 February 1898.
With the 1st Batallion at the Atbara
and Omdurman, and was Orderly
Officer to Brigadier General
Wauchope. Captain, 17 March 1900;
Brevet major, 22 August 1902. (07)

CHURCHILL, Winston Spencer
(1874 - 1965)
Commissioned into the 4th Queen's
Own Hussars as a Lieutenant, 20
February 1895. Saw action in Cuba
as a correspondent for *The Daily
Graphic*. Served with the Malakand
Field Force in 1897, and charged with
the 21st Lancers at Omdurman. (Also
Correspondent for *The Morning Post*)
During the South African War he was
captured but escaped. He went on to
become a Member of Parliament,
Cabinet Minister, and Prime Minister.
(05)

CLERK, Charles James
(22 June 1867 - ?)
Second Lieutenant in 21st Hussars,
5 October 1887; Lieutenant, 6
November 1889; Adjutant, 1898;
Captain, 30 May 1899. (05, 10)

CONOLLY, Thomas
(1 September 1870 - 11 July 1900)
Served in Egyptian Army: 1898 to
1899. Killed in action in Boer War.
Final British Rank: Lieutenant. (10)

COTTINGHAM, Charles Scarborough
(3 July 1868 - 10 October 1898)
Commissioned into Manchester
Regiment, 24 April 1889; Lieutenant,
10 September 1890, achieved the
rank of Captain. Served with the 10th
Soudanese Battalion of the Egyptian
Army from January 1898 until his
death from typhoid. (02)

COUTTS, Malcolm (Royal Scots Fusiliers
and Army Service Corps)
(1 January 1869 - 31 October 1922)
Served in Egyptian Army: 1899-1907.
Served in Nile campaign of 1898 and
World War I (OBE). Final British Rank:
Major. (10)

COWAN, Lieut. W. H.
Royal Navy; Commander of Nile Fleet.
(10)

COX, Samuel FitzGibbon
Lieutenant, 9 June 1892; Captain, 11
March 1898. Served with 1st
Battalion, Lincolnshire Regiment at
the Atbara where he was in charge of
Brigade Signallers, and at Omdurman,
in charge of Divisional Signallers. Saw
action in South Africa, 1899-1902.
Commanded 2nd Battalion in 1915,
retiring in 1920. (03)

CROLE-WYNDHAM, Walter George. See
WYNDHAM, Walter George Crole. (10)

CROMER, Lord. See Baring, Sir Evelyn

CROSS, Henry
Correspondent with *Manchester
Guardian*

CUMBERLAND, Richard Ormsby
Lieutenant, Lincolnshire Regiment,
14 May 1884; Captain, 5 May 1894.
Major, 1905. Present at the Atbara
and Omdurman. (02)

DAUNCEY, Thursby Henry Ernest
Lieutenant, 20 September 1884;
Captain, 26 October 1892. Served in
the Egyptian War, 1882, with the 7th
Dragoon Guards, and was present at
the engagements at El Magfar and
Mahsama, at the two actions at
Kassassin, and at the battle of Tel-el-
Kebir and the capture of Cairo. Served
with the 21st Lancers at Omdurman.
(06)

DE MONTMORENCY, Willoughby John
(3 May 1868 - 5 July 1917)
Served in Egyptian Army: 23
December 1898 to 1900. Prior to
service in Egypt, he served in Burma
and on the Northwest Frontier. Final
British Rank: Captain. (10)

DOUGHTY, Charles Hotham Montagu
(23 July 1867 - 28 April 1915)
Served in Egyptian Army: 22 May
1898 to 1 March 1900.
Present at final defeat of Khalifa at
Um Dibaykarat in November 1899.
Served in Boer War; killed at Gallipoli
during World War I. Final British
Rank: Lieutenant-Colonel. (10)

DOUGLAS, William Sholto (Royal
Engineers)
(18 September 1875 - After 1917)
Special Assignment to Egyptian Army:
20 December 1898 to 4 September
1899. Final British Rank: Major (10)

DOWHARD, ———
(Possibly servant to Lieut. Hamilton
Hodgson.) (03)

DOYNE, William Markham
Lieutenant in 21st Hussars, 27 January
1883; Captain, 9 September 1888;
Major, 26 October 1898. Served with
the 21st Lancers at Omdurman. (05)

DRAGE, William Henry (Commissary
and Transport Corps)
(25 November 1850 - 1915)
Served in Egyptian Army:
1 December 1886 to 1904. Director
of Supplies in Egyptian Army. Final
British Rank: Lieutenant-Colonel.
(01,10)

DYKE, Oswald Muirhead
Second Lieutenant, Lincolnshire
Regiment, 4 May 1898. Served with
the 1st Battalion from 1898 until
1902, when he transferred to the
Indian Army. Promoted Captain in
1907. Saw action at the Atbara and
Omdurman, and on the North West
Frontier of India in 1902 and 1908.
(02)

EADON, Frank Henry
(7 May 1861 - ?)
Lieutenant, 21st Hussars, 30 January
1884; Captain, 6 November 1889;
Brevet Major, 16 November 1898;

Major, 26 November 1899. Served
at Omdurman with the 21st Lancers.
(05, 10)

EARLE, Philip Douglas
Second Lieutenant, Lincolnshire
Regiment, 8 September 1897. Served
with the Lincolns from 1897 until his
resignation in 1906. [In Chapter Two,
Hubbard mentions that Earle became
ill and was left behind; he also refers
to a person named `Spider' who was
left behind due to illness. Earle and
`Spider' may be one and the same.]
(02)

ELGOOD, Percival George
(30 July 1863 - 20 December 1941)
Served in Egyptian Army: 28
December 1898 to 1903. Remained
in Egypt to serve in Ministries of
Interior and Finance. Final British
Rank: Lieutenant-Colonel. (10)

EMSLIE, ——— (Major) (08)

ENGLISH, A.
Sergeant-Major with the 21st Lancers
at Omdurman. (05)

ESCOMBE, Lieut. ——— (Royal Navy;
Gunboat Commander)(10)

FELL, ———
Lieut., Royal Navy; Gunboat
Commander. (10)

FINN, Harry (21st Lancers)
(6 December 1852 - 24 June 1924
Enlisted 1871 in 9th Lancers,
promoted in 21st Hussars to 2nd
Lieutenant in 1887, Major in 1894;
Lieutenant Colonel in 1900. Assigned
to Queensland, Australia in 1900,
transferred to New South Wales,
Inspector General for all
His Majesty's forces in Australia in
1905-1906. Promoted to Colonel in
1907, Brigadier-General in 1912;
retired to Australia. (See Introductory
notes to Chapters Five and Ten)

FITTON, Hugh Gregory
(15 November 1863 - 20 January
1916)
Served in Egyptian Army: 11 May
1894 to 17 December 1899. First Civil
Secretary of Sudan Government,
1898-1899. Served in Boer War; died
in combat during World War I. Final
British Rank: Brigadier-General. (10)

FLEMING, Dr. Charles Christie.
(1864-1917)
Commissioned into the Royal Army Medical Corps in 1892, and joined the Egyptian Army in September 1896. Sent to South Africa in December 1899. Served also in World War I; died of wounds received on the Western Front. (09)

FOWLE, John
(26 May 1862 - 25 September 1923) 2nd Lieutenant, 22 January 1881; Lieutenant, 1 July 1881; Captain, 23 November 1887; Major, 2 April 1898 with the 21st Lancers; Lieutenant-Colonel, 1902; Colonel, 1907. Saw action in the Soudan, 1884-95, 1898, and the South African War. (05; 07)

FRIEND, Sir Lovick Bransby
(25 April 1856 - 19 November 1944) Lieutenant in the Royal Engineers, 1873; Captain, 1885; Major, 1893; Lieutenant-Colonel, 1900. (05)

GAISFORD, Walter Thomas
2nd Lieutenant, Seaforth Highlanders, 23 May 1891; Lieutenant, 22 January 1894; Captain, 21 October 1899. Served in the occupation of Crete in 1897. (07)

GAMBLE, Richard Narrien
(10 March 1860 - 17 March 1937) Lieutenant in the 10th Foot, 2 April 1881; Captain, 3 August 1887. With the lst Battalion, Lincolnshire Regiment from 1879 until 1900; promoted Lieutenant-Colonel in 1907. Saw action in the Bechuanaland Expedition, 1884-85 under Sir Charles Warren as Adjutant of the 3rd Mounted Rifles, at the Atbara and Omdurman, in the operations against the Khalifa in 1899. Served on the staff during the South African War, winning a D.S.O. Retired in 1918 following his command of the 17th Brigade in Mesopotamia in 1915 (02)

GATACRE, Sir William Forbes
(3 December 1843 - 4 March 1906) Entered 77th Foot in 1862. Served in the Hazara Expedition of 1888, commanded the Mandalay Brigade in 1889-90 and participated in the Burma Tonhon Expedition. Saw action during the Chital Campaign. Went to Egypt in January 1898 with the local rank of Major-General to command the British brigade in the advance up the Nile for the recovery of Khartoum. At the Atbara, he was one of the first to reach the enemy Zareba and would have been speared if his orderly had not bayoneted his would-be assailant. During the Omdurman operation he commanded a division of two British brigades. He commanded the 3rd Division of the South African Field Force, 1899-1900. (02, 05)

GORRINGE, George Frederick (Royal Engineers)
(10 February 1868 - 24 October 1945) Served in Egyptian Army: 1893 to 1899 and 1902 to 1906. Responsible for rebuilding Palace at Khartoum and Gordon College. Military Governor of Sennar, 1902-1904; Military Governor of Blue Nile Province, 1905-1906. Served with distinction in Boer War and World War I. Final British Rank: Lieutenant-General. (10)

GOSSET, F. (Royal Engineers)(10)

GRAHAM, John Malise Anne
(19 July 1869 - ?)
Served in Egyptian Army: 1 January 1897 to 20 February 1900. Served in Boer War and World War I. Final British Rank: Lieutenant-Colonel. (10)

GREATWOOD, Francis William
Second Lieutenant, 28 September 1895. Joined the 1st Battalion, Lincolnshire Regiment in 1895; became Captain in 1904. Saw action at the Atbara and Omdurman, and in the South African War with Mounted Infantry Operations in 1902. (02)

GREGSON, Francis M.
Correspondent with *St. James Gazette*.

GRENFELL, Robert Septimus
(? - 2 September 1898) 2nd Lieutenant, 12th Lancers, 9 December 1896. Attached to the 21st Lancers and killed in the charge at Omdurman. (05, 06, 07)

GUEST, Frederick Edward (cousin of Winston Churchill)
(14 June 1875 - 28 April 1937)
Served in Egyptian Army: 7 July 1899 to 1 August 1901. Served in Boer War and World War I. Final British Rank: Captain. (10)

HAMILTON, Hubert Ian Wetherall
(20 February 1864 - 14 October 1914)
Lieutenant, Queen's West Surrey Regiment, 11 August 1880. Saw action in the Burma War of 1886-9. Served in Egyptian Army from 28 August 1897 to 3 December 1899, and was with the 14th Soudanese at Omdurman. Served in Boer War. Killed in action in World War I. Final British Rank: Major-General. (02, 10)

HENRY, St. George Charles
(29 December 1860 - 9 December 1909)
Served in Egyptian Army: 10 April 1896 - 2 December 1899. Served in Boer War, then returned to Egypt in 1902 as Military Governor of Kassala, then was Adjutant-General of the Egyptian Army until 1907. Final British Rank: Major-General. (10)

HOBBS, Frederick Manoli Baltazzi
(11 December 1867 - c. 1911)
Served in Egyptian Army: 1 July 1897 to 8 March 1902. Final British Rank: Captain. (10)

HODGSON, Lieutenant Hamilton
(6 July 1874 - 6 May 1915)
Commissioned as Lieutenant to Lincolnshire Regiment, 20 February 1895, serving in the Sudanese Campaign and was present at Battle of Omdurman. Promoted Captain in 1904. Served in Egyptian Army October 1899 to c. 1910. Served in Hampshire Regiment in World War I, killed at Gallipoli. (See Introductory Note to Chapter Three) (03)

HOLLINS, Charles Ernest
(1875 - 15 April 1939)
Second Lieutenant, 26 February 1896. Joined the 1st Battalion, Lincolnshire Regiment in 1896, becoming a Captain in 1904; was at the Atbara and Omdurman. Won the D.S.O. during World War I and attained the rank of Lieutenant-Colonel. (02)

HOPE, Lewis Anstruther
Lieutenant, Army Service Corps, 1 April 1874; Major, 11 December 1888; Lieutenant-Colonel, 17 June 1892; Colonel, 10 October 1900. Saw action in the Zulu War, the Nile Expedition of 1884-85, and in the 1898 Nile Expedition. [Hubbard described him as the "disembarking officer at Omdurman."] (02)

HORE-RUTHVEN, Alexander Gore Arkwright: See RUTHVEN, Alexander Gore Arkwright. (10)

HOSKINS, Arthur Reginald
(30 May 1871 - 7 February 1942)
Served in Egyptian Army: 20 March 1896 to 31 January 1900. Served in Boer War, Somaliland, World War I.

HOWARD, Hubert
(? - 2 September 1898)
Correspondent for *The Times*. Killed at Omdurman (after the battle) by a stray shell. (05)

HUBBARD, Alfred Edward
(6 September 1862 - 31 July 1921)
Lieutenant, 25 August 1883; Captain, 1st Battalion. Lincolnshire Regiment, 16 January 1894; present at the Atbara and Omdurman. Promoted to Major, 6 October 1904; retired 1912, but served in World War I as Major in Reserve. (03)(See Introductory Notes to Chap. 2)

HUNTER, Archibald (Staff).
(1856 - 28 June, 1936)
Served on Kitchener's staff in Sudanese Campaign of 1898, was present at Battle of Omdurman. (See Introductory Notes, Chapter Eight) (05, 08)

HUNTER, William Hugh
(8 July 1860 - 20 July 1902)
Served in Egyptian Army: 1898 to 1902. Military Governor of Bahr el Ghazal Province. Died in Egypt. Final British Rank: Major. (10)

INGLE, William Daly (Daley?)
(9 August 1871 - ?)
Served in Egyptian Army: 1 March 1899 to 5 March 1903.
Present at Um Dibaykarat for final defeat of Khalifa, November 1899. Served in World War I. Final British Rank: Lieutenant-Colonel. (10)

JACKSON, Ernest Somerville
(26 December 1872 - 10 March 1943)
Served in Egyptian Army: 1898 to
1914. Retired to a farm in the Sudan,
died there. Final British Rank:
Lieutenant-Colonel. (10)

JACKSON, Sir Herbert William
(5 February 1861 - 28 January 1931)
Entered Gordon Highlanders as
Lieutenant in 1881; Captain, 1
September 1891; Major, 18 November
1896.

JAMES, Lionel
(1871 - 1955)
Correspondent for Reuter's of London.
(See Introductory Note to Chapter
Four)

KENNA, Paul Aloysius.
(16 August 1862 - 30 August 1915)
Joined 2nd West Indian Regiment as
Lieutenant, 28 August 1886; served
two years in the West Indies and West
Africa, but transferred to the 21st
Hussars in 1889; Captain, 12 June
1895. Served with the 21st Lancers
at Omdurman and was awarded the
Victoria Cross for the following
service: "At the battle of Khartoum
on the 2nd September 1898, Captain
P. A. Kenna assisted Major Crole
Wyndham of the same regiment, by
taking him on his horse, behind the
saddle (Major Wyndham's horse
having been killed in the charge),
thus enabling him to reach a place of
safety; and after the charge of the
21st Lancers, Captain Kenna returned
to assist Lieutenant de Montmorency,
who was endeavouring to recover the
body of Second Lieutenant R. S.
Grenfell." Served in South Africa from
1899 until 1904. (06, 07)

KENNEDY, see Watson-Kennedy (07)

KITCHENER, Major General Horatio
Herbert
(1850-1916)
Commander-in-Chief (or Sirdar) of the
Egyptian Army from 1892 through
1899. (09)

LAWSON, Henry Merrick (Royal
Engineers)(1859-?)
(See Introductory Note to Chapter
Nine) (09)

LE GALLAIS, Philip Walter Jules
(17 August 1861 - 6 November 1900)
Served in Egyptian Army: 27
November 1896 to 1899. Died in
South Africa of wounds suffered in
combat during Boer War.
Final British Rank: Lieutenant-Colonel.
(10)

LEWIS, David Francis
(21 October 1855 - 1927)
Served in Egyptian Army: 1886 to
1900. Retired to become military
correspondent for The Times. Final
British Rank: Colonel. (10)

LIDDELL, John Stewart (Royal Engineers)
(11 October 1868 - 1934)
Served in Egyptian Army:
15 December 1898 to 1924.
Established the telegraph network
in the Sudan, 1898-1904; became
Director of Telegraphs of Egyptian
Government, 1904-1920. Final British
Rank: Lieutenant-Colonel. (10)

LOWTH, Frank Robert
(7 June 1850 - 24 January 1931)
Lieutenant, Lincolnshire Regiment,
28 October 1871; Captain, 11 March,
1881; Major, 17 February 1892;
Lieutenant-Colonel, 11 March 1898.
Officer Commmanding 1st Battalion
Lincolnshire Regiment. Joined the
regiment in 1870 and served until
1902; he retired in 1904. Saw action
in the Perak Expedition in 1875 and
was present when a combined naval
and military force attacked and
captured the stockades and five guns
at Passir Sala; and at Omdurman in
1898. His official report of
Omdurman is printed in Albert Lee,
History of the 10th Foot, Vol. II, pp.
216-217. (02)

LYALL, Charles George
Lieutenant, 28 March 1894. With the
Lincolnshire Regiment from 1892
until 1907. Served at the Atbara,
Omdurman and in South Africa. (02)

MACAULEY, George Bohun
(25 August 1869 - 6 January 1940)
Served in Egyptian Army: 1896-1906.
Director of Sudan Railways, 1899-
1906; Director-General of Egyptian
State Railways, 1906-1919.
Final British Rank: Brigadier-General.
(10)

MACDONALD, Sir Hector Archibald
(1853 - 25 March 1903)
Enlisted in the 92nd Highlanders in
1870 and served nine years in the
ranks. Saw action in the Afghan War
of 1879-1880 and accompanied Sir
Frederick Roberts in his march to
Cabul, and was present at the battle
of Candahar. Fought at Majuba Hill in
1881, and participated in the Nile
and Suakin Expeditions. In 1896 he
commanded the 2nd Infantry Brigade
of the Dongola Expeditionary Force.
Commanded the Egyptian Brigade at
the action of Abu Hamed and at the
Atbara. [The adroitness he displayed
at Omdurman in wheeling round his
brigade through a complete half circle,
half-battalion by half-battalion, to
meet an unexpected flank attack of
the Dervishes turned what might have
proved disaster into victory.]
Commanded the Highland Brigade
in the Boer War and was wounded
at Paardeberg. He committed suicide
in Paris.(02)

MACNEECE, Thomas Frederick.
Surgeon, Royal Army Medical Corps,
6 March 1880; Surgeon-Major, 6
March 1892. (05)

MAHON, Brian Thomas
(2 April 1862 - 24 September 1930)
Served in Egyptian Army: 20 January
1893 to 24 January 1900.
Commanded column which relieved
Ladysmith during Boer War. Military
Governor of Kordofan, 1899-1900 and
1901-1903. Served in World War I.
Final British Rank: Lieutenant-General.
(10)

MAINWARING, Henry Bolton
Lieutenant, 21 August 1878, Captain,
18 November 1884; Major, 17
February 1896. Served with the 1st
Battalion, Lincolnshire Regiment from
1878 until 1905, and saw action at
the Atbara and Omdurman. (02)

MAJENDIE, Henry Grylls
(28 March 1865 - 13 February 1900)
Served in Egyptian Army: 1898 to
1899. Died of wounds in Boer War.
Final British Rank: Captain. (10)

MARTIN, Rowland Hill
Cornet, 14 January 1875; Lieutenant,
28 October 1871; Captain, 16
December 1878; Major, 2 February
1884; Lieutenant-Colonel, 26 October
1892; Colonel in 21st Lancers, 26
October 1896. Served with the
Bechuanaland Expedition under Sir
Charles Warren, 1884-85, during the
latter part of which he commanded a
Regiment of Mounted Rifles. (07)

MATCHETT, Henry Gerald Keith
(1 March 1866 - 16 March 1932)
Served in Egyptian Army: 9 October
1896 to c. 1909. Final British Rank:
Lieutenant Colonel. (10)

MAUD, William Theobald
(September 1865 - 12 May 1903)
Correspondent, *The Daily Graphic*
(See Introductory Notes to Chapter
One)

MAXWELL, Robert Percy
Lieutenant, 22 October 1881; Captain,
25 April 1892. Joined the 1st
Battalion, Lincolnshire Regiment in
1881 and achieved the rank of
Lieutenant-Colonel in 1910. Was at
the Atbara and Omdurman. (02)

MAXWELL, Sir John Grenfell
(12 July 1859 - 21 February 1929)
Joined 42nd Highlanders in 1879.
Saw action at Tel-el-Kebir in 1882
with the 1st Battalion, The Black
Watch. Staff Captain during the 1884
Nile Expedition and A.D.C. to Major
General Grenfell in 1885-86, and won
the D.S.O. at the Battle of Giniss.
Served in the Dongola Expedition in
1896. Commanded 2nd Soudanese
Brigade at the battles of Atbara and
Omdurman. Served in Egyptian Army
from 7 September 1886 to 12
February 1900. Military Governor of
Omdurman, 1899-1900. Commanded
14th Brigade in South Africa, 1900-01.
Colonel of the Black Watch, 1914. (02;
10)

MAXWELL, William
Correspondent for *The Standard*.

McNEILL, Lieutenant Angus
(1874 - 1950)
Enlisted 1895 in Seaforth Highlanders,
served in Crete in 1897, to Sudan in
1898 and saw action at the Atbara

River and Omdurman. Served in South Africa in 1899 and 1900. Enlisted in Montmorency's Scouts in World War I, D.S.O. 1918. Served in British Gendarmerie in Palestine, 1922-1926. (07)(See introductory notes Chap. 7)

MICKLEM, Henry Andrew
(29 June 1872 - 9 March 1963)
Royal Engineers; served in Egyptian Army: 25 June 1897 to 3 October 1899. Served in Boer War and World War I. Final British Rank: Colonel.

MITFORD, Bertram Reverly
(6 February 1863 - 23 February 1936)
Served in Egyptian Army: 2 September 1886 to 6 October 1891, and 23 July 1898 to 10 November 1899. Served in Boer War and World War I. Final British Rank: Major-General. (10)

MOLYNEUX, ———
(21st Lancers) (07)

MONTMORENCY, Hon. Raymond Harvey Lodge Joseph de
(? - 1900)
Lieutenant, 6 November 1889. Served with the 21st Lancers at Omdurman and was awarded the Victoria Cross for the following service: "...Lieutenant de Montmorency, after the charge of the 21st Lancers, returned to assist Second Lieutenant R. S. Grenfell, who was lying surrounded by a large group of Dervishes. Lieutenant de Montmorency drove the Dervishes off, and finding Lieutenant Grenfell dead, put the body on his horse, which then broke away. Captain Kenna and Corporal Swarbrick then came to his assistance, and enabled him to rejoin the Regiment, which had begun to open a heavy fire on the enemy." During the South African War, he led the Montmorency Scouts and was killed early in 1900. (06, 07)

NESHAM, Cuthbert Spencer.
2nd Lieutenant, 21st Lancers, 26 March 1896; Lieutenant, 28 January 1899. Served with the 21st Lancers at Omdurman and was severely wounded. (06, 07)

NEWCOMBE, Edward Osborn Armstrong (Royal Engineers)
(30 August 1874 - 15 May 1941)
Served in Egyptian Army: 14 December 1896 to 12 November 1899. Served on Railway Staff in Sudan; returned to Sudan as Traffic Manager of Sudan Railways, 1914-1917. Served in Boer War and World War I. Final British Rank: Major. (10)

NICKERSON, George Snyder (Royal Army Medical Corps)
(1873 - 1911)
Served in Egyptian Army: 1898 to 1911. Transferred to Sudan Government in 1905; at his death, was Governor of Sennar. Final British Rank: Captain. (10)

NORBURY, Coningsby
(5 May 1865 - 1913 or earlier)
Served in Egyptian Army: 2 February 1899 to 14 March 1906. Present at Khalifa's final defeat, November 1899. Final British Rank: Major. (10)

OPPENHEIM, Lawrie C. F.
Correspondent.

PAGE, Charles Stanmore (10)

PARKER, Alfred Chevallier
(3 June 1874 - 27 December 1935)
Served in Egyptian Army: 1899 to 1924. Served in World War I. Final British Rank: Lieutenant-Colonel. (10)

PARSONS, Colonel Charles S. B.
Named Commander of Kassala November 1897; commanded the 16th Egyptians and a group of Arab Irregulars who had been transferred from Italy into the Egyptian Army. (09)

PEDLEY, Oswald Henry.
Lieutenant, Connaught Rangers, 11 October 1882; Captain, 21 December 1892 in the Northumberland Fusiliers; Brevet Major, 17 December 1898; Major, 11 February 1903. Served as Staff Officer on Line of Communication during the 1896 Dongola Expedition and also in 1897. Served with the Egyptian Army during the Omdurman campaign and again in 1899. Took part in the first advance against the Khalifa as Brigade Major of the 2nd Soudanese Brigade. Was a

INDEX OF NAMES

Special Service Officer during the war in South Africa. (05)

PERSSE, William Horsley
(16 October 1863 - ?)
Served in Egyptian Army: 1896 to [?]
Served in World War I. Final British
Rank: Honorary Lieutenant-Colonel.
(10)

PHIPPS, Pownall Ramsay
(2 April 1865 - 6 August 1932)
Served in Egyptian Army: 1899 to
1914. Present at Khalifa Defeat at Um
Dibaykarat in November 1899. Civil
Secretary of Sudan Government,
1905-1914.
Final British Rank: Lieutenant-Colonel.
(10)

PIRIE, Arthur Murray
(3 May 1869 - 21 November 1917)
Lieutenant, 6 November 1891.
Served with the 21st Lancers at
Omdurman and was wounded.
Mentioned in despatches and awarded
the D.S.O. Served in Egyptian Army:
7 October 1898 to 18 June 1904.
Killed in action in World War I. Final
British Rank: Lieutenant-Colonel.
(06, 10)(See introductory notes
Chap. 11)

PLUNKETT, Edward Abadie.
(1870 - 8 June 1926)
Lieutenant, 23 December 1893.
Served with 1st Battalion, Lincolnshire
Regiment at the Atbara and
Omdurman. Attached to the
Montenegrin Forces in the Balkan
War of 1912-13. Promoted Lieutenant-
Colonel in March 1918, and was
Military AttachÈ in Belgrade in
November 1918. Retired with
honorary rank of Brigadier-General
(03)

PRENDERGAST, Frederick Lenox
(3 August 1862 - c. 1900)
Served in Egyptian Army: 8 February
1899 to 1900. Died in the Sudan.
Final British Rank: Major.
(10)PROTHEROE-SMITH, Hugh
Bateman
(1872 - 26 November 1961)
2nd Lieutenant in Dorset Regiment,
1892; Lieutenant, 15 June 1895;
exchanged to the 21st Lancers in
1897. Took part in the 1898

Omdurman campaign; reached the
rank of Major, 1906. Served in South
Africa at the relief of Kimberley and
the battle of Paardeberg. Also served
in World War I. (07)

RAY, ———
(Possibly Captain Grattan George
O'Neil Ray, Royal Warwickshire
Regiment) (02)

RENNIE, Coverly James
(- 26 August 1901)
Lieutenant, Lincolnshire Regiment,
10 November 1897. With the Lincolns
from 1894 until 1901. Wounded at
the Atbara but recovered to fight at
Omdurman. Served in the South
African War and died of wounds
received in action. (02)

RHODES, Colonel Frank (Brother of Cecil
Rhodes)
(9 April 1851 - September 1905)
Served with 1st Dragoons. Present at
the ill-fated Jameson Raid in 1895.
Covered the Sudan campaign as a correspondent for *The Times*; wounded in
the Zareba at Omdurman. (06)

RITCHIE, Archibald Buchanan
(14 May 1869 - 9 July 1955)
2nd Lieutenant with Seaforth
Highlanders, 21 September 1889;
Lieutenant, 2 September 1891;
Captain, 2 May 1898. Achieved rank
of Brevet-Colonel in 1915.
Commanded the 26th Brigade, 9th
Division in 1915-1916 and was
dangerously wounded whilst
commanding the 16t Division in
1918. Retired in 1928, became
Colonel of the Seaforths from
1931-39. (07)

ROBERTS, Henry Bradley (Royal
Engineers)
(28 August 1860 - ?)(10)

RUNDLE, Sir Henry McLeod Lesley.
(6 January 1856 - 19 November 1934)
Lieutenant, Royal Artillery, 14 August
1876; saw action in the Zulu War, the
first Boer War (wounded), the
Egyptian War, the Nile Expedition,
the Dongola Expedition of 1896;
promoted to Major-General for
distinguished service. Adjutant-General
of the Egyptian Army during the
Omdurman campaign. Held various

commands following his service in South Africa, and was G.O.C. in Command 1st Class from 1915-1916. (08)

RUTHVEN, Alexander Gore Arkwright
(6 July 1872 - 2 May 1955)
Joined Highland Light Infantry in 1891. Attached to Egyptian Army, Sudan Campaign, 1898; Commander Camel Corps Detachment, Battle of Gedarif, 22 September 1898. Awarded Victoria Cross for Bravery. Served in Egyptian Army 7 July 1899 to 27 August 1903; present at final defeat of Khalifa at Um Dibaykarat, 1899. Present in Somaliland Campaign, 1903-1904. Served on Western Front, World War I; wounded at Gallipoli. Final British Rank: Brigadier-General. NOTE: Extensive listing in *Who Was Who* under Hore-Ruthven,(10)

SANDERS, Robert Muriel
(4 March 1866 - ?)
Served in Egyptian Army: 6 March 1899 to 24 June 1901. Military Governor of Fashoda, 1900-1901. Final British Rank: Major. (10)

SANDERSON, ———
Sergeant in A Company, lst Battalion, Lincolnshire Regiment. Wounded at Omdurman. (03; 10?)

SARGENT, Harry Neptune
(? - 6 February 1946)
Joined Army Service Corps as Lieutenant in 1890; Captain, 1892; Adjutant, 1895-97; Lieutenant-Colonel, 1906; Colonel, 1909. Staff Officer at Assouan during the 1898 Nile Expedition. During the South African War saw action at the relief of Ladysmith, Tugela Heights and Laing's Nek. During World War I he participated in the retreat from Mons, the battles of the Marne, Aisne, First Ypres, Loos and the Somme. (05)

SCOTT, Albert Charles (Royal Engineers)
(4 August 1871 - 29 October 1947)
Served in Egyptian Army: 2 April 1899 to 31 March 1901. Served in Boer War and World War I. Final British Rank: Lieutenant-Colonel. (10)

SCUDAMORE, Frank
Correspondent for *Daily News*.

SIMPSON, Charles Rudyard
(15 November 1856 - 7 December 1948)
Lieutenant, 10th Foot, 21 September 1874; Captain, 19 July 1882; Major, 7 June 1893. Served with the 1st Battalion, Lincolnshire Regiment from 1874 until 1900, including the actions at the Atbara and Omdurman. Became a Brigadier General in 1908. (02)

SMITH, Guy de Herrez
(27 August 1869 - 10 October 1904)
Served in Egyptian Army: 3 May 1896 to 10 October 1904. Military Governor of Khartoum at time of his death. Final British Rank: Captain. (10)

SMITH-DORIEN, Horace Lockwood
(26 May 1858 - 12 August 1930)
Lieutenant, Derbyshire Regiment, 26 February 1876; Captain, 22 August 1882; Major, 11 May 1892; Lieutenant-Colonel, 20 May 1898; Brevet-Colonel, 16 November 1898. Served in the Zulu War amd was present at the engagements at Isandhlwana and Ulundi. Served in the Egyptian War of 1882 in command of the Mounted Infantry (which he raised) with Sir Evelyn Wood's Brigade. Served in the Soudan Campaign of 1885 with the Mounted Infantry; also served with the Soudan Frontier Force in 1885-86, including the investment of Kosheh and the engagement at Giniss. Served in the Tirah Expeditionary Force under Sir William Lockhart in 1897-98 with the Lincolnshire Regiment, and was present at the capture of Sampagha and the Arhanga Pass, and in the operations in the Mastura, Waran, and Bazar Valleys. Promoted Major-General following his command of a division in the South African War. Commanded the British Expeditionary Force in 1914-1915 and was C-in-C, East African Forces, 1915-1916. (08)

SMYTH, Neville Maskelyne
(14 August 1868 -)
2nd Lieutenant, 2nd Dragoon Guards, 22 August 1888; Lieutenant, 26 April 1895; Captain, 8 December 1897.

Served with the Zhob Valley Expedition in 1890-91. Served with the Dongola Expeditionary Force under Sir Herbert Kitchener in 1896 including the engagement at Firket and the operations at Hafir. Served in the 1898 campaign attached to the Egyptian Army and was present at the cavalry reconnaissance of 4th April and at Omdurman. Awarded the Victoria Cross for the following action during the battle: He galloped forward and attacked a Dervish who had run amok among some camp followers, killing him, at the same time being wounded with a spear in the arm. He saved the life of at least one of the camp followers. (08)

SMYTH, Robert Napier
(26 June 1868 - 14 October 1947 Entered army 1890, promoted to Lieutenant, 16 February, 1892; to Captain in 1899, Mayor in 1905; Lieutenant-Colonel in 1910, Colonel in 1914. Served with the 21st Lancers at Omdurman. In South African War, D.A.A.G. Intelligence and served in 13th Hussars. In World War I, served as General Staff Officer and Brigade Commander. (05; 06)(See introductory notes Chap. 6)

SOWERBY, Maurice Eden
(Royal Engineers)
(15 December 1874 - 28 January 1920)
Served in Egyptian Army: 1898-1920. Chief Engineer of Sudan Railways, 1906-1915. Final British Rank: Colonel. (10)STANTON, Edward Alexander
(15 November 1867 - 2 December 1947)
Served in Egyptian Army 1896 to 1908. Military Governor of Khartoum 1904-1908. Final British Rank: Colonel. (10)

STEEVENS, George
Correspondent, *Daily Mail.*

STEVENSON, Alexander Gavin
(15 October 1871 - 13 March 1939)
Served in Egyptian Army: 13 September 1895 to 11 December 1899. Served in Boer War and World War I. Final British Rank: Major-General. (10)

SWABEY, Wilfred Spedding
(25 February 1871 - 13 September 1939)
Served in Egyptian Army: 31 December 1897 to 19 October 1899. Served in Boer War and World War I. Final British Rank: Colonel. (10)

TATCHELL, Edward
Lieutenant, 1 January 1896. Served with 1st Battalion, Lincolnshire Regiment at the Atbara and Omdurman. Served in South Africa, 1899-1901; retired 1908 but re-employed 1914 and won the D.S.O. during World War I. (02, 03)

VANDELEUR, Cecil Foster Seymour
(7 November 1869 - 31 August 1901)
Served in Egyptian Army: 1898 to 1899.
Killed in South Africa during Boer War. Final British Rank: Brevet Lieutenant-Colonel. (10)

VILLIERS, Frederic
(23 February 1851 - 3 April 1922)
Joined *The Graphic* in 1876 when he was sent to Serbia and to Turkey the following year. Covered the Egyptian War of 1882, the Nile Expedition of 1884, the war in Burma in 18876, and the Graeco-Turkish War of 1897. Sent to Sudan in 1898 on behalf of *The Illustrated London News* (although Hubbard refers to him as the *Graphic* artist.) Later covered the Russo-Japanese War and World War I. (02)

WANHILL, Charles Frederick
(Royal Army Medical Corps)
(4 September 1871 - 29 May 1958)
Served in Egyptian Army: 23 February 1898 to 23 February 1900. Served in Boer War. Final British Rank: Lieutenant-Colonel. (10)

WATSON, Rev. Alfred William Brown
Chaplain to the Forces (2nd Class), ranking as Lieutenant-Colonel, 14 December 1898. Served with the Dongola Field Force under Sir Herbert Kitchener in 1896. Participated in the Gordon Memorial Service, 1898. Retired 1906. (02, 03)

WATSON-KENNEDY, Thomas Francis Archibald
(12 November 1856 - 30 May 1935)
Lieutenant, 27 January 1875 with the

Queen's Own Cameron Highlanders; Captain, 20 January 1886; Major, 22 February 1893; Brevet Lieutenant-Colonel, 16 November 1898; Lieutenant-Colonel, 21 May 1899. Served with the Black Watch at Tel-el-Kebir in 1882, and in the Soudan Campaign of 1884 at Tamai and El Teb; he was severely wounded at Kirbekan. Served in South Africa, 1900-1901. (07)

WAUCHOPE, Andrew Gilbert
(1846 - 11 December 1899) Commanded brigade in expedition for the reconquest of Sudan and was promoted Major-General. Commanded the Highland Brigade in General Lord Methuen's column in Transvaal in 1899; mortally wounded at Magersfontein. (02, 06, 07)

WAYMOUTH, Ernest G.
2nd Lieutenant, 22 July 1888 in Royal Garrison Artillery; Lieutenant, 27 July 1891; Captain, 12 December 1898. Served in Omdurman campaign. (02)

WELDON, Hamilton
Correspondent, *Morning Post*.

WELLBY, Montagu Sinclair.
(10 October 1866 - 5 August 1900) Lieutenant, 18th Hussars, British Army, 1886; Captain, 1894. Expedition to Explore and Map Somaliland (1894); and Second Expedition to Somaliland (1895). Expedition to Central Asia (1896); published *Through Unknown Tibet* in 1896; served in Tirah Campaign, 1897. Accompanied British Agent Captain J. L. Harrington to Abyssinia in August 1898; account of this trip published posthumously as *'Twixt Sirdar and Menelik*. Mortally injured in action at Mertzicht, South Africa, 30 July 1900. (10)

WEMYSS, David Gillespie
(2 January 1863 - ?) Served in Egyptian Army: 19 July 1899 to 30 April 1901. Served in Boer War. Final British Rank: Lieutenant-Colonel. (10)

WHIGHAM, Robert Dundas
(5 August 1865 - 23 June 1950) Lieutenant, Royal Warwickshire Regiment, 9 May 1885; Captain,

3 March, 1892. During the 1898 campaign he was attached to the 13th Soudanese Battalion and saw action at the Atbara and Omdurman. Was on campaign in South Africa and commanded the 62nd West Riding Division in France in 1918. (08)

WILLIAMS, Charles
Correspondent, *Daily Chronicle*.

WOLLEN, William Russell Grant
(21 November 1874 - 7 April 1900) Royal Engineers; Served in Egyptian Army: 6 May 1898 to 7 April 1900. Served on Railway Staff. Died in the Sudan, buried at Khartoum. Final British Rank: Captain. (10)

WOLSELEY, John Francis (Nephew of Field Marshall Lord Wolseley)
(7 April 1862 - ?) Served in Egyptian Army: 30 January 1897 to 1 March 1900. Served in Boer War. Final British Rank: Major. (10)

WOODCOCK, Ernest Elborough
Second Lieutenant, 1 December 1897; served with the 1st Battalion, Lincolnshire Regiment from 1897 until 1900. Saw action at the Atbara and Omdurman. Captain in the Indian Army in 1906. (02)

WYNDHAM, Walter George Crole.
(9 August 1857 - 7 December 1948) Lieutenant, 21st Hussars, 11 February 1875; Major, 16 July 1884; Captain, 19 May 1890. Saw action in the Zulu War and the Nile Expedition. Served at Omdurman with the 21st Lancers where his horse was killed and he was saved by Captain Kenna. Promoted to Lieutenant-Colonel and Commander of the 21st Lancers, 26 October 1898. (05, 06, 10)

YOUNG, Norman Edward
(26 October 1862 - 26 February 1902) 2nd Lieutenant, 25 July 1882. Served in Egyptian Army from 14 July 1892 to 28 November 1898. Saw action at Abu Hemed and awarded the D.S.O. Served in 2nd Boer War, died of typhoid at Bloemfontein. Final British Rank: Major. (07)